Foodways and Daily Life in Medieval Anatolia

(BY NICOLAS TRÉPANIER)

Foodways and Daily Life in Medieval Anatolia

A NEW SOCIAL HISTORY

University of Texas Press AUSTIN

First edition, 2014
First paperback edition, 2015

♾ The paper used in this book meets the minimum requirements of ANSI/NISO Z39.48-1992 (R1997) (Permanence of Paper).

LIBRARY OF CONGRESS CATALOGING-IN-PUBLICATION DATA
Trépanier, Nicolas, 1976–
Foodways and daily life in medieval Anatolia : a new social history / by Nicolas Trépanier.
pages cm
Includes bibliographical references and index.
ISBN 978-0-292-75929-9 (cloth)
ISBN 978-0-292-76189-6 (ebook)
Acknowledgments—A Note on Transliteration—List of Abbreviations—Introduction—Chapter 1. Food Production—Chapter 2. Food Exchanges—Chapter 3. Food Consumption—Chapter 4. Food and Religion—Conclusion—Appendix: Sources—Notes—Bibliography—Index.
GT2853.T9 T74 2015
394.1′209561—dc23

2014012689

ISBN 978-1-4773-0992-6 (paperback)
doi:10.7560/759299

To R.Y.,
who shows me where to look
among the garbage and the flowers

Contents

Acknowledgments

I borrowed a lot of time and energy from many people over the ten years or so it took to bring this book into existence. As research turned into writing and then into revision, I kept borrowing from new people for new reasons, and I now find myself completely unable to pay back the accumulated debt. Let's be honest: I did not borrow the time and energy of so many friends and colleagues; I stole it.

Still, inability to repay debt does not prevent me from acknowledging it and from expressing gratitude to my victims. I should first mention my mentors, Cemal Kafadar, Amy Singer, and Scott Redford, who helped shape this research project from structure to fine grain. Each one has left a lasting imprint on my mind, using a different set of superpowers. Cemal Kafadar always listened to my ideas (some of them rather unorthodox) with an open mind, and on those occasions when he expressed his disagreement or suggested alternative ways of thinking, he probably saved me from myself. My education as a historian greatly benefited from Amy Singer's sharp mind, "natural-born mentor" character, and superhuman ability to focus on the big picture and the tiniest detail all at once. Scott Redford took me in as an archaeological orphan a number of years ago and ran me through the basics of a foreign discipline despite having no obligation whatsoever to do so. I owe each of them a debt of gratitude that is even deeper than the respect and admiration I have for them as scholars.

The methodology presented in this book requires a healthy degree of linguistic self-confidence. I had the immense privilege (and pleasure and, on occasion, pain) of learning Persian from Wheeler M. Thackston. If I were asked to list the best teachers I encountered through a quarter century as a student, Professor Thackston's name might be the very first to pop into my mind; if I were asked to list the least demanding, it would not. I was also blessed with the chance of studying Old Anatolian Turkish under the infinitely kind, infinitely patient supervision of the late Şinasi Tekin. I would add that, beyond languages, I also benefited from guidance and professional opportunities given to me by Hakan Karateke, Helga Anetshofer, Stefan Winter, Roy Mottahedeh, Roger Owen, and Laurel Thatcher Ulrich, if the resulting list of names did not sound so much like bragging.

I stumbled into archaeology late in the game, but archaeology is a place where they pick you up when you fall—and then make sure you don't have a scorpion in your boots. Besides Scott Redford, I met there a crew that welcomed my beginner's questions with smiles and inexhaustible patience. Joanita Vroom, Marie-Henriette Gates, Canan Çakırlar, Ekin Kozal, Allyson McDavid, Suna Çağatay, and many others all have, to different degrees, invested their time in making me a little more literate in their culture, and I thank them for it.

Part of what made this book possible is the time and space through which a number of institutions allowed me, directly or indirectly, to concentrate on my research and writing. These include le Fonds de Recherche du Québec—Société et Culture (then FCAR), the Vakıflar Genel Müdürlüğü in Ankara (with its tremendously friendly and helpful staff), the Başbakanlık Osmanlı Arşivleri in Istanbul, the library of the İslam Araştırmaları Merkezi (also in Istanbul), Harvard University, and the Radcliffe Institute for Advanced Study. McGill University's Library of Islamic Studies in Montréal has provided a refuge for most of the past fifteen or so summers. Yet my fondest memories will remain with the wonderful year I spent with the rowdy crew of Koç University's Research Center for Anatolian Civilizations in Istanbul, a year that was not only tremendously productive, but also the starting point of many precious professional connections and even more precious friendships.

Friends have done a lot to blow some life into this text. Some I encountered while a student, among whom İklil Erefe-Selçuk, Richard Wittman, Rachel Goshgarian, Giancarlo Casale, Murat Cem Mengüç, Deniz Karakaş, and Maria Cristina Carile stand out in a group of people that includes many others. My job at the University of Mississippi brought me both friends and colleagues, many of whom helped in the latter stages of this project becoming a book. Marc Lerner, Oliver Dinius, Deirdre Cooper-Owens, and Vivian Ibrahim as well as Joe Ward, Charles Eagles, Susan Grayzel, Kelly Brown Houston, and pretty much everybody else have done a lot to make me feel at home in Mississippi. And then there were a number of other friends pulled out from the real world, among whom I am especially thinking of David "un petit thé vert avec ça?" Jalbert, Mélissa Thériault, Nigel DeSouza, Marie-Ève Charron, Sakura Dogglett, Hardy Griffin, Georges-Rémy Fortin, Vincent Roy, Midori-san, and many others who got stuck with me for reasons unrelated to work. All of the above are guilty by association for my seeing this project through without losing any more of my mind than was necessary.

Finally, my highest expression of gratitude has to go to my family. To my parents, who are indirectly responsible for most of what this book turned out to be through the example they gave me of ceaseless hard work, egalitarian empathy, and thematic interests and, more than everything else, their constant yet never overbearing support. To the Trio de la rue St-Dominique and to Juliette Bourassa, forever the *révolutionnaire tranquille*, for giving me a sense of grounding even if they may not have been aware of it. And to Reiko, dearest Reiko, who has made my life a better place in more ways than she will ever know.

A Note on Transliteration

Transliteration is a recurrent problem in the historiography of the Middle East. In this study, the problem is compounded by the fact that the source material I use is almost evenly split among three languages: Turkish, Persian, and Arabic.

I have chosen to follow the transliteration system of the *International Journal of Middle Eastern Studies* (*IJMES*) (available at http://web.gc.cuny.edu/ijmes). Following one of the options that this system offers, I have chosen to transliterate passages from Old Anatolian Turkish sources in modern Turkish.

Because the *IJMES* system requires a different transliteration scheme for each language, I chose the language of transliteration of a word based on the text where it is found. When discussing words that simultaneously appear in sources in several languages (*bāgh* and *ḥalwāʾ*, for example), I chose according to the etymological origin of the word.

For the titles of the narrative sources, I followed the *IJMES* practice, including the removal of diacritics. When titles of primary sources were in a different language from the body of the text, I transliterated them according to the title's (rather than the content's) language; typically, Turkish sources have Persian titles, whereas the titles of Persian and Arabic sources are in Arabic. In bibliographical references to published texts, I have given the transliteration as it appears in the published version or, if it was published entirely in the Arabic alphabet, a full transliteration.

Unless there is a widely established practice for a particular name (e.g., Osman rather than ʿUthmān for the first Ottoman sultan), I chose the transliteration language for personal names according to the linguistic origin of these names (e.g., ʿĀrif in Arabic and Saru in Turkish).

I followed the "Word List" offered on the *IJMES* website to determine which words can be considered as having entered common English usage and which words required transliteration. Unless otherwise noted, I use modern place-names and give the dates in the Common Era calendar.

List of Abbreviations

References correspond to page numbers in the specified edition unless otherwise noted.

AE	Gülşehri, *Karamat-i Akhi Avran*
APZ	ʿĀşıkpaşazāde, *Tavarikh-i Al-i Osman* (references correspond to chapter [*bāb*] numbers)
AQ	Aqsarāyī, *Musamarat al-Akhbar*
AU	al-ʿUmarī, *Masalik al-Absar fi Mamalik al-Amsar*
BR	Astarābadī, *Bazm u Razm*
DN	Enverī, *Dustur-nama*
GN	ʿĀşıkpaşa, *Gharib-nama*
IB	Ibn Baṭṭūṭa, *Rihla*
IN	Ahmedī, *Iskandar-nama* (references correspond to line numbers)
MA	Aflākī, *Manaqib al-ʿArifin* (references correspond to Yazıcı's paragraph numbering)
MQ	Elvan Çelebi, *Manaqib al-Qudsiyya fi Manasib al-Unsiyya* (references correspond to line numbers)
QN	Kay Kāʾus b. Iskandar, *Qabus-nama* translations
RS	Sipahsālār, *Risāla*
SH	ʿAbd al-Karīm b. Shaykh Mūsa, *Maqalat-i Sayyid Harun* (references are given using the MS folio number, as provided by Kurnaz)
VN	*Vilayat-nama-yi Haji Baktash Veli* (references are given to the folio in the facsimile at the end of the 1995 edition, which is different from the one appearing in the 1958 edition)
WQ	*Waqfiyya* (the letters *WQ* are followed by a reference number corresponding to the table located in the bibliography)

YED Yûnus Emre, *Divan* (references correspond to the poem number, followed by the line number, in Tatcı's edition)
YER Yûnus Emre, *Risalah al-Nushiyyah* (references correspond to the line number, as given in Tatcı's edition)

Foodways and Daily Life in Medieval Anatolia

Introduction

Bir anda bütün dünyam karardı
Bu sesle sokaklar yankılandı
Domates biber patlıcan.

[At once my whole world turned to darkness
The streets echoed with this sound:
Tomato! Pepper! Eggplant!]

BARIŞ MANÇO, "DOMATES BIBER PATLICAN"

The history of Turkish reggae is a short and uneventful one. In fact, for a long time casual observers of Turkish popular music like myself could name only one song fitting the description, "Domates biber patlıcan" (Tomato, pepper, eggplant), by the late Barış Manço.

To the distracted listener, "Domates biber patlıcan" gives off the vibe of a cheerful song about vegetables, one that *Sesame Street* would use to teach toddlers the intricacies of the produce section at their local supermarket. Yet paying more attention to the lyrics, one discovers behind the lively tune (and the vegetables) a heart-wrenching story, that of a hopelessly shy man who finally musters the courage to confess his love to the woman of his dreams only to be interrupted, as he is about to utter the most important words of his life, by the calls of a produce seller on the street: "Tomato! Pepper! Eggplant!" Long after that tragic moment when, we are left to assume, the appeal of fresh vegetables annihilated the promise of marital bliss, the only thought keeping him alive is the hope of one day holding her in his arms. As the song fades out, all we hear are the echoes of the fateful street seller's calls: "Tomato! Pepper! Eggplant!"

Just as "Domates biber patlıcan" tells about more than vegetables, this book tells about more than food. It offers an investigation of the subjective experience, the "texture of daily life," of late-medieval Anatolians and, through this, of their worldviews. Food, in short, deserves its place in the title of this book because it is at the center of a much broader inquiry, in the same way that conductors deserve mention on the program of symphonic concerts in which they will not be heard.

OBJECTIVES

This book has four main objectives. At the most basic level, it offers a picture of daily life in fourteenth-century Anatolia. Beyond this narrow function, it is also meant to serve as a methodological model, using food as an organizing principle to present the general picture of a society. Third, it is also meant to show how a deep reading of narrative sources, together with archaeological data, can serve as the basis for social history in the absence of archival material. Finally, it raises some questions about our own cultural relationship with food by contrasting contemporary practice with an intensely foreign culture in a way that makes this book relevant and, I hope, interesting to readers outside academia.

The first objective of this book is to establish a "baseline," a general picture of society in the late-medieval Anatolian context, to serve as a frame of reference for studies whose subjects are more narrowly focused. The fourteenth century was a pivotal moment in the history of a region that includes most of the Middle East and eastern Europe. It saw the waning of Mongol power, which had profoundly reshaped the geography and political culture of the Muslim world. Perhaps more important, the fourteenth century also saw the realm of the last "Roman" rulers, the Byzantine emperors, slip into the hands of the Ottoman family. This moment is therefore located at the juncture of two millennia of imperial history.[1] Research on the social history of that period has tended to concentrate on a limited list of social organizations such as *ahi*-led groups, *gazi* volunteers, and Sufi orders. All of these presented unique configurations in late-medieval Anatolia, and I do not mean to deny the relevance of their study. For example, the debate around *ahi*-led groups, which were social structures that incorporated characteristics of both labor and religious organizations, has brought about a healthy questioning of the all too easily borrowed concepts of "religious order" and "craftsmen's guild." Likewise, a long-standing debate on the role of *gazis*, religious volunteers whose military operations greatly benefited the expansion of the young Ottoman state, has raised important questions on the relationship between religious heterodoxy, motivations for holy war, and the peculiarities of a frontier setting. Yet it remains difficult to understand a social institution without knowing much about the society in which it arose, from which it received its main influences, and, sometimes, to which it reacted. It is, after all, perfectly worthwhile to study the hippie movement or McCarthyism, but one cannot expect to gain much understanding of these phenomena without relating them to the broader post–World War II social developments in the United States. Providing a broader context is bound to bring insight not only to the discussions I just mentioned, but also to our understanding of the ways in which the early Ottomans turned from a sheepherding family to masters of most of the Balkans within a few generations. This book, in short, offers a new starting point for those studying the social and cultural context from which the Ottoman Empire arose.

My second objective is to show how one can use food as the organizing principle in painting the picture of an entire society. Food is more than the edibles we put into our mouths. It is a "total social fact," following the terminology of Marcel Mauss, that is, a single element that brings together virtually all aspects of human life, even those that at first glance seem unrelated to each other. As a topic, food can organize a survey of the entire experience of daily life within a culture ("daily life" being defined as the sum of all the practices and elements of the worldview that members of the middle and lower classes would have described as ordinary and usual). Thus, food's production, agriculture, constitutes the primary occupation of the great majority of the population in the period I study here and lets us, for instance, explore the ways in which the daily routine of a gardener differs from that of a pastoralist nomad. Food's exchange both establishes and reflects networks of power and information over the land and between groups of people, allowing us to examine the texture and frequency of the interactions between a villager and the tax collector, or any other representative of the state. The consumption of food typically follows time-honored rules of behavior, affording us a glimpse into worldviews that would otherwise remain unvocalized—for example, through the meaning ascribed to seating arrangements in a banquet. Furthermore, food and food-related practices are often endowed with value and meanings that reflect religion as it is practiced, rather than the official prescriptions of theological treatises—for instance, marking those engaged in extreme fasting with a social identity unlike any other. The following chapters will therefore strive to present food as a rare element that can bring together a large swath of the subjective experience of daily life in a given period.

Third, this book also presents a method of investigation into the social history of a period where archival material is essentially nonexistent. The research presented here relies first and foremost on deep textual analysis of a wide array of narrative texts (primarily hagiographies), as well as a study of endowment deeds and archaeology. I will discuss the nature of these sources and the method I employ to approach them in greater detail later in this introduction and in the appendix. For the time being, however, I simply want to emphasize that this material does not share the systematic, serial organization of the archival documents on which most social historians rely when researching later periods in the Ottoman Empire or other times and places.

Finally, at a more abstract level but also closer to the reasons that made me a historian in the first place, the fourth and final objective of this book is to present historiography as an intercultural endeavor. I wish, in other words, to look into the worldviews that prevailed in a society as culturally distant as can be from my own, a land unreached by even the faintest echo of cultural influences that we today deem universal, from movable type to popular sovereignty. Learning about alternative perceptions and conceptions of the world, in turn, allows for a rich infusion of perspective in our own worldviews. This explains (and, I hope, justifies) the many references, examples, and comparisons to our contemporary world that are scattered about the following chapters.

FOURTEENTH-CENTURY CENTRAL ANATOLIA

As I pointed out above, the period discussed here is interesting in its own right, in no small part because it saw the birth of a state that would lead the destinies of a good part of the Middle East and eastern Europe all the way down to World War I. So what do we talk about when we talk about fourteenth-century central Anatolia?

The best way to give a feel of central Anatolia's appearance might be through its colors, a palette ranging from yellow to gray, with short-lived patches of green at the beginning of the summer and a white blanket of snow lasting for most of the winter. The land is dry but not barren, with gentle slopes curving up into rocky spines—the only areas truly inhospitable to cereal cultivation.[2] Rivers are few and tend to follow deeply eroded beds. Summer rain pours down in short and infrequent bursts. Trees never seem to gather in large-enough numbers to deserve the title of forest.

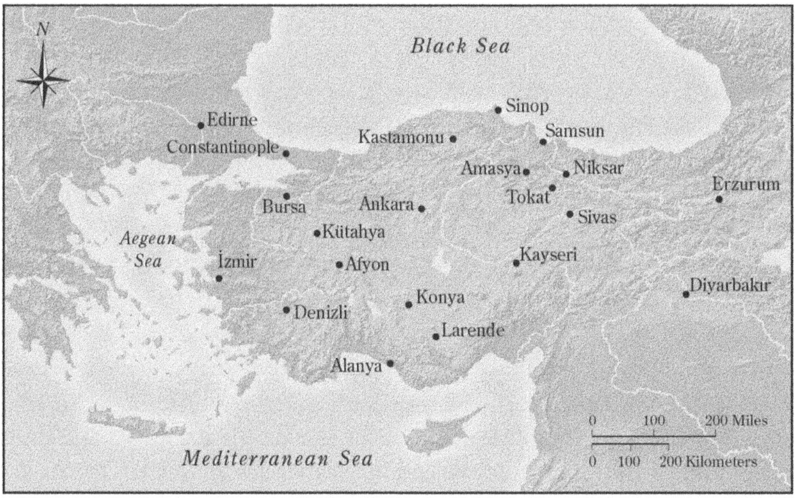

Medieval Anatolia

Although not entirely flat, the plateau that is central Anatolia (which I roughly define as extending from Kütahya to Sivas and from Larende—today's Karaman—to Kastamonu) is surrounded by land more mountainous than itself. To the north, its edge is pleated to form the southern half of the Pontic range, whose northern slopes catch most of the Black Sea rain before it can make its way inland. To the west, it melts into increasingly well-watered valleys, ultimately becoming the horticultural heaven that is the Aegean coast. To the south, it quickly rises into the Taurus range, through which Anatolia shoulders the Mediterranean. To the east, valleys become deeper and mountains higher, as if to channel those traveling from the Caucasus and Iran into narrow highways. All of these "sharp edges" create a dramatic ecological contrast with the surrounding coastal regions, whose direct consequences will become obvious as we discuss the political evolution of the region throughout the Middle Ages.

Impressionistic evidence concerning the identity of the people who lived in Anatolia in the fourteenth century strongly suggests a heterogeneous ethnocultural makeup that, in its simplest form, can be divided in two on the basis of origins. The first category, the locals, had its roots in the numerous Anatolian peoples one can trace back to antiquity (such as Isaurians and Cappadocians), together with a few groups that Byzantine authorities had forcefully settled in the region. By the time the Byzantines no longer ruled over central Anatolia, in 1071, these populations had been undergoing a millennium-long and still partially incomplete process of assimilation into a Greek-speaking, Christian mainstream. Perhaps as diverse as the first, the people of the second category were descendants of immigrants who came to Anatolia from various regions of central Asia and Iran in successive waves between the late tenth and the thirteenth centuries. Mostly nomads, these newcomers spoke a number of Turkic (and, to a lesser extent, Mongolian, Persian, and Kurdish) dialects, and most can be described as Muslim. The religious map was as fragmented as the ethnolinguistic one, with a myriad of groups claiming to follow "real Christianity" and "real Islam"—and a few more who did not even try.

The sources I use refer to a number of groups (using name tags such as Rūm, Armenians, Jews, Turks, and Tatars), and they do suggest that Persian was the common language among the educated urban elite, itself overwhelmingly Muslim. However, how these groups interacted on a daily basis is less obvious. Regional differences, the interplay between various levels of identity (religious, linguistic, ethnic, economic), and the importance of the "cultural survivals" probably still attested to the multiplicity of backgrounds that had come together to form this society. In other words, although it is clear that late-medieval central Anatolians were fully aware that their neighbors had languages, accents, religious practices, and other cultural traits different from their own, we remain in the dark concerning the particular ways in which they dealt with these differences, both in terms of mental classification and in terms of quality of interaction.

It seems reasonable to estimate the population of fourteenth-century Anatolia as a whole (including the coastal areas, which fall outside the scope of this book) at somewhere between five and ten million people.[3] Perhaps more striking for the modern reader, and certainly more important for the analyses I put forward in the following chapters, was the size of the cities, which seldom exceeded ten thousand inhabitants; the largest ones probably had a population of thirty-five thousand or so.[4] The relative anonymity that most readers of this book enjoy as they live in cities of several hundred thousands or even millions of inhabitants, in other words, was simply absent from daily life.

From a political perspective, the fourteenth century in Anatolia can be termed the "age of the *beylik*s," or emirates—regional polities that divided the land between themselves for most of the century. At a superficial level, the *beylik*s seem to constitute a fragmented episode contrasting with a succession of unified rules over Anatolia: Byzantine until the end of the eleventh century, Seljuk from the late eleventh century, and then Ilkhanid Mongol for the second half of the thirteenth century. As Ilkhanid rule imploded, local *beylik*s arose to fill the political void, and it is only at the end of the fourteenth century that one of these *beyliks*, that of the Ottomans, began to reunify Anatolia through conquest.[5]

Although it corresponds to the typical timeline offered when presenting the transition from Byzantine to Ottoman times, this chronological sketch is an oversimplification at best, and in many respects wholly inaccurate. It obscures the role of lesser-known and ultimately unsuccessful polities that coexisted and sometimes rivaled those empires, such as the Danishmendids in the eleventh century. It also gives the wrong impression of "centralized" political power when most rulers could in fact not aspire to much more than loose and indirect control over the local authorities in cities where they did not reside. In many instances, the difference between "overlord" and "rival neighbor" was in fact unclear even to those it involved—or the subject of bloody disagreement.

This sketch also misleads by giving the impression of an evolution that unfolded evenly over Anatolia as a whole, whereas the rise of the *beyliks* to the rank of independent polities took place at an irregular pace and spans several decades, from the late thirteenth to the early fourteenth centuries. The eastern half of central Anatolia clung to the fiction of central imperial authority for more than half of the fourteenth century, long after the *beyliks* located on the Aegean coast, acting as de facto independent units, had amassed unparalleled riches and glory through war and commerce.

From the longer-term social perspective of this book, the main consequence of this political evolution is the fundamentally different social dynamics between the central plateau and coastal areas. The latter remained under Byzantine rule (and thus in close cultural and economic relation to Constantinople) for much longer than central Anatolia, in some cases well into the period discussed here. Most of central Anatolia, on the other hand, had been under the influence of Muslim institutions and subject to massive immigration for more than two centuries, since the second half of the eleventh century.

Such longer history of social and political integration resulted in a much more stable (though not homogenous) social makeup in central Anatolia than on the coasts. In other words, no matter if a recipe or agricultural sheep-rearing technique made its way into fourteenth-century central Anatolia through the mother-to-daughter teachings within an Armenian family of Sivas or on the back of a horse arriving from central Asia, it was more likely to be familiar to all those present and remain unmodified throughout the fourteenth century on the central Anatolian plateau than in the rapidly changing coastal regions. Given the kind of snapshot this book intends to offer, and given the limited source material available to serve as its basis, the relatively stable sociocultural background this entails is simply invaluable.

That being said, "fourteenth-century central Anatolia," as it appears in this book, should be understood as a guideline in the selection of the sources rather than a sharply defined geographical and chronological scope. This is because most of the information available cannot be reliably linked to a particular time or place, for two main reasons: the passages I use are often geographically or chronologically unspecific (or both), and the written accounts we have are often the last link in an otherwise oral chain of transmission. I therefore include the texts that, through the setting of their subject matter or the background of their authors, were likely to contain material reflecting life in fourteenth-century central Anatolia.

I also rarely identify an element of information with a specific city or decade within this broader framework. I obviously do not mean to suggest that the society I describe was entirely unchanging and homogeneous. But given that many of my conclusions are based on the comparison of an extremely limited number of passages, to give too much importance to a handful of chronological hints would have resulted in suggesting a host of (often contradictory) historical trends where there may have been differences of perspective between only two or three authors. As a result, I have strived as much as possible to settle on conclusions that best account for all variations between the various sources I use.

SCHOLARSHIP

This book is an attempt at opening up a hitherto disregarded realm of considerations, and not a response or contribution to a preexisting historiographical debate. A widespread belief that pre-Ottoman Anatolia offers historians limited source material has kept scholars of social history away from the Anatolian fourteenth century. Such a characterization is, of course, all relative (scholars of the Bronze Age would dream of the written sources I browsed through as part of this research project), but it is true that the dozen or so narrative sources and the few dozen endowment deeds (*waqfiyyas*) surviving from fourteenth-century Anatolia create a tougher set of challenges than those facing historians who can draw from millions of archival documents in their work on later Ottoman centuries. I will discuss the primary sources I used in the next section and present each one of them individually, its unique strengths and weaknesses, in the appendix.

Most historians who have worked on the period have concentrated on the twenty-odd *beylik*s that coexisted at the time,[6] especially the one that was to become the Ottoman Empire. In the latter case, their discussions have dwelled at length on the so-called *gazi* debate, concerning the motivations (religious, materialistic, or both) of a group of volunteer soldiers who seem to have played a central part in the early expansion of the Ottomans.[7]

As far as social history is concerned, it is more accurate to talk of a handful of isolated (though sometimes very good) studies than of a significant body of literature. Perhaps the broadest in scope among them is a major opus on the Turkification and Islamization of Anatolia from Byzantine to Ottoman times.[8] One can also find a few studies of social phenomena such as religious organizations,[9] the *ahi*-led groups,[10] and nomadism.[11] In addition, a number of pieces on indirectly related subjects also contain references to social history.[12] Yet I could find only one article, based on a single source, that even remotely resembles an attempt at describing daily life during that period.[13] This book, in short, appears in a very dry historiographical landscape.

SOURCES

Yet it *is* possible to produce meaningful research on fourteenth-century Anatolian society, with the help of some creative questions and tools of source criticism. In order to do so, one must, however, cast a wide net, essentially covering all the original source material produced in late-medieval Anatolia, both textual and nontextual.

Concretely, this material falls in three broad categories. The first and substantively most important category is that of narrative texts. Among these, chronicles are the oldest companions of medievalists, but hagiographies and other religious texts have consistently yielded the wealthiest harvest of details about daily life. The second category is that of the *waqfiyya*s, the foundation documents for endowments (*waqf*s) that funded pious and charitable institutions ranging from mosques to soup kitchens. Along the way, these documents describe not just the directives on how these resources should be used (which sometimes include food distribution), but also the specific origins of the endowment's revenues, typically agricultural land. *Waqfiyya*s were drawn up by private individuals rather than the state and show no trace of a sequential or systematic character, but their relatively formulaic format does make them the closest equivalent to "archival documents" that fourteenth-century Anatolia has to offer. The third and final category is composed of archaeological studies. These give us insight into a wide array of themes that go from specific animal productions to cooking techniques.[14]

Covering this broad pool of sources in a single study is more realistic than it may seem. Not counting the numerous translations of earlier works (primarily to Turkish, a new literary language at the time), a dozen or so extant narrative texts can be considered "original products" of this time and place. Likewise, copies of about three dozen of the (no doubt much more numerous) *waqfiyya*s that were drawn up during this period survive to this day. As for archaeology, Anatolia of course has a long history of excavations; one need recall only the infamous work on Troy by Heinrich Schliemann, in the late nineteenth century. Although these excavators used to approach medieval layers as rubbish to be discarded on the way to "the good stuff" (mainly the Hellenistic layers), such habits are a thing of the past. As excavation methods have become more systematic, massive amounts of medieval archaeological material have accumulated in university vaults. A small but growing number of scholars have begun to specialize in the analysis of this material, yielding extremely important results that historians have yet to fully acknowledge. Since my own expertise makes me dependent on the publications of these scholars, and because only a modest proportion of the raw material has been analyzed at this time, here again the volume of data remains manageable. A relatively exhaustive approach to the source material is, therefore, a realistic ambition for this project.

Of course, not all of these sources provided the same volume or type of usable contents. This uneven distribution of information actually strengthens the method used here, as sources complement each other, allowing me to cover a broader array of topics than studies based on a single type of source. For example, some texts carry greater authority when describing agricultural productions, while others tell us more reliably about the seating arrangements at a ruler's banquet. I will address these questions in much greater detail in the appendix, which presents and evaluates each source in detail.

I should add that none of these sources was specifically intended by its author to be "about food." Some texts exist that specifically address the topic of food, but they were produced outside the time and place that this book covers, and geographical and chronological relevance is extremely important when talking about food and society. Different areas mean different ecological conditions, so the plants and animals available to be eaten vary widely from place to place. Likewise, the social and cultural landscape of Anatolia changed dramatically between the Byzantine and Ottoman periods, and it would be foolish to assume that food practices did not change as well. Still, because methodological questions are of particular interest to this study, it is worth spending some time surveying the kind of thematically relevant texts that neighboring times and places produced.

Cookbooks are the most obvious type of food-related sources, and they were not completely absent in the Middle Ages. Thus, the first known Ottoman cookbook, the fifteenth-century work of one Meḥmed b. Maḥmūd Shirvānī, is in fact the Turkish translation of a thirteenth-century Abbasid (i.e., Iraqi) Arabic-language cookbook to which the translator seems to have added a number of recipes of his own.[15] One could also mention a half-dozen Abbasid cookbooks from between the tenth and thirteenth centuries,[16] as well as the two Safavid cookbooks (sixteenth and early seventeenth centuries) published by Iraj Afshar, once again composed in geographical settings (respectively, Iraq and Iran) that fall outside the scope of this study.[17] Research on later periods would have to jump all the way down to the nineteenth century, when the printing of cookbooks rather suddenly became a regular occurrence in the Ottoman Empire.[18]

Medical literature also has some bearing on food-related practices and beliefs, and fourteenth-century Anatolia did in fact produce a number of medical treatises. However, it would have been difficult to integrate them in this research project. For one, many of these works are adaptations of Arabic and Persian originals, usually translated into Turkish. Furthermore, those that can be considered to be "original texts" deserve this status not so much by virtue of being entirely original works, but because they are the result of a more extensive process of adaptation, as they are all very much part of a long tradition of medical thought that can be traced back to ancient Greece. The degree and nature of this adaptation to local conditions are certainly significant and meaningful in themselves, but can be identified only by someone who already possesses a thorough knowledge of the history of the medical discourse. I have deemed it preferable to concentrate my efforts on other categories of sources, although there is no doubt that late-medieval Anatolian history would greatly benefit from such a survey by a specialist of medical history.[19]

Dictionaries open another, if slightly trickier, path to knowledge about food. The first Turkish (to Arabic) dictionary, the famed *Diwan Lughat al-Turk*, does in fact contain relevant food-related material. Once again, however, its chronological location (the eleventh century) and geographical associations (it was written in Baghdad by a scholar for whom Turkic peoples had much to do with central Asia and nothing at all with Anatolia) create the same problems as would be caused by using a dictionary from the Elizabethan period to discuss nineteenth-century American society. In other words, while a significant portion of the vocabulary the author includes was still current in fourteenth-century central Anatolia, it is far from obvious that the same words still meant the same thing after three centuries and a migration of thousands of miles. The shifting meaning of words is a constant problem, but in this case the risk of falsely assuming the relevance of (even carefully selected) data from the *Diwan* was simply too high.

In other contexts, archival documents provide a natural gateway to a wide array of data on social history. When discussing food in particular, we can, for example, think of reports of taxes collected on food production and exchanges, just to name the most obvious. Yet as far as the fourteenth century is concerned, no body of state archival documents remains in existence. This situation primarily derives from political history: the fourteenth century represents a period of reconstruction for administrative structures in Anatolia, after the institutions of the Seljuk and Ilkhanid Empires had collapsed in the thirteenth century. The states that took over (*beylik*s, or emirates), including the Ottoman one, were at this stage rather diminutive in scale and probably organized in large part on the basis of tribal principles, two factors contributing to a limited production of archival documents. Whatever state records may have existed were in any case lost sometime during the Ottoman conquest of most of these *beylik*s in the late fourteenth and early fifteenth centuries or during the various transfers of the Ottoman capital until the mid-fifteenth century.[20]

Finally, unusual texts appear here and there that squarely address the relationship between food and social or cultural issues. Examples show up in contexts neighboring the scope of this book, though in all cases they involve equally unique reasons that would have made their use here questionable. There is, for example, a short treatise written in 1405 by Maqrīzī on the topic of famines in Egypt,[21] but when Maqrīzī denounces the Egyptian rulers' attitudes in times of food scarcity, he tells us little about Anatolian history, especially if we consider the importance he gives to the Nile's influence on such scarcity. Likewise, Muṣṭafā ʿĀlī's *Mawaʾid al-Nafaʾis fi Qawaʾid al-Majalis*, a treatise devoting much attention to banquets at the Ottoman court, is thematically relevant to this study, but its chronological location (the sixteenth century) reflects traditions that in large part developed well after the period covered here.[22]

METHODOLOGY

Any study of the life experiences of late-medieval Anatolian peasants or craftsmen needs to be indirect, insofar as they left no testimony for us to dissect. All the written sources that remain from the period originate, in one way or another, with the learned elite. In this book, it is therefore by reconstructing the world surrounding them (the "texture" of their daily life) that I try to extrapolate on their worldviews. Just like any historical scholarship, albeit to a higher degree, the conclusions presented in this book are therefore hypothetical in nature.

In the following pages, I will present both the methodological challenges that this project brings about and the choices I made in order to overcome them. These challenges fall into three broad categories: the identification of ordinary life in sources that explicitly concentrate on extraordinary characters and occurrences, source criticism taking into account the context of composition, and the identification of purely literary influences.

The Typical and the Exceptional

In a field where research is still largely driven toward outstanding historical events and exceptional processes (e.g., the early Ottoman expansion), interest in the "typical" and the "ordinary" may be one of the defining features of this study. Yet in late-medieval Anatolia, just like today, things that are most obvious are also the least likely to be committed to paper. For example, one would be hard-pressed to find, in the entire body of modern literary fiction, a single description of a toothbrush that would make sense to someone who has never seen this object, precisely *because* any potential reader assumedly knows what a toothbrush looks like. The same logic prevailed in the fourteenth century: Why describe a typical meal? After all, everybody experiences it on a daily basis. This challenge is in fact even greater in medieval sources, whose narrative-driven style devotes little attention to descriptions.

This is a significant obstacle, but one that we can bypass by reading textual sources "against the grain." Let us take the example of one episode found in the *Manaqib al-ʿArifin*: After the spiritual master Mavlānā Jalāl al-Dīn Rūmī passes away, a cat that had previously lived in his house begins fasting and starves itself to death. Rūmī's daughter then takes it upon herself to put the cat's corpse in a shroud, bury it near her father's mausoleum, and distribute *ḥalwāʾ* to Rūmī's other disciples.[23]

Whether this mourning cat ever existed—or experienced spiritual distress—may be of some importance for Rūmī's followers. But for the purposes of this study, the anecdote is most interesting because the depiction of a cat that is treated like a human being, as unusual as it may be, constitutes a unique opportunity to infer how a human being would be treated. Given that the narrative here tries to emphasize the high respect given to this cat, the passage therefore suggests that bodies of the deceased were shrouded and buried and that *ḥalwāʾ* was offered at funerals.[24]

Every assertion I present in this book is based on a "compatibility check" between all relevant passages I could find. Of course, the story of Rūmī's cat is an isolated episode. But some observations offer a better ground for generalization than others, and one way to flesh out the strongest hypothesis is to consider as wide an array of evidence as possible. Thus, in this particular case, another passage of the same source presents a religious master who orders *ḥalwāʾ* to be prepared for a man who just died.[25] Although they contain no hard proof that this was a generalized practice, it is the compatibility between these two passages that strengthens the idea of an association between funerals and the consumption of *ḥalwāʾ*.

Obviously, unlike the case presented here, some hypotheses turn out to be incompatible with other passages. In such cases, we can infer that the hypothesis relies on a spurious (or overextended) interpretation of the passage, a divergence in the outlook or circumstances of the authors involved (when incompatible passages come from different sources), or even cases where linguistic quirks can make the hypothesis simultaneously true and false (such as claiming that the verb *to drink*, in modern English, entails the consumption of alcohol).

As the following chapters make abundantly clear, the resulting picture leaves plenty of room for debate and imprecision. Yet it does also bring about a broad picture of daily life practices, the "typical" fabric of ordinary people's experiences. Furthermore, an entire supplemental layer of evidence can be added when we integrate the context of composition into our discussion of sources.

Context of Composition

When approaching textual evidence, we must also take into account the context in which a given source was written. This not only increases the degree of reliability of our conclusions, but also lets us reach a deeper level whence to extract information. More specifically, paying attention to the context of textual production entails four components: identifying the intended audience, approaching orally transmitted texts as evolving organisms, remaining particularly critical of passages set in "olden times," and avoiding the all too common temptation to conflate "traditional" and "medieval" practices.

Any process of source criticism and analysis can be made much more efficient by taking into account intended audience. Many hints exist that suggest the identity of the people whom the author intended to reach.[26] For example, in the context studied here, the choice of language is a good indicator: whereas Persian was the preferred language of written communication among the cultural elite, the authors who produced the first examples of written Turkish language in Anatolia explicitly mention that they were aiming for a broader (and assumedly less educated) audience. With the exception of Ibn Baṭṭūṭa and al-ʿUmarī, furthermore, the only Arabic texts appearing in this pool of sources are the *waqfiyyas*, technical documents meant to be read by people trained in Islamic law. It is also clear that chronicles, so often dedicated to the ruler himself, were intended for an audience well acquainted with courtly settings, that Enverī imagined his *Dustur-nama* to be consumed by soldiers and sailors (just like those from whom he heard the stories he used in writing it), and that ʿĀşıkpaşa did not target an audience with advanced religious education with his *Gharib-nama*.

Making educated guesses concerning the intended audiences for each source is thus possible, and it provides us with one further tool to evaluate the reliability of any given piece of information. The basic principle I have followed here is simply that a source will generally be most reliable when mentioning elements with which the intended audience was best acquainted. For example, if contradictory data concerning agricultural techniques were to appear in the *Manaqib al-ʿArifin* and the *Vilayat-nama*, the latter would likely be more accurate, insofar as peasants probably made up a significant portion of its intended audience, whereas they were—at best—a marginal minority among those who received the *Manaqib*.

The second task related to compositional context is to take into account the effects of oral transmission when we approach a text. After all, an oral text is in many ways an evolving organism whose life, lasting longer than the consciousness of any single individual transmitter, sometimes spanned several centuries before it reached the fossilized, written form in which we can now access it. The texts I use thus include, for example, the *Manaqib al-ʿArifin* (describing thirteenth-century events, but written in the fourteenth century) and the *Dustur-nama-yi Anvari* (describing fourteenth-century events, but written more than a century later). All these texts reflect the experience of the fourteenth century, but relate to it in different ways, and we must take into account the habit of oral transmitters—storytellers—to embellish and modify the details of the stories they tell. For this reason, I have ascribed a higher level of reliability to the core narrative elements (bits that need to be part of the story in order for it to make sense at all) from anecdotes set in the fourteenth century but committed to paper later on and to textural elements (details that can be readily modified without affecting the meaning of the story) in passages set in earlier centuries but written in the fourteenth. All of this, to be sure, is a matter of degree, but the importance of the "life story" of a text is the main reason that pushed me to provide detail on the pedigree of each of my sources in the appendix.

The third task, to remain particularly critical of stories set in "olden times," is in some ways an extreme version of the previous. Medieval texts frequently contain material borrowed from other sources, whether they acknowledge it or not. Even a casual reading uncovers a number of passages clearly set in a different time frame from that of the main narrative. This includes, for example, Rūmī's narration of the story of two kings "in past times" (*dar zamān-i māżī*),[27] but also episodes from the life of the prophet Muhammad and even the biographical sketches of some of the parents and grandparents of the saints celebrated in hagiographies. In many cases, these passages are written in a different, rather sketchy, tone that offers even less detail than the main narrative. But whether this is the case or not, the fact remains that they partly originate from a sociocultural context independent from that of the source as a whole (drawing from an older literary or religious tradition, or even from memories obtained from too long a string of informers). As it turns out, most of these passages contain very little information of relevance for the present study. In cases where they do, I have remained extremely critical in my reading, and in any case made sure to indicate the lower degree of reliability of the statements I make on the basis of these passages.

Finally, it is imperative that sources describing a medieval society actually originate from the Middle Ages. As obvious as it may sound, this rule is often overlooked on the basis of the all too common (and misguided) binary construct opposing "the modern" (educated, urban, technologically advanced, morally liberal) and "the traditional" (ignorant, rural, primitive, conservative), with the implication that the latter barely changed from the Middle Ages to the advent of mechanized agriculture. But historical evolution is not the private preserve of the urban, the rich, and the famous, and we should not confuse our inability or unwillingness to see change take place in the countryside for an actual absence, at least from the *longue durée*. For this reason, a fundamental methodological principle of this study has been to avoid using nineteenth- or early-twentieth-century ethnological observations as core source material. After all, no living human being, Turkish or otherwise, has memories of a grandmother born in the fourteenth century. So even if the following pages contain references to contemporary or near-contemporary observations, they typically serve as points of contrast to my descriptions of the daily life of fourteenth-century Anatolians.

Literary Concerns

Before closing this discussion of methodology, we should address a number of issues related to the literary character of the core source material for this study. After all, literary rules and usage contribute to shaping the way in which food appears in these texts. This is visible in the choice of vocabulary, of course, but also in the metaphorical uses of food, sometimes taking the shape of literary motifs.

First, we should remember that the food-related lexicon (the words in use and the meanings they carry) is one that does change over time. In the absence of sufficient historical studies on the topic, the available dictionaries simply cannot account for these variations in a satisfactory fashion.[28] What remains, then, is to look for hints of definition in the passages that use a given word and approach such semantic quests as an integral part of the set of questions raised in this study.[29]

Furthermore, we need to keep in mind that a multitude of factors influence vocabulary choices, from the aesthetics of rhyming prose to religious metaphors. Of particular concern for this study, because they can be mistaken for reflections of daily life practices, are set literary motifs, cases where a food reference is used as a short and conventional metaphor.[30] Such literary uses do not contribute to the purposes of this study. After all, once an expression becomes common enough, it is used at the outcome of a cognitive process in which the original image receives little if any attention at all, short-circuited, as it were, by force of habit. For example, the expression "straight from the horse's mouth" may be quite striking for those encountering it for the first time, but upon hearing it most native English speakers register its abstract meaning without ever conjuring the vivid image of a horse. Such expressions are very often based on archaic practices or uses of a word, growing independent from their original meaning to the point that many people will use an expression without even being cognizant of its original meaning.

Let us, for example, examine the passage where Gülşehrī states, at the beginning of his *Karamat-i Akhi Avran*, "Like the parrot, let us eat honey and sugar" (Tuti gibi şehd ü sükker [*sic*] yiyelüm).[31] Besides the fact that the Arabic word *şehd* (or *shahd*) is a rather unusual one for honey (the more common being *ʿasal* in Arabic and Persian and *bal* in Turkish), one should know that the parrot eating sugar is a common literary motif in Persian literature. Using this passage to lay any claim that honey and sugar were produced for parrot consumption in late-medieval Anatolia would thus be entirely off the mark. I have clearly identified passages that might be less reliable because they fall in this category.

Spotting literary motifs is not always that easy. Take, for example, Ibn Baṭṭūṭa's descriptions of Anatolian cities. At first glance, any one of these instances appears to be the short depiction of what he had witnessed during his visit. Yet putting all of his descriptions side by side, one notices suspiciously repetitive comments and formulations, in which fruits,[32] gardens,[33] and water provisioning[34] play the part of literary instruments used to praise a city or region. That a number of these agricultural elements were indeed present and visible in the cities he visited is beyond any reasonable doubt. Yet the literary concerns that seem to have governed Ibn Baṭṭūṭa's thoughts as he was telling of his visit to Anatolia should make us wary of taking his depictions too literally and assuming, as many have done, that he correctly describes every individual city as it was when he visited it.

Considering each source as a whole rather than examining individual passages in isolation, though not foolproof, is the best way to prevent the most obvious mistakes. The reader should therefore keep this caveat in mind before pointing out the absence of too literal an interpretation of certain passages.

THE BREAKDOWN

As I stated earlier, food provides not only a sampling device for the evidence on daily life, but also a way to organize the presentation of the findings derived from this evidence. A broad categorization of the many roles that food plays in human life thus provides the chapter breakdown for this book.

The investigation begins in chapter 1, devoted to the production phase of the food cycle. This chapter will be divided into three main sections: gardens, field cultures, and animal productions. In each of these, I will pay particular attention to agriculture as a professional activity, the peculiarities of life in the countryside, and the relationship that people entertained with the land. This survey will show that peasants had a much higher degree of agency and control over their lives than we might expect.

Chapter 2 will approach food as the object of exchanges, in two broadly defined categories of cases. The first is commercial exchanges, including, of course, local markets and long-distance trade, but also the particular instances of water distribution and grain milling. The second category will include cases in which food acts as a point of contact between the population and state institutions through taxes, army logistics, and plunder. Through these discussions, we will see that, as much as the general population was excluded from the political decision-making process, it nevertheless very much felt the effects of this process, more often than not in fairly painful ways.

Chapter 3 will address the issue that most readily comes to mind when mentioning the title of this book, food consumption. This chapter, the most substantial in this study, will cover a large number of issues that include the very act of eating, of course, as well as the social practices surrounding the meal. But it will also discuss the steps leading to that moment (from food acquisition to cooking and service), survey the various foods that appear in the sources, and investigate a number of more abstract concepts that relate to the central theme of the chapter, such as charity, taste, health, and mind-altering substances. Most apparent among the multiple conclusions of this survey will be the rigidity of the social hierarchy that prevailed in the region.

Chapter 4 will look at the intersection between food and religion. It will do so by surveying religious rituals that involved food, among which the best documented is the practice of fasting, and canonical festivals as ways to determine the extent to which formal Islam was integrated into daily life. This chapter will also include a discussion of the mental associations that existed between certain food items and religious concepts, paying particular attention to the question of religious identity. Beyond the straightforward division of the population between roughly equal numbers of Muslims and Christians, we will see that painting a picture of the religious landscape requires a lot of nuance to fully convey the diversity of experiences in late-medieval Anatolia.

The general conclusion will consist first and foremost in an evaluation of the extent to which this book *did* and *could* shed light on the daily life and worldviews of late-medieval central Anatolians. In order to do so, it will compare the results of this investigation with the medium that might offer the most efficient means to communicate a subjective experience: literature.

In the appendix, the reader will find a detailed discussion of the origin, nature, contents, and limitations of the sources used in this study: religious texts, chronicles, and geographical and other narrative works, as well as endowment deeds (*waqfiyya*s) and archaeological publications. The method I employ in my analysis makes a detailed discussion of the source material necessary: many of the statements that form the core of this book rely heavily on considerations pertaining to the perspective of the authors of the various texts and to their intended audiences. It would, in short, be impossible for the reader to judge the quality of this research without being presented with an extensive discussion of each one of the texts I have used and how I approached it.

(ONE)

Food Production

In one of the most vivid passages of the *Manaqib al-ʿArifin*, Rūmī's famed friend and master, Shams Tabrīzī, uses a country road as a metaphor for the religious life. "If you go on the road of faith," he says, "often you come to no village and no caravanserai, you see no sign, the sound of neither dog nor rooster comes to your ear. Often, as you go on this strange road, you pass by the same places where the cow and the donkey have passed before."[1]

Few are the passages that offer such a vivid picture of the rural expanse unfolding between late-medieval Anatolian cities that pay such attention to the sights and sounds that would have been so familiar to the people inhabiting that world. The late-medieval Anatolian countryside was a world in which the most basic form of food production, agriculture, held center stage: agricultural land occupied most of the space, and agricultural tasks occupied most of the time. Beyond the obvious chronological priority that agriculture holds in the human food cycle, it is such pervasiveness that places agriculture at the beginning of this book.

This chapter is thematically divided between the three main forms of agricultural production: gardening, field cultivation, and animal husbandry. Each one of these entailed a different set of practices and, especially in the case of gardens, involved a different category of people. Each one of them also appears in a host of anecdotes, with very little overlap between the three categories, affording us more than a glimpse into the daily life as well as the ideas and concerns of the people whose lives touched—or even revolved around—agriculture.

PART I: THE GARDENS

The Gardeners

Because this chapter approaches agriculture primarily as a professional activity, my discussion of gardens will concentrate on people, that is, the gardeners and the owners of the gardens in which they worked. The most common agricultural occupation to appear in all the narrative sources I use is that of a gardener. They appear under different names (*bāghbān*, *bāghchivān*, *būstānbān*, *bostancı*) in Turkish and Persian texts, especially in hagiographies, though the Arabic-language sources I consulted contain no direct references to them. All of these terms seem to refer to a single category of people, since there appears no obvious difference between the tasks performed by individuals bearing the various names. In fact, one passage even praises a *būstānbān* for his talents in "the art of being a *bāghbān*."[2]

The duties of a gardener were limited to agricultural production, in the broadest sense. Entertainment activities and social intercourse, including the social elite sport of hunting, did take place in many gardens.[3] However, while these could entail household-type duties, gardeners never appear performing tasks associated with household servants. At most do we see them, in a handful of cases, deliver their products (fruits or honey) to visitors coming to the garden.[4] The partakers in these activities, furthermore, seem to have considered the presence of the gardeners as a nuisance more than anything else.[5]

Such limited presence of gardeners in elite entertainment indeed closely reflects a geographical division in the garden: agricultural production, at least in the case of vegetable gardens and vineyards (and perhaps, to a lesser extent, orchards), would be confined to a part of the garden where no one would hold social activities. Considering that visitors were first and foremost members of the high society, this may further be interpreted as a general tendency to forcefully limit direct contact between the upper and lower classes, a division that also seems to have been enforced beyond the particular case of gardens and gardeners.[6]

Outside of the fruit harvest season, these gardener duties were assumedly concentrated in the more labor-intensive vegetable gardens (*būstāns*).[7] Sources include clear indications that a certain degree of horticultural expertise was important and that this expertise could extend to knowledge about the health effects of the various types of produce.[8]

Yet besides these strictly agricultural duties, a significant part of the work of a gardener seems to have pertained to control over the produce. At the most obvious level, this included the retail sale of the garden's yield on behalf of the owner, something that was often (perhaps even systematically) done at the production site. This, in turn, entails that there was regular traffic between urban centers and their periphery, since fruit-producing gardens appear to have been located at some distance outside the city.[9]

At least in the case of the less labor-intensive orchards, gardeners were also in charge of the security of the garden, protecting the crops from thieves. This is apparent in numerous anecdotes, including one in which the gardener (who turns out to be the semilegendary figure Ahi Evren) is asked to bring grapes from a given trellis. He gives an answer reminiscent of Nasreddin Hoca (and apparently with the same comic intent), stating that even though he has been in the garden for years, he was hired to guard it and had nothing to do with the planting, so he would not know where the trellis is located.[10] The importance of ensuring security against theft can be further illustrated through contrast, in the mention by al-ʿUmarī's informant that a particular mountainous region in western Anatolia was filled with wild-growing trees whose fruits are freely available to anyone who may care to pick them. The obvious astonishment that frames this affirmation strongly hints that, for this informant, the norm indeed revolved around a tight control over the produce.[11] Redford also points out that the gardens owned by thirteenth-century Seljuk grandees in Alanya were typically surrounded by walls between 3 and 4.5 meters (11–13 feet) in height, which can hardly be interpreted as mere boundary markers.[12]

There is obviously no way to determine the relative importance—in terms of time or energy spent—of protection and horticulturalism for a gardener. Yet when depicting these individuals, narrative sources put the emphasis on their control over ready-to-eat produce, through either sale or theft prevention, rather than on their planting and taking care of the crops. This is largely due to the fact that the security duties constitute a form of social interaction (whereas tasks such as planting seeds or pruning trees would have been solitary), making them relevant for the purposes of these sources. Because they involved interaction, however, security-related tasks probably also were the most important in defining the social identity of gardeners. If this hypothesis is correct, it would thus seem that the image of a gardener was indeed closer to the hardened security guard protecting a luxury property than to some meditative plant lover isolated from civilization.[13]

This emphasis on security may explain why gardeners fall in the category of "unskilled labor," or at least makes gardening the kind of occupation that did not require lifelong learning and commitment, a situation best illustrated by the story of Ahi Evren, who gives up his job as a gardener and later becomes a tanner.[14] Far from limited to gardening, other examples suggest that, indeed, changes of profession were regular occurrences, arguing for a "job market" in which following the professional footsteps of one's father may not have been the norm.[15]

This professional mobility (lateral, though not necessarily vertical) may have been helped by the fact that gardening was not tied to the ownership of the land. In fact, several anecdotes show that those who owned gardens and those who worked in them were not the same people and that the owners would not normally be physically present in their gardens, apart from those occasions when the place was used for entertainment purposes.[16] It is very difficult to determine the exact status of gardeners in relation to the owner of the garden in which they worked. It is clear, however, that decisional power on management ultimately rested with the owners, who could give orders to their gardeners when the two interacted.[17] It also seems that the latter would normally not be slaves, a claim that can be made based on both a narrative passage in which a gardener freely leaves the *bāgh* where he is working[18] and the near absence of slaves endowed along with gardens in the *waqfiyya*s.[19]

All of this, then, suggests that most gardeners were employees. And while the nature and value of their wages remains impossible to determine, quite a lot can be said about their employers.

Ownership

As I stated above, owners would normally not find themselves physically present in their gardens. This absentee character can be observed through direct mentions in narrative sources and through the ability of some individuals to own several gardens at once, perhaps even in various cities.[20] More important, however, we can also observe ownership on the part of people who, for a number of reasons, were quite unlikely to spend most of their time planting cucumbers and looking out for apple thieves. These included craftsmen (who had other professional duties to attend to),[21] but also—and mostly—religious and political grandees, the latter category including a minority of women.[22] Elite ownership of gardens is indeed one of the most salient points of overlap between narrative sources and *waqfiyya*s: numerous anecdotes in hagiographies directly refer to such ownership,[23] and many of the *waqf* endowers (who had to own property, including gardens, in freehold in order to endow it) are known through other sources as high-ranking historical characters.

All of this leads to the conclusion that gardens were associated with wealth. This association can be assumed both based on the owners' status and from more or less direct references in narrative sources, such as the mention in the *Gharib-nama* that "whoever has a garden, a farm, silver and gold / His heart is busy every day with those."[24] Yet the clearest example is perhaps that of Ḥusām al-Dīn Çelebi, a close disciple and successor of Rūmī. In his youth, Ḥusām al-Dīn approached Rūmī's notoriously ascetic master, Shams al-Dīn Tabrīzī, who asked him to get rid of his worldly possessions. Among those, a "heaven-like garden" that Ḥusām al-Dīn owned is the only piece of property that the author specifically mentions.[25] Even though the followers of Rūmī may not, in actuality, have been the most renunciative bunch to inhabit late-medieval Anatolia, this particular story clearly tries to contrast the spiritual path and financial excesses, the latter taking in this case the shape of a luxurious garden.

This wealth was not symbolic, nor did it rest primarily in the value of the real estate (as would be the case, to take an extreme example, of an acre of land devoted to cabbage cultivation in downtown New York). In fact, some indications also exist of the plentiful existence of land that would have been proper for horticultural purposes, but left for other, less profitable, uses, due to the limited availability of labor. In one instance, for example, a religious master tells his disciple to go somewhere along a major road and set up a *bostān*, paying no apparent heed to the issue of acquiring the land.[26] Rather than the real estate value, then, garden-based wealth was the outcome of the efforts put into working the land, concretized in the shape of the sale revenues from the garden's produce.[27]

In all this talk of wealth and commercial revenues, the poorer folk appear to be left aside. Although it is clear that the rich could and did own gardens, does this mean that lower-class people did not? There is only limited evidence that can help answer this question, both because medieval sources tend to pay little attention to poorer classes and because, obviously, the *absence* of a phenomenon makes the said phenomenon invisible in the sources. Yet it is striking that the only suggestion of garden ownership spreading across social classes falls outside the geographical scope of this study, in cities known to have been depopulated at the time they are described,[28] and that a source as close to the peasantry as the *Vilayat-nama* would not include references to subsistence gardening. It is therefore very likely that subsistence gardening (and, a fortiori, garden ownership) was least prevalent (if not downright marginal) among the lower classes.

Finally, both the identification of (at least grandee-owned) gardens as revenue-producing property and the apparently widespread practice of fruit exports from Anatolia[29] point to the identification of produce (in societal practice and, therefore, popular view) as commodities that could be bought and sold.[30] Put together with the large-scale production that actually was sold and turned into revenues, this view of produce as tradable goods necessarily entails that there were also people actually buying it. There is thus every reason to believe that, in this overwhelmingly rural society, a significant proportion of the households were not self-sufficient in terms of fruit and vegetable production.

Irrigation

Before closing this section, I should add a few words about garden irrigation. To begin with, it is clear and, given the rather dry climate of central Anatolia, rather unsurprising that efforts were made to irrigate cultures in order to supplement rainfall.[31] For example, the presence of water springs certainly was a major consideration in the site selection for some of the gardens of the thirteenth-century Seljuk elite near the coastal town of Alanya.[32] Yet given the apparent concentration of many gardens found in *waqfiyya*s (very often immediately bordering other gardens), it is unlikely that there would be a spring in each one of them.

In some cases, irrigation wheels (Persian: *dūlāb*) would take water from streams and bring it to gardens as well as, if we are to trust Ibn Baṭṭūṭa, to houses.[33] One should note, however, that among the ten gardens for which *waqfiyya*s list the neighboring elements, nine are bordered by neither river nor stream on which water wheels could be set up.[34] The lists of bordering elements obviously include only what could serve to delineate the endowed property. Thus, an irrigation ditch, for example, that would run from the middle of one garden to the middle of the neighboring one could not serve as a border and would not receive mention. An irrigation system that would justify the side-by-side location of gardens could thus very well be invisible in the *waqfiyyas*.[35] There probably was a water-distribution apparatus that included pools and ditches, making it unnecessary for each garden to have its own spring or river access. Details about the workings of this system (the extent of this water-distribution network, the frequency of irrigation devices, whether the water wheels were self-propelling or not, and so forth) are rather difficult to ascertain with any degree of precision.[36]

Yet the very existence of such an irrigation scheme shared between gardens in turn entails that an intense form of communal life occurred in a location that clearly lies outside urban areas.[37] It is also clear that the concern for watering gardens was very real and that setting up and maintaining this system entailed major expenses of time and energy, thus contributing to the high value ascribed to gardens in popular opinion.[38]

PART 2: FIELD CULTURES

As could be seen in the previous section, gardens are much more visible than field cultures in sources.[39] Yet in terms of sheer acreage, production volume, and dietary importance, cereals held a much larger space than produce in late-medieval Anatolia, just like in most agrarian societies.

This visibility of gardens largely originates from their close association with the upper classes, be it because of the grandees' visits to the gardens, the luxury status of gardens as real estate property, or the connotation of wealth that fruits carried, as well as their frequent appearance in religious and poetic imagery.[40] Religious leaders or the ruler's courtiers, on the other hand, never met to enjoy themselves in a field of wheat, and no one would admire the sight or the taste of a handful of high-quality barley. Incidentally, the *Vilayat-nama*, with its unusually strong associations with peasant culture, is the only source to devote significantly more space to cereal production than to gardens.

Yet despite the lower profile of field cultures, it is possible to gather information about them, as will be seen in this section. Thus, after presenting individual productions and their peculiarities (wheat, barley, rice, and others), I will discuss the agricultural techniques that were involved from plowing to harvest, ending with a few words on the ownership of agricultural fields.[41]

Wheat and Barley

Wheat and barley were the most widespread cultures in late-medieval central Anatolia. As a matter of fact, in Turkish the words *arpa buğday* (barley [and] wheat, always in the same order and without the *ve* conjunction) appear often enough to be deemed a consecrated expression, and it would seem that the same peasants could cultivate both cereals simultaneously.[42]

Sources have relatively little to say about wheat itself. Apart from a few rather inconsequential metaphorical uses,[43] references do little more than indicate that, quite unsurprisingly, wheat was grown in regions such as Cappadocia and the surroundings of Konya,[44] but offer no hints that could help distinguish between the different varieties of wheat. Price indications are likewise scarce, at most limited to a few general statements such as the claim by both al-ʿUmarī and Ibn Baṭṭūṭa (the only two authors who could really make "international" comparisons) that the price of goods, including cereals, was relatively low in Anatolia.[45]

Barley, on the other hand, is in many ways a much more interesting cereal. This is in no small part due to the fact that, whereas wheat was intended for human consumption, barley was generally perceived as a lower-status cereal that was largely, though not exclusively, cultivated as high-quality feed for animals (primarily horses, but also oxen and camels).[46]

Several sources associate human consumption of barley with poverty, which may seem surprising given that, under normal circumstances, barley sold for a price similar to that of wheat.[47] One should note, however, that water deprivation has a much greater negative effect on wheat than barley.[48] In the Anatolian context, with precipitations standing then as they do now just above the minimum required for cultivating cereals without irrigation, a drier than usual summer could have a major effect on the balance between the productivity—and thus availability and price—of wheat and of barley. Barley was therefore associated with dire times rather than "usual" poverty, with marginal periods rather than marginal people.[49] This also suggests that, when given the choice (same price, same availability), people would choose to consume wheat rather than barley. It was, in other words, a "matter of taste," affording us rare concrete evidence to support the commonsense assumption that taste had an impact on the economics of food production.

The *Manaqib al-ʿArifin* makes some references to bread made of barley, leaving no doubt about the low esteem in which it was held. In fact, barley bread in this text is nothing short of a culinary symbol of asceticism.[50] Insofar as the arguments I made above (concerning the relatively equal price of wheat and barley and the choice of the former as resulting of taste) are correct, this also shows that the asceticism depicted in the *Manaqib al-ʿArifin* was understood not so much to mimic the living conditions of the poor classes (to show solidarity, as the fast of Ramadan is often interpreted in contemporary Turkish society) but rather to counteract the inclination of the *nafs* (carnal soul) by deliberately choosing a course of action going against one's taste.

Rice

Fifteenth-century Ottoman archival documents suggest that rice was cultivated in Anatolia (and the neighboring regions of the Balkans) in the fourteenth century and perhaps even earlier. The production sites to which they refer, however, are concentrated in coastal and western Anatolia, since the large amounts of water that rice cultivation requires are hardly compatible with the dry climate of central Anatolia.[51]

Although it was not a common local production, rice was nevertheless known as a consumption product in fourteenth- (and probably even thirteenth-) century central Anatolia and was a high-end commodity.[52] This luxury status, making rice the polar opposite of barley among cereals, can be attributed, at least in part, to transportation costs. Of course, distances are fairly short from coastal to central Anatolia, but the economic advantage that this relative proximity constituted was probably more than offset by the use of overland transportation along mountainous routes and the likely absence of wheeled vehicles.[53]

Still, there are strong indications that infrastructures existed that were devoted to the storage, processing, and sale of rice. Besides a "*khān* of the rice-sellers" in Konya,[54] two *waqfiyya*s also mention a total of four "rice houses" (*bayt al-aruzz*) in Niksar, in three separate mentions.[55] Although documents do not provide any elements of definition for "rice house," it seems reasonable to imagine that the term refers to rice granaries. Rather strikingly, three of these structures are geographically (and, based on the formulations, perhaps functionally) connected to mills. One should know that rice requires some milling in order to remove the hull and make the grain edible (and not just, as in the case of wheat, to turn it into flour). This suggests that the mills discussed here would have been dedicated to rice only, at the exclusion of other cereals.[56]

It is unclear to what extent these structures were peculiar to Niksar. Still, the way they appear in the *waqfiyya*s suggests a close integration of processing structures, something we do not see for other cereals. Furthermore, at least three of these four mills appear in a clearly urban environment, which seems to stand in contrast to water-powered, flour-making mills.[57] These factors—the concentration of location and ownership of rice-processing structures along with the apparent use of labor-intensive human- or animal-powered milling techniques—strengthen the idea of rice as a high-priced luxury good produced and processed in relatively small quantities.

Other Field Cultures

Sources mention a few other field cultures, albeit much more rarely than barley and wheat. Rye (*çavdar*), for example, appears twice, along with just enough information to suggest that it could be made into bread of much lower quality than wheat bread.[58] Another cereal, millet (*dare*), also appears on two occasions, though both of them fall outside the geographical scope of this study, and neither of them gives any significant information.[59]

But cereals, in the strictest sense, were not the only field cultures. Lentil cultivation appears once, when the saintly figure Hacı Bektaş Velī, walking in the countryside, encounters villagers who are busy harvesting their fields and asks them for charity. When they refuse, he turns their grain into stone.

He then promises that, if they make penance, those who eat one of the wheat seeds that he turned into stone will have a son, and those who choose the lentil will have a daughter.[60]

This passage is interesting for two reasons. First, it attributes a "feminine" connotation to lentils and a masculine one to wheat, an association with gender whose origins or implications I have, unfortunately, been unable to document. And second, it mentions wheat, barley, rye, and lentils next to each other in a single episode that incidentally includes the most detailed harvest scene in any source from that period.[61] The formulation strongly suggests that these four crops were cultivated in similar ways, which in turn shows both that lentils were conceptualized as cereals (grown in fields rather than in some kind of garden) and that the same people would cultivate all of these crops. This provides us with a strong hint that the peasants discussed here performed complex crop rotations.[62]

Vetch (*burçak*), another noncereal, likewise appears only once, when a saintly old man undertakes the burdensome task of harvesting it by himself.[63] Although the extent to which it was "cultivated" is unclear,[64] the lonely work of this character clearly contrasts with the collective harvests of cereals, and for a good reason: unlike barley, wheat, and other similar crops that require basic processing (threshing and winnowing) within a relatively short time period after harvest, vetch is used untransformed as animal fodder. This passage also puts much emphasis on the weight of the product thus collected, strongly hinting that it was harvested while still green.[65] Vetch may have been collected when needed rather than all at once when the plant was deemed ready for harvest (as was the case for cereals, fruits, and vegetables). However, it remains unclear whether the main character in this episode, a "saint" (*eren*) living with his wife off agriculture, is involved in other types of cultures (and therefore produces vetch for his own oxen) and whether this was the usual model of production for all fodder (including the fodder that would complement barley for horses).[66]

I should point out, before closing this section, the absence of oats from this list of field crops. This might seem a striking omission given that oats are considered the horse feed par excellence in most places where they are cultivated. One should note, however, that this reputation is partially biased by the prevalence of oats in European (and, later on, North American) agriculture. Still, while at least one variety of oats indeed originates from Anatolia and absence of evidence is by no means evidence of absence, it is more than likely that oats cultivation in fourteenth-century central Anatolia at most remained relatively marginal in comparison to the place held by wheat and barley.[67]

Agricultural Practices

PEOPLE AND PLACES It is difficult to determine the precise identity of the people who worked in cereal production, in no small part because farmworkers appear much less often than gardeners in *waqfiyyas* and in other written sources. It is clear that some of these peasants held a position akin to that of an employee (as opposed to that of "owner-cultivators"), since *waqfiyyas* show that wealthy absentee owners did own a significant amount of land in freehold. However, extant references seldom mention the relationship between workers and landowners. Whatever that relationship may have been, it was indeed probably a rather distant one.[68]

It is clear that individual ownership by peasants was possible for some types of property, such as livestock.[69] However, in order to determine the extent to which such individual ownership was also possible in the case of land ("ownership" here being taken in the broader sense, i.e., whether a given plot was associated with a given individual), we must look into the way that *waqfiyyas* refer to countryside real estate. The latter appears both as "land" or "land plots" (*qiṭʿa al-arḍ, arḍa, arāḍī*) and as "villages" (*qariya*).[70] Although most *waqfiyyas* that include villages do not include land, and vice versa, I would nevertheless argue that the two types of references correspond to different forms of property (a "piece of land" being only one of the many fields surrounding a "village," and the latter comprising both the central agglomeration and the surrounding farmland), rather than two different ways to refer to a single concept.[71]

There are several reasons to make such a claim. First, the documents provide us with toponyms for villages but generally not for land plots.[72] Furthermore, in the cases where the property element is delineated, the bordering elements given for a village are almost always other villages,[73] whereas in the case of land plots these elements comprise much more specific geographical markers (such as roads, rivers, other pieces of land, and even buildings and cemeteries) that evoke a much smaller scale.[74] This suggests that endowed "land" provided revenues from the cereal harvest of specific fields, whereas endowed "villages" also brought in revenues exacted from other activities in the village.[75]

Whether the revenues of endowments were organized in such a fashion or not, it is nevertheless clear that villages were collective spaces of habitation but did not constitute single units of production in which the various plots of land would have been worked by all villagers collectively (like kolkhozes or kibbutzim). Insofar as the quality of agricultural land is never fully equal, in turn this also entails a slew of opportunities for inequalities among peasants, serving as a good reminder that a variety of individuals, each one with a different status and life experience, is hidden in the undifferentiated mass that comes to mind when one mentions medieval peasantry.[76]

Apart from "land" and "villages," *waqfiyya*s also mention a small number of endowed elements under the name *mazraʿa*, a word usually translated as "farm."[77] Given the pattern of the bordering elements (including both villages and smaller-scale geographical features such as rivers and roads), their relative size appears to have been halfway between villages and land plots. References by al-ʿUmarī to the "villages and estates" (*qarī wa ḍiyāʾ*) that economically supported Denizli provide another hint, however tenuous, that these might have been agricultural production units geographically independent from villages.[78]

Both their low frequency in *waqfiyya*s and their near absence from other sources suggest that these units were rather unusual. Still, it is worth pointing out that, following a long-standing historiographical tradition, Ottoman historians have primarily studied agricultural units from an administrative and economic point of view, often without paying attention to their social implications for the people inhabiting them. Insofar as these *mazraʿa*s were indeed small demographic units geographically set apart from villages, it would, for example, be extremely interesting to compare the respective identities of villagers and farmstead workers or the nature and intensity of farmstead-village communications to the interactions between two villages. In view of the availability of sources, however, such a task would need to be conducted with a larger scope (and later focus) than the fourteenth century.

WORKING THE LAND Sources are fairly quiet with respect to actual agricultural practices, probably in large part because of the relative absence of social interaction that such activities generated with the literate classes. Although it is, for example, impossible to say anything about the agricultural calendar or the number of annual harvests, a few observations can still be made. Hence, as I pointed out above, there seems to have been a practice of complex crop rotations involving several types of productions, and, quite unsurprisingly, seeds for sowing the fields were taken from previous harvests.[79]

There are very few references to irrigation in relation to field cultures. Given the immediate association that sources make between drought and its negative (or downright tragic) impact on cereal harvests, it is rather easy to assume that the watering of field cultures primarily relied on rain.[80] Yet it is striking to note how often cereal fields endowed in *waqfiyya*s are located along waterways, considering the relative scarcity of rivers in central Anatolia.[81] This most probably relates to a combination of socioeconomic and geomorphological factors: endowers were more likely to be part of the elite, the land owned by the elite to be the most productive, the most productive land to enjoy better natural underground irrigation, and the better-irrigated land to be located near rivers. Both the practice in later periods and the very occasional presence of what appears to be irrigation ditches, however, suggest the possibility that some cereal fields were irrigated, if only to a very limited extent.[82]

Sources also refer to the use of animal work in agriculture. It is, of course, well known that the Turkish word *çiftlik*, referring to a single-family farm, derives from the area that can be exploited with the help of a pair (*çift*) of oxen, and indeed my sources do use the word *çiftlik* to refer to agricultural exploitations.[83] They also clearly mention the use of pairs of oxen for plowing,[84] showing that the term used to designate farms was not antiquated.[85] Oxen are not presented as having other uses than plowing (a tedious task to be sure, but one that needs to be performed only in preparation for sowing, usually twice a year),[86] and horses do not appear to have played any part in agricultural exploitation.[87] The latter point indeed supports the idea that horses were expensive properties.

Harvest scenes often leave us with the impression, by their use of narrative devices such as an imprecise plural designation for the actors ("the villagers"), that harvesting was a collective task.[88] It was clearly a labor-intensive process that would bring people together in an environment (the fields) that was different from the one in which they would normally interact (the village) in an activity that would require very close collaboration. It is not hard, for this reason, to imagine that the harvest periods would bring about a peak of sorts in the intensity of social interactions.[89]

Although no source elaborates on techniques used, it also seems that threshing and winnowing were both performed on a dedicated threshing floor in the vicinity of inhabited spaces, rather than out in the fields.[90] As I stated earlier, there is no direct reference to the use of animals when discussing threshing (and, conversely, no mention of anything but plowing when referring to the work of farm animals); one passage, however, strongly hints at the use of a threshing sledge (a wooden board under which pieces of stone or metal are affixed that is pulled over the newly harvested cereal in order to chop the straw and detach the grain from it). After threshing and winnowing, the resulting grain was then kept in the same place, under a fabric tarp, until taxes were collected and the remaining product could be sent away.[91]

Sources depict the grain thus produced as a freely traded commodity and, as will be seen in chapter 2, a worthy object of plunder.[92] There are also clear indications that straw and husk, too, were products that were bought and sold, although they were much less valuable than grain.[93]

OWNERSHIP OF AGRICULTURAL LAND As I stated earlier, one of the main differences between the way sources present gardens and cereal fields is the fact that garden owners interacted much more often with their properties, primarily when using them as places of entertainment. In the case of cereal land, by contrast, the idea of ownership seems to have been more purely financial, creating much fewer opportunities for us to access details about the interactions that owners had with the land itself or with the people working on it. Narrative passages referring to the ownership and, a fortiori, acquisition of countryside real estate therefore do not mention the people inhabiting or working the land, but often refer to political authorities.[94]

The picture becomes even more complex, but also potentially more interesting, in the case of land belonging to an endowment (*waqf*) established for the benefit of a religious community. There is very little in the source material that can tell us about the interaction between the two sides of this equation or, to put it more clearly, *whether* and, if applicable, *how*, *when*, and *why* the cultivators would interact with the members of the religious community for the benefit of which their work produced revenues.[95] Of the three anecdotes making passing references to such a relationship, one emphasizes the "accounting" aspect of the interaction, as it presents the spotless honesty of a disciple of Rūmī who was put in charge of administering one of those endowments.[96] Yet the other two suggest that there was a significant degree of interaction (or at least consciousness of each other's presence) between the producers and the beneficiaries. In the first case, the feeling of "integration" between the revenue-producing structure and the benefiting institution chiefly resides in the formulation at the beginning of the passage, which refers to "the *çiftlik* of Hacı Bektaş."[97] The second passage, taken from the *Maqalat-i Sayyid Harun*, is linguistically more challenging, but appears to be a rebuttal by a religious master to those of his disciples who want to derive revenues from renting out endowed mosques and madrasas as living spaces, on the pretext that such rent is already obtained from endowed agricultural property:

> Some people said: "[Seyyid Hārūn, the religious master for the benefit of whom a large *waqf* was recently constituted], our mosques are your mosques, these lands are endowed to you. What if we asked for a rent on

> some of these places?" [Seyyid Hārūn] replied: "Shame on the one who comes and makes a house out of [what was donated to me]. But it is legal to ask for rent on some of the cultivated lands. There are many cases like this."[98]

If this reading is correct, it betrays a high degree of association between the various parts of a *waqf*, such a high degree, in fact, that the religious master has to remind his people of the different purposes of the revenue-producing property and service-giving property that combine to make up the *waqf*. This, in turn, entails that the association with the religious community was widely known in the population, rather than remaining a mere accounting fact or technical legal status of which only administrators would be aware.

Given that legal owners of cereal fields were much farther removed from the physical location of their properties than in the case of gardens, it may be misguided to take the concept of "property" in the strictest legal sense. It is likely, rather, that an individual's association with (and control over) a given plot of land played a much more important role than the identity of the legal owner in such respects as self-image, fears and concerns, material and psychological well-being, social status, and the like—all of which were major building blocks in the construction of worldviews and the "texture of daily life."

The nature of such associations between individual plots of land and individual peasants (or peasant households) is difficult to characterize with any degree of precision. Yet, as I stated earlier, cereal-producing land was clearly, legally divided into individual fields, and the existence of different owners entailed different treatment at the moment of tax collection. This fact could not have been ignored by workers farming plots belonging to different owners. Furthermore, sources indeed suggest a widespread awareness of the ownership status of endowed land, which could include one field but not the bordering one within a given village. Finally, very simple names appear among the owners of plots bordering some endowed fields, and these names could not have referred to people holding any significant social position, therefore suggesting the existence of owner-cultivators.[99] All of this clearly shows that the differentiation of fields that appears in *waqfiyya*s did reflect a division of the land that was apparent to those working it and strongly suggests that this division was also accompanied by a geographically based division of agricultural labor. In other words, independently of the legal authorities' opinion on the subject, it is more than likely that individual peasants could identify a certain field as their "own" field.

PART 3: THE ANIMALS

Fields and gardens may have figured prominently in the sources, but the economic and cultural importance of animals in the late-medieval Anatolian countryside is equally hard to overstate. Various animals entertained various types of relationships with plant cultivation, some contributing to the production process, others consuming the products, still others damaging the crops. In most cases, farm animals constituted a rather large investment of work and money for their owners.

This section will discuss the status, use, and other aspects of domestic animals; as will be seen below, these are widely variable from one species to the next. We will also examine how animals shaped the relationship between the people and the land on (and off) which they lived.

Care, Use, and Ownership

SHEEP Perhaps because of their association with pastoral nomadism, sheep are often seen as a symbol of late-medieval Anatolia. This view is actually not a recent one: al-ʿUmarī, following his local informer, indeed claims that sheep ownership was widespread among the population.[100]

Available sources are, by nature, sedentary-centric.[101] Although it is clear that large pastoral movements among the nomads were taking place ("large" in terms of both the human and animal populations that were involved and the distances they covered), the information that sources offer on sheep rearing is largely limited to sedentary people. For the latter, the shepherd's task of grazing the sheep was a solitary one that was organized on a daily basis, with animals being brought back to the village every night.[102] Shepherd dogs seem absent, even from passages where the authors would have had every reason to mention them if they had been in use, including one where a shepherd has trouble controlling his flock and another that contrasts the usefulness of sheep to the uselessness of (city) dogs.[103]

Sheep were raised, in part, for milk production.[104] Although, biologically speaking, a ewe can give birth at any time of the year, it seems that flock management led to most lambs being born in late winter, prompting al-ʿUmarī to point out that milk was so plentiful in the spring that it was neither bought nor sold.[105] This in turn suggests that sheep-milk production was limited to part of the year (although, as will be seen below, cow milk was also available). But this also means that, in order to save some of the milk for human consumption, lambs had to be kept apart from their mothers for at least part of the day, thus increasing the burden of the shepherd and, conversely, decreasing the size of the flock that an individual could manage. There was, in other words, a trade-off between the extra amount of work put into the management of sheep and the increased return on investment. This attempt at maximizing returns suggests that the animals themselves, as capital, were worth quite a lot in comparison to the value of a shepherd's work.[106]

Sheep also provided meat. The separate mention of lamb and (adult) sheep meat in some sources hints at an awareness of the former's higher quality. But it also is consistent with a practice that helped control the lambing patterns: limiting the number of rams by slaughtering most male lambs helped flock managers to control mating while at the same time ensuring the availability of lamb meat for the consumers.[107] Some wool production must also have taken place, although it is interesting to note the absence of direct reference to shearing in sources.[108]

The question of ownership is even more muddied for sheep than in the previously discussed cases of gardens and cereal fields. Although it is clear that upper-class people *could* own sheep, it is more difficult to determine the status of the shepherds and whether they would take care of an absentee owner's property, of their own sheep, or of flocks that could include animals falling into both categories. The way sources present sheep ownership, however, suggests that it was a sign of wealth only when it involved large flocks.[109] Given further indications of the relatively low price of sheep in relation to oxen, whose ownership was widespread among peasants, it would thus seem realistic that many shepherds indeed owned at least a good proportion of the sheep they tended.[110]

The attested flock ownership by members of the urban elite suggests one more fact: although historians often mention that the perspective of sedentary political authorities on pastoral nomads was heavily influenced both by the sheep's destructive effects on plant agriculture (and, in turn, on the revenues that these would bring) and by the trouble that the ruling elite had to secure control over nomads as subjects, the part that flocks played in the sedentary wealth also means that nomadic pastoralists could be seen as direct economic rivals.[111] The relationship between nomadic pastoralism and agents of political centralization in the medieval Middle East is complex and much discussed. Even a summary of the issue would require a thorough description of economic structures, environmental setting, topography, and cultural factors that do not equally apply to all of central Anatolia—too large a task to be undertaken in this thematic section. Nevertheless, the evidence I put forward here suggests that a desire to shut down the competition may, at least in certain cases, have also been a factor encouraging central authorities to enact repressive policies toward nomadic groups.[112]

BOVINES For all the symbolic load that sheep carried, bovines (cattle and water buffalo) occur rather more frequently in sources.[113] Their primary function, at least in the case of oxen, was to be a source of power for plowing; several references confirm the direct relationship between the word *çiftlik* and the pair (*çift*) of oxen that constituted its defining element.[114] As I stated earlier, however, there is no clear evidence that this animal power was tapped for other agricultural purposes, except perhaps for sporadic use as pack animals.[115] It thus appears that oxen were relatively idle for most of the year, justifying the organization of a collective system in which an individual (called in Turkish *sığırtmaç*, ox drover) was hired to lead all the oxen of a village to graze.[116]

Cows were also raised for milk production, and as such had to be kept apart from their calves for most of the day.[117] In this system, the production of meat should not be seen as a primary objective or concern. Of course, sources mention the slaughter of bovines on several occasions, both as religious sacrifices and for commercial meat production.[118] But an optimal use of the animal for its traction power (mostly or exclusively males) and milk production (females) required approximately one calving a year per cow (to ensure near-constant milk production). Even accounting for sickness and accidents, such a reproduction rate was far above what is necessary in order to maintain the population, hence allowing for the slaughter of some of the young animals for the owner's profit. Adding to this the (documented) practice of disposing of animals too old to be of other use by turning them into meat, it becomes clear that slaughtering the bovines did not need to be anything more than the by-product of other uses of the animal in order for significant amounts of meat to become available.[119]

All of this may have entailed that the connotations and implications of ownership were different for cows and for oxen. On the one hand, a pair of oxen appears to have been a requirement to work the land. More than two would have been a rather unproductive burden on the owners, and, as a previously mentioned passage in the *Vilayat-nama* points out, villagers organized structures to take care of the animals collectively when they were not in use.[120] A household's ownership of a pair of oxen was, in other words, the standard.

On the other hand, ownership of cows was more flexible. Whereas poorer farmers could very well perform all their agricultural duties without owning cows, involvement in dairy production would require better-off farmers to milk the cows and to look after them (both to protect the herd and to keep the calves from "stealing" the milk), which could in turn result in the need for hiring labor.[121] From this we can tell that owning cows would have been a more direct indicator of peasant wealth than owning oxen. Furthermore, this also shows that a peasant family had the opportunity to accumulate capital and generate increased revenues. Whether cow ownership was the only way to do so or rather one among many others is unclear, yet from a psychological point of view, the important element to retain here is that a relative improvement of the economic status *was* possible and that individual peasants were not lifelong prisoners of the economic level at which they were born, at least within the range of variation that existed between the poorer and richer individuals in a given village.

ANIMALS FOR TRANSPORTATION Although the fact that horses, mules, and donkeys were domestic animals justifies their appearance in this chapter, they seem to have had little to do with peasant life or agriculture except as consumers of agricultural productions.[122] All three animals appear to have been seen primarily as mounts; horses often appear in military contexts,[123] and at least one passage presents a mule used as a pack animal, in this case by the "public water-seller."[124]

Written sources associate horses and mules (which seem to have been of relatively equal standing in this respect) with people of higher status.[125] The level of skill and specialization that seems to have been required for horse breeding further strengthens this association by attributing to these animals an aura of "quality craftsmanship."[126] Horses further appear as a semantic point of contact between connotations of high status and the military world.[127] Of course, this was at most a possible mental association and says nothing of the lower-ranking soldiery. Yet it suggests that, for a peasant witnessing a troop of soldiers on horseback passing by, the presence of horses would be an element that increased, rather than limited, the impression of "otherness" that the military class projected.

SWINE, FOWL, CAMELS, AND GOATS Although pigs have been present in Anatolia since prehistoric times, zooarchaeological studies point to a sharp, unambiguous decrease in their population after the beginning of the Turkish immigration to the region, in the late eleventh century. Still, a (very limited) number of pig bones appear in the medieval and postmedieval layers of most excavated sites.[128] It is also clear that the animal was known to medieval authors in part because of its status as a marker of religious difference between Christians and Muslims and in part because wild boars roamed the countryside and were hunted.[129]

The sharp decline in popularity for swine as farm animals can obviously be attributed to the introduction of Islam in the region, and to the capture of political power by Muslims. Unsurprisingly, the sources consulted clearly associate the raising of pigs with Christian realms. Thus, one anecdote tells of a shepherd who is punished for his disrespect toward a religious figure by being sent to keep the pigs belonging to a monk in "Frengistan."[130] Both the way in which this story presents the task of pig keeping as essentially the same as sheep keeping (even though, in actual practice, a herd of pigs can be and typically is left to forage for itself, without the supervision that a flock of sheep requires) and the handy appearance of "Frengistan" in the anecdote (as "a land far far away") strengthen the impression of exoticism surrounding pigs.

The factors explaining the small-scale, continued appearance of pig bones in the period discussed here and beyond are not perfectly clear. It is, of course, possible that Christians continued to raise pigs, albeit on a much smaller scale and perhaps more or less secretly, even after they began to have Muslim neighbors. This hypothesis entails that most sites excavated retained a Christian minority, something that remains to be proven.[131] But one should not discount the possibility that these pig bones merely reflect occasional hunting of (or even self-defense against) wild boar, whose bones differ only by size from those of domestic pigs[132] or, perhaps more frequently, the contamination of medieval layers with pig bones from earlier periods when medieval Anatolians dug out those refuse pits whose traces dot most excavation sites.

There are a few hints that unspecified "birds" (presumably chickens) were raised, though the handful of occasions on which they appear give little information as to the connotations they would have had as a source of meat.[133] It is quite possible that the scarcity of details on the agricultural (as opposed to culinary) aspects of the subject suggests a rather small place for chickens in terms of the care they required and financial value they had for the peasants, even though archaeological evidence does suggest that both chicken meat and eggs were consumed.[134] Geese, ducks, and "flying birds" (assumedly wildfowl), on the other hand, were more clearly luxury foods, and most signs of their presence reside in consumption and farm-based production rather than hunting.[135]

Two animals, finally, hold a much smaller place in textual sources than one would have expected. Camels are all but absent, appearing either in scenes set outside of Anatolia or as metaphors that by no means imply knowledge of the animal beyond literary references, an observation that squares well with their limited compatibility with Anatolia's winter weather.[136] As for goats, they make only two very short appearances that cannot serve as a basis for much further discussion, through the mention that al-ʿUmari makes of "silky-haired goats" in Anatolia[137] and in a reference to the flock of goats that Ottoman soldiers used as decoys in preparing a sneak attack.[138] As I have already stated, absence from sources is by no means proof of absence from reality. Yet in view of the comparatively large number of references to other domestic animals, it is not impossible that camels and goats could in fact seldom be seen in Anatolia, or at least that their economic and cultural importance was relatively limited.

Animals and the Land

HOUSING AND HOLDING ANIMALS Although sources never describe barns or stables, there are some indications that buildings were indeed used to house animals overnight as well as, assumedly, during the winter.[139] Besides protection against the climate, these structures would also offer security against the flight of animals, theft, and the dangers of wild predators such as wolves.[140]

When they were grazing (a good part of most summer days at least), animals were kept under active human supervision, rather than being held by fences.[141] Several reasons might explain this, chief among them the limited availability of wood to build effective fences. But a number of other factors may have also contributed to make the use of fences impractical, including the relatively high economic value of animals as investments (in comparison with that of the manpower required to oversee them), the very large grazing area that such enclosures would need to contain (at least in the case of sheep), the fairly extensive effort required to build and maintain the structure (needing repair on a regular basis), and the far from perfect efficiency of enclosures (by no means a foolproof guarantee against animals bent on fleeing, especially where tasty-looking cereal fields may be present nearby). In any case, the oversight of animals was an essential task in order to avoid damage to both plant cultures and the livestock itself. Whatever the justification may have been for entrusting it to people rather than to fences, it had the effect of making land use fluid and adaptable—for example, by allowing the manuring of fallow fields used as pastures.

This also means that the people involved in watching over these animals thoroughly occupied the land surrounding their village and had every opportunity to develop a very intimate knowledge of even its most subtle features.[142] Our own contemporaries often look down upon medieval peasants, pitying them for the limited exposure they had to the world beyond their immediate environment. Such a view, however, fails to take into account the depth and intensity of the relationship that peasants had with the landscape they inhabited, a relationship that is difficult for us to even begin imagining.

NOMADISM, PASTORALISM, AND GEOGRAPHY The sources I use do not allow us to reconstruct a nomad's point of view and could hardly form the basis of a revolution in the debate over nomadic pastoralism in late-medieval Anatolia. They nevertheless offer some hints about the way peasants perceived and dealt with nomads and nomadism.

It is clear, to begin with, that there were pasture areas (*maṣīf* or *yayla*[*k*]) that were inhabited during the summer but inaccessible during the winter.[143] Taking the concept of "nomadic people" in its most literal understanding, sources leave no doubt about the existence of groups that traveled significant distances according to the seasons and would constitute a large-enough population to make them politically significant not only because of their sheer size, but also because they were organized as autonomous political structures.[144] Members of these "nomad" groups, often designated in sources as "Turkish," "Tatar," or "Mongol," would come under the authority of a state not as individuals, families, or village-size subunits, but rather through their own leader's allegiance to the (sedentary) state ruler.[145]

For sedentary peasants, the sheer size of these migrations may have constituted a significant obstacle to interaction with the nomads, because of both the logistical implications of periodically moving an entire society and the natural tendency to see a large "foreign" population as an undifferentiated mass (making them an "other") rather than a collection of individuals with whom communication was possible.[146] Such limitations on interaction (and, in turn, on intercultural understanding) must have contributed to the often negative view that sedentary people had of the nomads.[147]

Besides massive groups covering large distances, sedentary (or, as will be seen below, semisedentary) villagers also used the concept of *yayla*. In the case of "village *yaylas*," the distances involved were certainly much shorter than when talking about fully nomadic societies. At least one passage leaves no doubt that the word could be used to designate a location that could be reached and then returned from within a day while driving a flock of sheep.[148] Furthermore, whereas passages that associate *yaylas* with large nomadic groups tend to refer to seasonal migrations, references to the term in relation to sedentary people mostly center on day-to-day sheep grazing.

It might actually be significant that the word *yayla* is *not* used in reference to animals other than sheep. The term is absent, for example, from the one scene where oxen are led to graze, even though the reader is left with a strong impression that the animals spent the day at some significant distance from the village.[149] Since the sedentary Anatolian population was at least partially from nomadic descent, the continued use of the word *yayla* in particular association with sheep may be interpreted as a case of cultural transmission where a word was kept in use even though the scale of the reality it depicts shrank as the population became sedentarized over time.[150]

Between the village's grazing land and the large nomadic confederations, a few scattered hints also suggest the presence of a form of what could be called "settled seminomadism," in which a village-size group would live in permanent houses during the winter months and then move, still as a group, to another location a significant distance away during the summer. This is best illustrated by an anecdote of the *Vilayat-nama*, in the course of which a character enters a village entirely deserted by its inhabitants, who had "gone to the *yayla*."[151] It seems to be the same phenomenon that is evoked in two other passages, one using the expression "nomad's houses" (*göçer evleri*),[152] and the other mentioning a "village and tribe" (*karye ve kabile*) at the beginning of an anecdote and then later referring to what appears to be the same element with the word *kışlak* (winter pasture).[153] This admittedly limited amount of evidence may suggest that, even though the people it involved perceived such seminomadism as a more or less permanent status ("this is the way we live"), their lifestyle was an intermediary step in a process of sedentarization that spanned several generations.

CONCLUSION

At the end of this survey of agriculture and the countryside, it is already possible to shed some light on the life and worldviews of the people it discusses. It appears, for example, that although those living in the countryside concentrated their attention on a tiny piece of the universe, they also had ways to come in contact with the outside world. Sedentary villagers would see the nomads passing by when their season came, gardeners could witness the enjoyments of visiting VIPs, farmers would know who—between the political authorities and Sufi communities—was to benefit from their toil. The people of the countryside, in other words, were very much aware that their world was not the only world in existence.

Other worlds were not theirs, however, and a number of symbols reminded everybody of the strongly hierarchical division between social classes. The gardeners could certainly not participate in the leisure meetings of the owners of the gardens and their guests. Horses, likewise, were creatures belonging to another realm, that of the rich folk, the military, and probably some of the nomads.

Such a hierarchy may seem dreadful for a reader living in a world where it is relatively common for a powerful leader to rise from a working-class family. Yet several factors mitigated what may otherwise seem like the shackles of a predetermined fate. For one, the people of the countryside enjoyed in their work something that is slowly fading away in our world of factories and offices: autonomy. Although it is unclear whether, from a legal standpoint, gardeners were slaves or cultivators who owned their fields, in practical terms they could very much behave as if they were self-employed. They certainly had somebody standing above them, but that somebody was on most days nowhere to be seen. Being in charge of their own work no doubt contributed in pushing the peasant's overall lowly social status to the background of their daily experience—though without, of course, obliterating it.

Furthermore, whereas a rags-to-riches story may not have been everyone's life plan, as often seems to be the case in the United States of the twenty-first century, there were ways through which individuals were responsible for their own lot and could, to some extent, improve in status. Owning and milking cows or acquiring land to cultivate, for example, allowed a peasant family to make its status different from that of the neighbors. On the other hand, a number of collective tasks were undertaken, and these no doubt limited the possibility of savagely selfish behavior. "Grassroots-level" organization was required, for example, to hire someone who would lead all the villagers' oxen to graze, to coordinate the collective effort that took place during the harvest season, and to maintain the irrigation schemes running between gardens. But the point here is that there was nothing fatalistic in the view countryside dwellers had about their life: earning one's livelihood was the result of hard work. Even harder work was necessary to improve one's status, but, while the ambitions they had for themselves had little to do with those floating high on the American dream, the prospect of concrete improvement in living conditions and in one's place within the local hierarchy was not an illusion.

This awareness of the outside world, this control over their own destiny, was by no means foreign to fourteenth-century Anatolian villagers. And, to return to the words of Shams Tabrīzī, while they passed "by the same places where the cow and the donkey have passed before," they knew where they were going and could set their own pace.

(TWO)

Food Exchanges

Food binds. As a product, food requires distribution and exchange, if only because its producers are not its only consumers. These operations are part of networks of human interactions that are made even more complex because food, just like any other useful good in limited supply, has economic value. When food behaves as a commodity, the paths it traces reveal economic networks such as those that crisscrossed the human and geographical landscape of Anatolia. These economic exchanges are part of the subjective daily experience of most human beings. In the absence of the consistent and reliable quantitative data that would allow for a more classical economic history of food in medieval Anatolia, these exchanges and the ways in which they affected the texture of daily life provide the crux of this chapter.

Beyond such concrete incarnations of abstract economic phenomena also lies another, even more pervasive, concept: power. The influence of postmodernist thought in the past thirty or forty years has led to a reconceptualization of power, seen not as a resource in limited supply but rather as a fundamental component of all human interactions. From a perspective that acknowledges every human interaction as a power relation, to depict food as a widely exchanged commodity therefore entails that to talk about food is to talk about power.

The exchange of food takes many shapes and forms. This heterogeneous character explains the wide scope of this chapter, in which I cover both commercial and political interactions. I thus begin with a look at trade and transportation as well as the market scene, before concentrating on the particular issues that surround mills and water provisioning. I will then dwell at more length on the various incarnations of the state and the ways in which food played the part of a point of contact between the rulers and the ruled, in the shape of taxes but also as part of military operations. This broad survey will reveal that even the most disenfranchised peasants may have had a much greater awareness of the world governing them than we might suspect.

TRADE AND TRANSPORTATION

Active trade networks linked medieval Anatolia and the neighboring regions. Among a variety of factors encouraging trade, historians have emphasized the importance of the caravanserai network developed under Seljuk rule (in the twelfth and especially thirteenth centuries) as well as the favorable atmosphere that the Pax Mongolica created in the second half of the thirteenth century. The traveler Ibn Baṭṭūṭa and the encyclopaedist al-ʿUmarī,[1] writing in or about the 1330s, seem to confirm that trade was still healthy well into the fourteenth century, despite the collapse of Ilkhanid power and subsequent breakdown of Anatolia into small polities. Both authors point out the general cheapness of prices in comparison to other areas, helping the region in its role as an exporter, and they mention a number of export products. Sheep, a form of meat that provided its own transportation, certainly ranked high in this list of exports,[2] as probably did dried fruits.[3] On the import side, archaeology provides plentiful evidence of a steady (if small-scale) import of luxury wares from Syria to the southeastern edge of the area discussed in this book up to the late thirteenth and, in some cases, the fourteenth centuries.[4] Similar evidence also exists for an equivalent pattern of trade with Byzantium on the western edge of central Anatolia.[5]

Concerning the concrete incarnations of trade, a few impressions stand out. One of them is the fairly small-scale, individual-level character of the process by which traders acquired goods. This impression first arises from several scenes depicting producers selling products such as cereals either to merchant intermediaries or directly to the consumers.[6] For example, we see the Ottoman sultan creating an opportunity for his soldiers to buy cereals from the besieged people of Konya, without himself taking part in the trade,[7] and people do not hesitate to haggle directly with a man who is transporting grain from one town to the next.[8] Likewise, when Ibn Baṭṭūṭa enters a village where the sole agricultural production is saffron, he is met by a woman who, falsely assuming that he is a trader, tries to sell him her production, following what appears to be a common local habit.[9]

Towns primarily devoted to monocultural, cash-crop productions such as saffron or rice were unusual enough to be singled out in the sources.[10] This suggests that, in most other villages, merchants acquired either the excess amounts of the central production of the peasant families they encountered or the peripheral productions of these same peasants—and thus that merchants had to visit a large number of producers in order to build up their stock. It is also clear that large cities such as Konya had *khāns* (urban caravanserais) where traders dealing in a particular type of good would temporarily settle in individual rooms they could lock, and from where they presumably would sell their merchandise. Sources mention, for example, the *khān* of the sugar sellers[11] and that of the rice sellers.[12]

All of this, combined with the distribution pattern of camel bones in archaeological excavations across the region,[13] suggests that traders interacted directly with a large number of people and, in an export-oriented region such as Anatolia, especially with peasant producers. In other words, even villagers had a direct opportunity to have conversations with individuals who had traveled, sometimes to fairly distant lands, thus directly expanding the awareness and even knowledge they had of the world beyond the immediate boundaries of their own living environments.

Having said that, it is also clear that differences in social status limited the interactions between peasants and merchants. Although merchants are a discreet presence in sources, which usually concentrate on political or religious characters, the few appearances they make strongly suggest that they could hold a relatively high social status,[14] and that they were readily identifiable by their clothes and behavior. It seems significant, for example, that saintly figure Shams Tabrīzī would stay in *khāns* and adopt "the ways and clothes of merchants" when he wished to travel incognito.[15]

As for transportation, there is ample evidence that the preferred method would be to put the goods directly on the backs of animals—mules, donkeys, horses, oxen, and camels.[16] Conversely, I could find only one reference to wheeled vehicles that falls within both the geographical and the chronological scope of this study, as part of a scene where the followers of spiritual leader Sayyid Hārūn are building a city and see miraculous "cartloads of *helvas* and various bounties pouring in."[17] On the other hand, a passage from the *Gharib-nama* categorizing animals according to their use makes no mention of vehicles, but includes animals that "carry loads from region to region."[18] The word *yük*, sometimes used in the abstract sense of *load*, is indeed sometimes used to refer to a saddle-like contraption put on the animal's back in order to contain what was to be transported.[19]

This absence or near absence of carts or other wheeled vehicles might be attributed to the general state of disrepair of the roads,[20] which would, in turn, have limited the incentive to transport products with a relatively low price-to-weight ratio such as cereals over longer distances. After all, the ports of the Mediterranean and Black Seas (and, to a lesser extent, the Aegean) were accessible but through fairly steep mountain roads.[21] It thus comes as no surprise that al-ʿUmarī, despite his mercantile sensibility and the emphasis he puts on the cheapness of Anatolian cereals, makes no reference to any cereal export to other regions. The suggestion that central Anatolia did not export cereals abroad is further strengthened by two scenes depicting the transportation of unthreshed cereals—a normal practice when cereals are produced for local consumption that becomes wasteful nonsense in the case of long-distance trade.[22]

For peasants, the absence of export had a direct impact on the demand for cereals, both pushing down the prices and closing off a possible outlet for extra production. One would therefore expect that peasants able and willing to invest extra time and resources to improve their lot probably did so in ways that diversified their production rather than increasing the acreage devoted to their main activity, the production of cereals. This does not mean, of course, that foreign lands hosted the only possible outlet of agricultural production. In fact, the very existence of cities depends on gathering surplus food from the surrounding countryside. The distribution of such surplus, in turn, happened in the marketplace.

MARKETS AND CRAFTSMEN

The market, usually called *bāzār* in Turkish and Persian sources and *sūq* in Arabic ones, served as the central locus of food exchange. Hints appear to suggest that people from outside the city would occasionally come to the market to sell their wares, such as in a reference to "a Turk" (presumably a poor, rural, and perhaps nomadic Turkish speaker) standing in the middle of the market and auctioning a fox's pelt.[23] More important, markets appear as a meeting point for the majority of the urban population. A reference to the "mardum-i bāzārī" (men of the market) in the eleventh-century Persian *Qabus-nama* is rendered in the earliest Anatolian Turkish translation as "şehr kavmı" (the people of the city). That the translator understood both expressions as synonymous implies that a large proportion of city folk worked in the markets.[24] To the centrality of the market for the population of medieval towns, we should oppose the composition of modern urban society, which tends to be divided between people of the working class, manning factories that have no counterpart in the context discussed here, and white-collar workers, whose late-medieval counterparts, state administrators and religious clerics, were demographically marginal.

Furthermore, the appearance of individual shops as revenue-producing properties in *waqfiyyas* shows that ownership of real estate in the marketplace was broken down into tiny chunks. Because of this, the symbolic presence or social influence of individual grandees was necessarily likewise broken down as well—much more so than in the vicinity of a caravanserai bearing the name of a ruler or in a village whose revenues belonged entirely to a military leader. Finally, there are clear indications that a notion of "being in public" (in the sight of a whole array of people, in a place that belongs to no one in particular) was associated with the marketplace.[25] Put together, these elements reveal the market as a locus of interactions over which no single political authority had enough of a monopoly to control comments about politics and censor selected perspectives. The marketplace, in other words, could be likened to our concept of "public space."

Sources often talk about the presence of numerous markets in major cities, identifying each of them with a given trade: the market of the butchers, that of the cloth sellers, of the goldsmiths, and so on.[26] Some geographical indications, mostly found in *waqfiyyas*, suggest that these were concentrations of a particular trade within a continuous commercial urban fabric, rather than commercial "islands" geographically isolated from each other.[27] Although most shops clearly were located near other shops of the same trade (hence the trade-specific designations), sources do not suggest an otherwise thematic organization of the commercial spaces, and one can easily find a *baqqāl* (grocer's) shop standing next to the presumably unrelated market of the blacksmiths.[28] However, how the location of markets related to other parts of the city, and especially to residential quarters, remains very much unclear.[29] The few indications available suggest that there was no significant difference in social status between food-related and non-food-related craftsmen, all of them being conceptualized within a single social category.[30]

Archaeology is of little help in studying urban markets, because their sites are constantly reused, without the benefit of continuity like monumental buildings, or the stability of rural sites where alternation between periods of continuous use and sudden abandonment often divides the occupational phases into clearly legible strata. However, textual information suggests that the shops were buildings large enough for customers to enter and exit them, such as when Ibn Baṭṭūṭa mentions that one of his fellow travelers settled down in an empty shop to watch over the horses on a winter night. The existence of enclosed structures (as opposed to mere counters or niches) would indeed seem almost essential for the conduct of commercial activities during the Anatolian cold season.[31] Most references to shops appearing in *waqfiyyas* make no mention of the particular trade of the folk who rented them, thus also implying that these structures were architecturally simple or standard rather than optimized for a particular purpose.[32]

Whatever they may have looked like, it appears that these shops were of a relatively small size, and while Ibn Baṭṭūṭa mentions one case where a shopkeeper seems to have a young apprentice,[33] most other references present—without paying much attention to the issue—shopkeepers as working alone, or at least not as part of a crew of employees. There are some hints that, given the small scale of these commercial operations, the various craftsmen in a given trade collaborated with each other. While there is no direct reference to guild-like structures (though it is conceivable that such organizations existed without attracting the attention of the various authors),[34] the grammar of two passages concerning the slaughter of animals (sheep, bovines) hints at a team effort from a number of butchers.[35] Furthermore, a number of anecdotes refer to craftsmen specialized in cooking and selling sheep heads, designated with several different names (*ravvāsī, sar-paz, ṭabbākh*). The authors appear to have considered these individuals as different from the butchers who had slaughtered the animals in the first place, thereby revealing a division of labor very well adapted to small commercial units[36] and to the production of ready-to-eat food.[37]

The slaughter of animals seems to have taken place directly in the marketplace. This, of course, makes perfect sense in a setting where no refrigeration could stretch the time available between slaughter and consumption. It also limited the transportation expenditures, since the product itself (animals' muscles) provided its own transport. The exact opposite situation appears to have prevailed in the case of produce, which, as I pointed out earlier, seems to have been sold primarily or exclusively at production sites, probably in the cities' suburbs.[38] The combination of these two sets of selling practices is important insofar as it must have at least attenuated (if not reversed) the price contrast that prevails today between (relatively cheap) prices of produce and (comparatively expensive) meat, therefore assumedly making the consumption of meat more accessible to the lower layers of the social hierarchy than a twenty-first-century observer would expect.[39]

This is far from the only difference between the setting described here and the foods that sustain us, twenty-first-century humans. Much, if not most, of the food we eat undergoes a host of automated processes, whereas only one step of the food-production-and-transformation cycle in late-medieval Anatolia was truly mechanized: grain milling.

MILLS

Grain milling is an essential operation in the production of bread, perhaps the most central food item of the late-medieval Anatolian diet.[40] Sources point to the existence of water mills (but none to mills using either wind, animal, or human power), with the clearest example appearing when the *Gharib-nama* states that water "grinds the wheat and waters the *bāgh*."[41]

Two main types of water mills existed at the time. The first model is a simpler, more primitive and sturdy, but also less efficient design, in which water falls down on the obliquely set paddles of a wheel that is laid horizontally, supported by a vertical axis. The second, better-known, type of mill sets the wheel vertically, a much more efficient method to capture hydraulic power, but also one that requires a relatively complex mechanism to translate the power of the waterwheel's horizontal axis to the millstone's vertical axis. Which of these two setups was in use in the medieval Anatolian context is uncertain, but the horizontal type is a more likely guess, both because this was the only type in existence during the Byzantine period and because it squares better with the formulation of some passages in fourteenth-century sources.[42]

Either way, these mills required water to strike the paddles while falling down vertically.[43] The water had to build up some head before reaching the mill, and indeed sources do mention the channels thus constructed in order to bring water to the mill at a height.[44] One should remember, however, that the relatively flat topography, deeply eroded riverbeds, and scarcity of waterfalls in central Anatolia offered a limited number of natural mill locations. One can therefore surmise that the geographical relation between inhabited spaces and mills changed quite a lot from town to town, thus preventing the mills from acquiring a homogenous sociocultural image and function that would parallel, for example, those of marketplaces (always located in town) throughout central Anatolia.

The *Gharib-nama*, as part of a lengthy metaphor, describes the workings of a mill with such detail that it is worth translating in full:[45]

[102a]
I saw [the mill], which of a total of nine things
Is made; the noble and the humble know this.

One is the paddle, one the axle, one the stone,
One is water, one the ground and the stone

One is the gutter, from which the water comes down
When this one comes down, oh, the mill turns.

[102b]
One is the wheat, the basket is also one,
When it is ground, this is the place [where] the wheat [goes].

The clapper is also one, oh, it makes a clap
This is the one that always drives the wheat.[46]

Those nine things thus named,
They make up the mill, o friend.

Of those nine, if one is missing,
It shall not work anymore, but remain broken.

It is the paddle, ultimately, [that] both turns
The axle stands up and sends [power to the millstone] and makes [the mill] turn

It is the paddle that turns and makes [the mill] turn,
When the water strikes it, it both turns and makes [the mill] turn.

If the paddle does not turn, how could the stone turn?
Then know that if there is no such paddle, [the mill] is not [working].

If the axle does not stand straight up,
If it does not carry the stone on its head,

The stone, by itself, cannot keep hanging [in the air],
[The two stones] stick to one another, and do not move.

Once these are there, now [if] there is no stone
No outcomes occur anymore.

It is the stone that, night and day, runs;
When this one runs, this wheat is ground.[47]

[103a]
One turns, [but if] there is none that stays still,
How could it run and make the wheat into flour?

This turning stone, as it turns night and day,
All the wheat falls and flour comes out of it.

The stone is fine, but now [if] there is no water,
Which is the one that makes all of these move?

It is this water itself that gives motion in the mill,
It is the only one that makes it move, gives it motion.

Now a gutter is necessary for the water to come down,
To fall straight down on the paddle so that it may turn.

If there is no gutter, the water scatters,
The flour is not ground, the whole remains inoperant.

[Once] there are all of these, now wheat is necessary,
So that it may become flour, so that warm *çörek*[48] may always bake.

If there is no wheat, these serve no purpose;
All of these came in motion for the wheat.

There is wheat, this time a basket is necessary,
So that this wheat can fall little by little from it.

If there is no basket, the wheat cannot stay,
It is a great instrument for this wheat, that basket.

If there is no clapper with all of these,
The wheat cannot fall down and come, little by little.

[103b]
As it moves in various ways, now this one
It is the one that pours the wheat in its measure.

These details, of course, concern the mechanics of the mill rather than its socioeconomic characteristics. But they do convey a sense that the intended audience of the author, ordinary (rural) people, would have been familiar not only with the rhythmic sound coming out of the mill, but also with the complexity and fragility of the mechanical apparatus that produced flour.

A small number of short references suggest that the dealings the population had with mills occurred on a household-by-household basis, with a certain delay taking place between the moment one would bring grain and the moment when one would come back to pick up the flour.[49] The presence of mills in *waqfiyya*s also shows that mills could be the personal property of individuals and that fees must have been extracted for milling services, since these structures appear as sources of revenues for the endowments. Grain milling was, in other words, a for-profit enterprise.[50] This observation is quite consistent with a context in which privately funded foundations (*waqf*s), unevenly distributed across the region, were in charge of providing "services" to the population.

Grain milling is not the only service we would be wrong to expect seeing provided by the state authorities. The distribution of water was also a private enterprise, whether it was organized for profit or for more or less charitable purposes.

WATER PROVISIONING

Let us state the obvious: water is the most fundamental component of human nutrition. In many ways, water distribution constituted the greatest challenge of medieval urban organization, itself a work in progress; in fourteenth-century Anatolia, few city dwellers had access to as much running water as they wanted, and those who did may have considered it a luxury.[51] An episode depicting water distribution on donkey back in a small town gives us a hint of the systems that may have been used in places where no aqueduct flowed, as does the presence of a water well (*chāh-i ābī*) in the garden surrounding a madrasa in Konya. The stagnant water thus made available no doubt left people dreaming of water flowing out of fountains.[52]

As was the case with mills for the countryside folk, then, no state institution or policy existed that was intended to provide the urban population with running water. Fountains appear on a number of occasions as part of endowments (*waqf*s), always the product of a rich individual's generosity. The presence of an endowment further reveals that the upkeep of the fountain entailed regular expenses. No document, however, offers any detail on the source of this water or how it was brought into town.[53]

Such a system served the needs of the endowers at least as much as those of the water consumers. This is most obvious when we look at the list of locations for the fountains appearing in a 1323 endowment deed: in the *dār al-ṣulaḥā'* (a Sufi convent) that is supported by the same *waqf*, in a madrasa also part of the *waqf*, in the house of the endower, beside the door of the endower's house, and near a vineyard in a village. Even the most naive observer can see that the needs of the population, while they may have been served by such infrastructure, were by no means central in the choice of locations for these fountains.[54] Uneven access to water across social strata also appears through the story of a beggar asking for water at a rich man's house.[55]

The observations I just made about the water-distribution systems, together with others on food distribution,[56] reveal the importance that patronage had in creating a relationship between the population at large and the political authorities. For one thing, almost any service offered to the population was deemed a "privilege" rather than a fundamental right of the population or obligation on the part of the state. But at least equally interesting is the role of individual political figures, whose names were attached to the endowments, and thus to the endowed structures that provided services to the population. These individuals, and presumably the members of their families, incarnated political power in the absence from popular view of an abstract agent that we today would call "the state." From the perspective of the population, we can therefore assume that the political world had a much more personal and much less abstract or legalistic character than what we moderns have in mind when thinking of the affairs of state. The political world, in short, was populated by recognizable characters, whereas the state itself amounted, to a large extent, to a rather barebones tax-collection operation.

TAXES ON FOOD

In the absence of income tax (or of a significant population of wage workers, for that matter), most of the revenues of the medieval state were collected from food production. For late-medieval Anatolians, tax collection must therefore have been one of the most frequent, tangible, and psychologically significant forms of state presence.

I encountered only one scene depicting the very act of tax collection from peasants. The expression "their habit was to" (*ʿādetleri bu idi kim*) introduces this anecdote, therefore suggesting that the practice changed significantly between the moment when the story took place (sometime in the thirteenth century) and the time it was written down (late fifteenth). This implies that at least some tax-collection practices of the Seljuk era did not survive into the Ottoman period.[57] In any case, the scene shows that an official bearing the title of *şahne* traveled from the administrative center that was the city of Kırşehir to a Cappadocian village. There, he met with peasants who had already harvested, threshed, and winnowed the various field cultures (wheat, barley, lentils, and rye), then covered them with a tarpaulin while awaiting his arrival. The *şahne* then measured the grain and collected from it an unspecified proportion as taxes. One should note, along the way, that the less than optimal form of protection that the tarpaulin offered, leaving cereals partially vulnerable to vermin and bad weather, could cause both crop loss and discontent toward the tax collector when the latter took a little too long to arrive.

As I noted earlier, *waqfiyya*s include, among the properties endowed to provide revenues, entire villages, individual pieces of land, and *mazraʿa*s (possibly small-size agricultural communities).[58] That the first two types of property should seldom appear side by side in a single document raises the possibility that these in fact reflect different fiscal models. Roughly speaking, the revenues of these tax-exempt endowments correspond to what would otherwise be collected as taxes. One can thus assume that different types of land tenure appearing in different endowment deeds reflected different systems of tax collection.[59]

As far as markets are concerned, documents also reveal their taxation only once, in a rather exquisite scene reported by ʿĀşıkpaşazāde:

> Someone came from [the neighboring *beylik* of] Germiyan. He said: "Sell me the *bac* [tax revenues] on this market." The people said: "Go to the lord." This person went to the lord [Ottoman ruler Osman] and presented his request. Osman Gazi said: "What is the *bac*?" This person said "Whoever comes to this market, I get one *akçe* [coin] from them." Osman Gazi said: "Do you have some right over the people of this market, for which you would ask an *akçe*?" This person said "My lord! This is a tradition! It exists in all regions, and the one who is the ruler takes it." Osman Gazi said "Did God order it, or did the princes create it themselves?" This person repeated "This is a tradition, my lord! It is [an ancient practice]." Osman Gazi got very angry, and said: "What one earns, does it belong to another? It is one's own property. What did I put into their goods that I would ask them [to] give me an *akçe*? Leave, go away. Don't repeat this to me anymore or I shall punish you!" And the people said "Lord, it is a tradition that a little something be given to those who protect the market." Osman said: "Now since you are saying so, every person who shall bring a load and sell it, let them give two *akçe*s, [but] whoever does not sell, let them not give anything."[60]

The claim that the first Ottoman ruler was unaware that tax could be collected on a market may very well be apocryphal, or at least slanted in such a way as to support the author's admiration for early Ottoman simplicity and dislike for the wealth-accumulating tendencies of institutionalized states. But the short passage in which the protagonist makes his initial request might be more reliable than other parts of this anecdote, insofar as it is less ideologically laden. As such, it raises interesting questions not only because it suggests that it was a common practice to farm out the collection of market taxes, but more important because it also shows that someone from one *beylik* (principality) could imagine going to another *beylik* to acquire such a privilege. This is a startling proposition, at least if one assumes that the various *beylik*s were entirely independent polities from the very beginning of their existence (which, in most cases, means the early fourteenth century). However, we must remember that political power was rather fractured in the second half of the thirteenth century, a period during which "the state" was consistently weaker than the sum of its parts (the latter comprising a handful of political and military grandees). It would therefore make sense to conceptualize the early *beylik* period as one where lower-level, provincial state institutions continued to survive, develop, and flourish after the decapitation of higher-level, imperial power. This perspective would transform the incongruous overlap of independent states' power in some locales into more readily understandable rivalries between administrative units that had not yet started regarding themselves as political rivals and neighbors.

More concretely, positing that lower-level administrative units survived with variable degrees of continuity through the numerous changes that brought Anatolia from the rule of Seljuk and Ilkhanid oligarchs into that of the *bey*s (rulers of *beylik*s) and, ultimately, to the Ottoman era entails that this transition was, from the point of view of the population at large, a smooth one if perceptible at all. In any case, it seems clear that the average Anatolian peasant's experience was light-years away from the dramatic shift in political structures that the representations of his period, often amounting to no more than rather desperate attempts at map painting, would lead us to believe.

The few references to taxes that appear in the sources surveyed as part of this study present the issue from the point of view of those *collecting* rather than *paying* the taxes. Historians have covered this question, especially for the Ottoman period, with the help of a much more extensive documentation than what is available for the fourteenth century. However, the present survey, as superficial as it may seem, makes it absolutely clear that tax collection was not simply an abstract administrative operation, but rather that its modalities very much shaped the texture of the relations between the population at large and the political authorities. The same can be said for the way in which the population interacted with the other major component of the medieval state besides tax collection: the army.

ARMY LOGISTICS

In a world where "state institutions" were little more than a combination of military forces and tax-collection and management structures, feeding the army created a point of contact between the rulers and the ruled that may have been more sporadic than regular tax collection, but was at least equally intense. Sources leave us with the impression that armies were generally independent from supply lines, precisely because they fed directly off the land.

The military actively sought interaction with the farming segment of the population, as we can see from a village being designated as a choice place for an army to alight.[61] Once the army alighted, soldiers would scatter in order to gather supplies for themselves and their horses.[62] Although they would probably not go farther than an hour's walk away from the main camp, such collection of supplies left the army particularly vulnerable to enemy attacks and significantly slowed down the movement rate.[63] Soldiers would then do the cooking for themselves, thus completing a picture of armies that had a relatively low level of specialization.[64]

Though it remains unclear to what extent food was acquired through exchange or confiscation, the fact that individual soldiers rather than groups were sent to forage suggests that consent and compensation were, at least to some extent, part of the deal. This suggestion is strengthened by two factors. First, political leaders, who would often lead the army in person, had an interest in leaving peasants in good-enough shape to pay their taxes. Second, the few references that sources make to invading foreign armies almost systematically associate the latter with a destructive impact on the land, with one anecdote bluntly presenting a high-ranking military commander who, discussing strategy with his ruler, suggests taking his underfed army to enemy land in order to provision it through plunder.[65]

In any case, the inconvenience created by logistics—both the vulnerability to attacks and the burden on local populations—could be at least partially alleviated by advance planning and provisioning by allies or subaltern polities. For this reason, logistical agreements sometimes appeared as topics of diplomatic discussion. In one scene, the Ottoman ruler thus requires logistical support from an allied polity when planning a campaign on a common enemy, and the points of passage that the Ottoman mentions suggest that campaigns could be planned in stages roughly 150 kilometers (100 miles) in length.[66]

It is rather unlikely that the peasant population perceived the passage of any army, friend or foe, as good news. Even if they received financial compensation for the foods taken, the locals obviously had no choice in letting their products go. Furthermore, security considerations required that the soldiers take care of this business in a swift fashion, and the fact that only one of the two parties in the transaction was trained in the art of fighting (and carried weapons) suggests that such interactions leaned toward the rougher end of the spectrum of human relations. As we will see in the next section, it was nevertheless fairly benign in comparison to plunder.

There was one aspect of military food provisioning in which interaction with the civilian population took place in a longer-term perspective: fortified places. Stockpiling played an absolutely crucial role in the strategic use of these military structures. No matter how thick its walls, no matter how well-trained and numerous its garrison, a castle or fortress without significant food reserves was as good as lost.[67] Likewise, a castle's water supplies were nothing short of a military secret. It is therefore not surprising, for example, that archaeological excavations at the Tavas fortress uncovered an underground water tank of a type common in Anatolia that was designed to be invisible from the surface.[68]

Fortunately, some factors facilitated fortress food provisioning. For one, stockpiles could be preserved over a very long period. Although the figure of "a hundred years" given by ʿĀşıkpaşazāde might be a tad excessive, it is clear that grain could be kept edible for at least several years.[69] The garrison of a stronghold may also have participated, at least in peacetime, in the agricultural exploitation of the surrounding countryside, thus drawing from a readily available workforce rather than depleting cash reserves in order to develop a secure source of food.[70] Finally, some passages suggest that sieges may not have been as systematically airtight as the modern imagination would have it and that the import of food from outside defense walls (and even trade with the enemy) may have been possible in the presence of a besieging force.[71] Fragmentary information prevents us from distinguishing different sets of practices for walled cities and strictly military fortresses, but one can at least see that the level of activity and the upkeep requirements of fortified places made them living entities in ways that do contrast with the still, empty shells that we can visit as tourists today.

On the whole, the civilian population could have more or less pleasant, more or less tolerable interactions with "friendly" armies. But as ironic as the term *friendly* may seem in this context, it does entail that some armies did not fall in this category, and, indeed, the situation would take a turn for the worse when the enemy arrived.

Plunder

Perhaps the form of interaction between the army and the population that most prominently figures in sources is plunder, the forceful appropriation of property from enemy civilians, which seems to have taken place more or less every time an army led a successful campaign into enemy lands. The latter point must be emphasized, insofar as damage on a similar scale does not seem to have taken place in "friendly territory"—the area from which the leaders of the army in question could hope to extract taxes.[72]

A few scenes depict soldiers plundering kitchen and table utensils made of precious metals.[73] This type of booty, however, may have made up a minority of cases, taking a disproportionate place in the source material because authors such as ʿĀşıkpaşazāde concentrate their attention on these types of goods, the most glamorous riches, in order to give a rosy picture of the "*gazi*" lifestyle. Probably much more common was the enslavement of defeated non-Muslims as well as the plunder of agricultural products such as cereals and, more frequently, farm animals (whose transportation was "part of the package").[74] As I pointed out in chapter 1, most peasants probably considered livestock as essential work instruments and savings accounts rolled into one; it is therefore easy to imagine the dramatic consequences that plunder may have had on peasant life. No source ever mentions local authorities offering any form of compensation for plundered property, although this omission may at least partially be an attempt to avoid admitting weakness (the confession that the ruler couldn't prevent an enemy force from raping his land). We are thus left to conjecture whether peasants could rebuild capital that was taken away by a visiting army or whether such a dramatic event would lead them to abandon the land. Likewise, sources are all but silent on the mechanics of plunder—such as the extent to which it was organized or spontaneous and whether the division of the spoils between leaders and troops would follow a shariʿa-inspired or home-brewed system. The most we can find are references to the fact that plunder could take place over anything between a few hours and two months, depending on the area discussed.[75]

Insofar as brigands sought many of the same prizes as plundering armies, it is against this backdrop that we should see a handful of "peacetime" scenes where a local ruler directly employs his military apparatus for the defense of agricultural property—for example, when Ibn Baṭṭūṭa depicts the commander of the Tavas castle (south of Denizli) in his habit of coming out of the castle with his troops every morning in order to inspect the area and ensure that no brigand is present before the farm animals are let out of the walls.[76]

During military campaigns, dealings between "friendly" forces and peasants were probably of the rough and heavy kind, but the harm they caused remained relatively benign when compared with the outright theft of a farmer's livestock capital and cereal production. In politically (and therefore militarily) unstable contexts, the appearance of a "friendly" army must thus have been for the average peasant something akin to a very strong antibiotic medicine, plagued with highly unpleasant or even hurtful side effects, but still preferable to the sickness it was meant to cure. But if plunder is a self-interested act of appropriation, it does not cover all the damage caused to the property of civilians in enemy territory.

Destruction

Given my discussion of the previous sections, one need not ponder for a long time the lessons of the Stanford prison experiment in order to imagine how individual soldiers and peasants may have interacted. Indeed, a few scenes leave no doubt about a certain degree of amused contempt—if not downright schadenfreude—that the military crowd entertained toward the victims of their plunder. For example, the *Dustur-nama* takes an unambiguously humorous tone when it describes the horrified reaction of enemy captives who are falsely convinced that they were fed human flesh.[77]

Whether this contempt is enough to inspire gratuitous destruction or not, many scenes refer to such an outcome for the local population's property, and most authors relish their emphasis of the wealth that soldiers could capture. In one significant exception to this rule, a lieutenant receives direct orders to destroy a region's villages *but only if* he cannot conquer a castle.[78] The author of the passage, ʿĀşıkpaşazāde, further mentions that this destruction was to be performed in such a way as to render it impossible to repopulate the region for a long time. Given this author's tendency to get to the point without stating the obvious, the need he felt to add the latter specification strongly suggests that such a policy of deliberate destruction was rather unusual.

Another case depicting a policy of destruction, in somewhat different circumstances, raises another set of interesting questions.[79] Toward the middle of the fourteenth century, a central Anatolian ruler by the name of ʿAli Beg (the son of Eretna, a onetime Ilkhanid lieutenant turned local ruler) marched against the city of Erzincan. The city's leadership was refusing to recognize his authority, and, when he arrived with his army, ʿAli Beg was faced with closed gates and no local spokesmen to talk to. Then, "ʿAli Beg consulted with the amirs on the way they should enter the city, and the way they should set battle. They agreed to settle on the east side, in between the city and the countryside, and to busy themselves destroying the cultivated land, cutting the trees, and beating down the gardens and vineyards."[80]

The combination of siege and crop destruction immediately suggests that these actions were meant to starve the besieged city into submission. Yet a number of factors indicate that the intention was in fact something else. First, it is striking that the plan should be geographically concentrated on one side of the city. It would, of course, be counterproductive to attack food-production structures in one location if goods and people retained free passage on the other side of the city. An enlightening parallel can be found in a similar case involving early Ottoman operations against İznik, a few decades earlier. There, a band of a few dozen—at most a few hundred—soldiers likewise repeatedly destroyed the gardens as part of siege operations, and the anecdote does not include any hint that the besieging force intended to consume the food thus targeted. Yet the same city, two hundred years earlier, had used its lakeside location to maintain outside access for a long period during a siege laid by an army of somewhere between sixty and one hundred thousand Crusaders—a force approximately *a thousand* times larger than the Ottoman one. Clearly, then, sealing off the enemy from outside provisioning could not have realistically been the objective in the Ottoman case.[81]

Furthermore, fruits and vegetables were of very secondary nutritional importance in comparison with cereals and livestock.[82] Under such circumstances, attacking the gardens and especially cutting down the trees (as if it were not just one but several years' worth of dessert that had to be taken away from the rebel city) seem like a rather unpleasant and life-threatening waste of time and energy—all the more so if they had to be done within firing range of the defenders on the city walls.

A better explanation for the tactical choice of ʿAli Beg and his amirs can be found by adopting a comparative perspective. In ancient Greece, "Long invasions not only meant much more complete destruction of the crops and the buildings in the countryside, they also posed a great threat to the unity of the citizen body. Long invasions created internal pressures, partly because they did not affect all alike (farmers were hit harder than those without land, and some farmers were hit harder than others), and partly because in a city under siege there was considerable scope for treacherous action and suspicion of treachery."[83]

Such a description fits the late-medieval Anatolian context particularly well, since ownership of gardens was closely associated with wealth and prestige.[84] It was the local grandees who were rejecting ʿAli Beg's authority; it was also them (much more than the population as a whole) that ʿAli Beg's forces targeted as they set out to destroy the gardens. In other words, this policy of destruction was primarily political, intended to pressure a key segment of the population into action. Whether this action was to be a military one (a sortie against the besieging force) or a diplomatic one (representatives coming out to start negotiations), such destruction aimed to break a stalemate that began with the gates of Erzincan being sealed off and its authorities refusing any dialogue.

This anecdote might seem remote from the daily concerns of ordinary people, but this is precisely why it should be mentioned here. It sheds light on the extent to which war and politics were, in late-medieval Anatolia, the exclusive playground of the elite. It suggests an at least partially conscious attempt to leave the general population out of the conflict, in this case by concentrating on property in which the lower social classes had at most a limited stake. This situation stands in stark contrast to the contemporary Western notion of popular sovereignty as a self-evident truth; here, political and military decisions belonged to an altogether different class of beings. Markets may have offered a neutral ground, echoing to some extent our idea of public sphere, but for most late-medieval Anatolians, to use the marketplace as a forum for discussions of the affairs of state would have entailed as much decision making as discussions of professional sports.[85]

CONCLUSION

In this short survey of food as a tie that binds, one element turns out to be more important than it would have seemed at first: the awareness that ordinary people had of the world beyond their immediate lives. Contact with long-distance merchants must have contributed to this awareness, as did interactions in the marketplace and a number of other circumstances, perhaps none as dreadful as the cloud of dust raised by an incoming army. The very existence of these channels of communication is reason enough to raise the question of popular involvement in politics—or the apparent absence thereof. Two observations help us gain some perspective on this question.

First, politics was a game to be played by the elite, between members of the elite. Looking at the way garden plundering was handled in the case discussed above, there are even reasons to believe that the elite may have actively tried to exclude the rest of the population from the consequences of these decisions whenever possible.

Second, a common pattern seems to run through all the moments that put the lower classes in contact with political processes. From the collection of taxes on cereal productions to the rough wrenching of supplies by a "friendly" army and the plunder of oxen and cereals, all these interactions tend to involve only the outcome of the political process and, more important, to fall somewhere along a spectrum of unpleasantness ranging from mere discomfort (at best) to horrible pain, enslavement, and death (at worst).[86]

Throughout the sources I consulted for this study, no clear example of a commoner actively attempting to influence the decision making of the elite ever appears. Absence from representation is, of course, no proof of absence from reality, and it is possible that some such practices, perhaps even common ones, remained undocumented. But caught between an elite bent on excluding commoners from its "internal" debates and a succession of painful experiences, it does not seem too extravagant to suggest that, for the bulk of the population, the struggles of the elite may have appeared at once difficult to understand and difficult to bear—and that those commoners found in such combination reason enough not to get involved in the first place.

Food was, of course, not the only category of goods to be traded. Its exchange may in fact have constituted but a small proportion of the activity in an urban market, although it did hold a central place in the interactions between the population at large and the political authorities. After all, the latter's main source of revenue was the taxation of agriculture, and their primary expense revolved around military activity, including campaigns where the army lived "off the land" of the peasants. This study of food as something that changes hands reveals a broad network of interactions that encompassed almost everyone in society—from peasants to the ruling elite, from soldier to long-distance trader.

Furthermore, this perspective humanizes politics and power relations. It lets us see, for example, that the presentation of the *beylik* period as one when political power over Anatolia was highly fragmented ignores the fact that, for most of the population, the rapidly changing colors on a political map left a remarkably light trace on the ground, if any at all. Perhaps more important, it allows us to examine power not at the flat, abstract level of analysis that a strictly administrative, economic, or even sociological approach would allow, but rather endowed with a richness of texture that would have been familiar to those who were the living nodes of this network.

(THREE)

Food Consumption

The great poet and spiritual master Rūmī one day encountered an Armenian butcher named Tanyīl. When Tanyīl bowed to him seven times, the spiritual master bowed back. This is how the anecdote begins and ends, in a formulation bound to puzzle most of today's readers—all the more so because it occurs as part of a discussion of Rūmī's qualities. Yes, he bowed back. But he bowed only once! Why is this worth mentioning? Is there any bragging ground at all in this story?

But of course a sentence often carries more than its superficial meaning. The context of this passage makes it clear that Aflākī, the author of the text, understood Rūmī's action as a display of kindness and consideration toward someone of much lower social standing. Yet to understand this scene fully, one needs to take a broader look at the norms that governed social interactions at the time. This is precisely what this chapter intends to do.

Food consumption provides an ideal angle to study such a topic. Historians often discuss rather abstract concepts such as social stratifications, but in our experience of daily life these considerations remain latent most of the time. Yes, identity or status can occupy or even shape the mind of an individual, but an external observer could follow that individual for most of the day without receiving any indication about what goes on inside that mind. Food consumption creates moments of social interaction where these considerations take a concrete form, where rituals uncover broader worldviews. When a number of people find themselves eating in a space where others are present, they necessarily have to sit either together or apart, all eating or some serving and others eating, and either eating simultaneously or in succession. These choices are unavoidable and they cannot be neutral, but rather betray much deeper, complex underlying structures of social statuses and relations.

This chapter attempts to tackle the issue of food consumption in as broad a perspective as possible.[1] Meals, of course, form the core of the topic. But I will begin with a discussion of the steps that precede the meal, from the acquisition and storage of food to the various circumstances of cooking. After covering meals themselves and the food that was consumed, I will conclude by addressing a number of important related concepts that surrounded the consumption of food.

THE FOOD BEFORE THE MEAL

Meals may hold a considerable importance and carry a lot of meaning, but the dishes that compose them do not appear out of thin air. Rather, they are the end result of a process spanning several months, if not more, that begins with the plowing of a field or the birth of a lamb. I have already discussed the initial phases of food production in chapter 1 and the different paths taken by these products in order to reach the households that consumed them in chapter 2. Before the moment of consumption, however, food had to undergo one final transformation, this time under the supervision of the household members. This last step begins with the acquisition, sometimes followed by a period of storage, and goes on to the cooking of these foodstuffs.

Acquiring the Food

Food intended for meals would generally enter a house untransformed or semitransformed. As I will explain below, buying ready-made dishes, let alone consuming them in a public space, was unusual.[2] Furthermore, it seems that acquisition took place at the site of the last step of production. For example, gardeners appear to have sold produce directly in the gardens,[3] and food-related craftsmen would sell their products themselves rather than handing over this task to third-party shopkeepers.[4] This situation, no doubt, reflects the limitations of transport and distribution technologies that had nothing of the scale or efficiency that we know today. But it also entailed that the people involved in the food-related economic networks all made a very visible contribution to the final product, thus limiting what in Marxian thought has been termed the "alienation" of work division.

Baked goods (various types of breads and cakes) constitute a notable exception to such unavailability of ready-to-eat foods.[5] There certainly were bakeries in urban settings,[6] and it is clear that bread makers would bake on a relatively large scale.[7] Interestingly, however, all these references mention only the baking process and say nothing of the earlier stages of bread making. They thus do not exclude the possibility that professional bread makers might in fact have been oven attendants, whose task was limited to baking the dough that their "customers" brought them.[8]

In one of the few direct references to food acquisition that sources present, a male head of household, probably from the lower elite or upper middle class, describes himself as "in charge" of the house's food provisioning. The formulation of this passage also suggests that the acquisition of foodstuffs (he refers to "bread and meat") would take place not on a daily basis but rather once every few days at most.[9] In a separate anecdote, another man claims that having "brought a new wife to the house" increased his own expenses.[10] Yet it is quite possible that this association between the responsibility of food provisioning and the male gender applies only to the financial side of things, without implying an exclusion of women from the practice of food acquisition.[11]

Once food was brought to the house, in any case, control over the food seemed to shift away from the males. We have anecdotes that include references to in-house food stores in both peasant and upper-class urban families, and, in all cases, control over these stores rests with women.[12] Furthermore, on one occasion a man also uses the expression "ev bekçisi" (house overseer) to refer to his wife.[13] All of this betrays a gender shift in responsibilities between the moment when the food is acquired and the moment it is stored in the house. Although this observation obviously refers only to the management of food reserves, it also opens the door to seeing household affairs as a gendered dominion, where men had limited influence over the decisions made.

This brings us to a topic closely associated with the acquisition of food: its storage.

Storing the Food

Storage prolongs the availability of foodstuffs beyond the production periods. In places like Anatolia, where plant production essentially ceases during the winter, storage is absolutely essential in order to ensure survival. But as necessary as it was, storage could be practiced in a number of ways.

It is clear that some of the food storage was undertaken for profit at the commercial level,[14] but also that palaces and houses belonging to the urban elite could have their own stockpiles.[15] Although sources do not specifically address the practices among nomads or in lower urban classes, a number of passages also suggest that it was common for a peasant household to stock up on basic products such as oil (or fat) and flour.[16] Archaeological research has uncovered a great number of large underground pits (up to ten feet in depth) dug in villages to contain harvests. Conical in shape, with a wide base and a narrow surface opening, these pits had the advantage of being discrete, and could conceivably have protected grain reserves not only from decay, but also from hostile intruders and even tax collectors.[17] These would have been complemented, at least in the urban context, by what sources call *anbārs*, which could have been domestic cellars or vessels (large pots, amphorae, and the like).[18]

A number of contextual factors must be considered when analyzing the contrast between urban and rural practices of food storage. Thus, the revenues of craftspeople are more evenly distributed over the year than those of peasants (therefore allowing them to buy smaller amounts more often), population density makes commercial storage more practical (and profitable) in the city, rural settlements offer more space to dig pits between buildings, and as producers peasants had to deal with large quantities of grain requiring storage all at once. Given these factors, it would make sense that urban lower classes relied more heavily than their rural counterparts on commercial food storage. The kind of interactions that accompany small-scale commercial transactions would therefore have occurred much more frequently in the urban context, endowing food with an economic value associated with its acquisition in the minds of the city dwellers, whereas peasants would have associated food's economic value with production and sale (or loss to the tax collector). Between the city and the countryside, therefore, stood a divide between food as something one buys and food as something one sells.

As for the methods of preservation used for other foodstuffs, it is easier to identify those that could have been used than the degree of typicality of any one of them. It is clear that some vegetables were pickled. One witnesses, for example, a nanny cleaning carrots and beets (*jazar va shaljam*), in an anecdote whose formulation suggests that she was processing a rather large amount of these vegetables, probably to prepare homemade pickles.[19] There seems to have been some use of spices as preservatives, perhaps even at the lower levels of the social ladder, although it remains unclear whether they were used on a large, commercial scale or rather within households.[20] Blocks of ice were also available in a city such as Konya, probably well after the end of the winter.[21] Finally, in the case of fruits, it is clear that drying was widely practiced and allowed for year-round consumption.[22]

It is worth noticing, at least en passant, that most if not all of these preservation methods induced a change in the nature of the foodstuff that also altered the experience of its consumption. For example, fresh fruits were consumed in a different way from dried ones (as snacks rather than as part of a meal), and pickled vegetables were appreciated precisely because they were pickled. Preferences in taste and the need for preservation thus had to accommodate each other. As I stated above, food preservation in central Anatolia was needed first and foremost because of seasonal changes, therefore creating an association between particular seasons and the availability of particular foods in particular forms. Since smell and taste—as Proust so famously expressed—carry an exceptional power of emotional evocation, late-medieval Anatolian society as a whole must have experienced the cycle of seasonal changes with a degree of intensity that no amount of intellectual effort could allow us, who grew up in the age of refrigeration and long-distance imports of fresh foods, to understand.

Yet along the lengthy path that leads food from seedling to digestion, preservation is not the step that carries the greatest potential of emotional expression. This distinction, rather, belongs to cooking.

Cooking

The family home is the setting that first comes to mind when we evoke cooking. But the preparation of meals can take place in a number of settings and involve a variable number of people, ranging from an isolated individual to a handful of courtiers in a palace to an entire army on campaign.

COOKS OUTSIDE THE HOUSE Before turning back to the house, it may be worth saying a few words about those individuals whose professional lives concentrated on the preparation of food for people outside their own immediate families. Such individuals indeed existed, falling in a number of different categories.

At the most obvious level, there were cooks who were in charge of preparing meals in elite households. Later Ottoman centuries provide us with large numbers of archives pertaining to the palace kitchens. The period surveyed here, on the other hand, offers only enough material to confirm that there indeed was such a category of people, that a high-ranking individual could employ more than one cook,[23] and that these cooks were not the same people as the employees responsible for serving the food.[24] A rather lengthy passage in which the son of a palace cook discusses his own professional background—he seems to have been a personal attendant to a female member of the royal family, then the ruler's furrier (*pūstīn-dūz*)—shows that it needed not be a lifelong or hereditary profession.[25] Put in a broader perspective, and in conjunction with my earlier discussion of gardeners, it does indeed seem that individuals—males in all the cases I could find—would select their profession rather independently from the trade of their fathers and experienced an apparent freedom of choice, at least within the boundaries of what we would call their social class. This impression is further strengthened by the case of the son of a top-ranking Ottoman official whose excessive spending habits forced him to become, among other things, a *kebab* turner in Bursa.[26]

A number of *waqfiyya*s include provisions for the employment of cooks in dervish convents. Apart from the odd mention that the person should be able to cook, these documents do not include references to the identity of the individual to be hired. Narrative sources, for their part, depict dervishes cooking for their own communities on several occasions.[27] There is thus every reason to assume that the various jobs in dervish convents—not only cook, but also sweeper, doorman, and the like—would indeed be held by members of the dervish community rather than "outsider civilians" employed by the religious community.[28] Conversely, this also means that there was a degree of specialization within these communities, in which few if any individuals would devote their entire schedule to spiritual pursuits.

It is also clear that the position of cook (always designated as *ṭabbākh*) was not an overly prestigious one. *Waqfiyya*s often prescribe salaries for the various employees of the institution endowed, and four documents allow us to compare the salaries of cooks to those of a total of seventeen other wage earners. The results are quite telling: thirteen of these seventeen individuals receive a salary equal or higher than that of the cook (often twice or even three times as much), and only four others receive less.[29] Of course, these figures concern only the cooks who are employed in a particular type of institution, and they should not be taken as an exact image of the cooking profession at large—especially given the very small size of the sample. Nevertheless, they do suggest a general trend that makes it hard to imagine that cooks commanded extremely high salaries elsewhere if they earned less than the average when employed by dervish convents.

A modern observer acquainted with such institutions as the Mavlāvī or Bektaşi Sufi orders through later sources or historical museums would, at this point, add a note on the symbolic status of food-related positions (such as cook and food buyer). Nineteenth- and early-twentieth-century observers point out that these assignments played a central part in the hierarchical progression of members of these orders and that food-related implements such as cauldrons often held great symbolic and ceremonial importance.

However, early narrative sources do *not* contain any reference to a set hierarchical level or symbolic meaning that the status of cook may have held within these orders. In fact, one passage characterizes one particular Mavlāvī dervish as particularly skilled at cooking tasty meals, hence strongly suggesting that it was his personal abilities (rather than preestablished stages of disciple progression for the order) that put him in charge of the cooking among his group. Likewise, another passage points out that two newly accepted disciples were put in charge of feeding the dervishes, one having been a bread maker and the other a butcher before joining the order.[30] It is clear that the structures and functioning of religious orders (as well as other social institutions, such as the Janissary corps) underwent a long process of institutionalization that may have continued down to the nineteenth or, in some cases, twentieth century. From my observations in these sources, and especially given the calculations that *waqfiyya* prescriptions let us make, it would thus seem that the symbolic status and significance given to cooks were late, formal recognitions of institutional structures that began as purely practical arrangements.[31]

Going back to the marketplace, there were also food-related crafts that involved some limited form of cooking, perhaps better characterized as "advanced ingredient preparation," without producing complete meals. It might have been the case, for example, with a *mayvapāz* (fruit boiler)[32] and certainly was for the cook (*ṭabbākh*) who worked in a (sheep's) head-selling shop (*dukkān-i ravvāsī*).[33] As we will see below, however, the marketplace does not seem to have offered any dishes that could have, without further transformation, constituted the central element of a meal.

The potential impact of the transformation of food on the quality of the final product tends to increase at every step of the process. A talented chef can prepare a great meal from average ingredients, whereas prime-quality produce will go to waste in the hands of a bad cook. Likewise, a piece of meat will suffer more from a mistake of the cook than from the incompetence of the farmer who raised the animal. Insofar as foods could be sold in semitransformed form (which could involve some cooking), it would thus make sense to expect that some sellers were preferred over others because of the quality of their products. Sources show, in any case, that there was a common acknowledgment that not all cooks are equally talented, and that this inequality could be reflected in the taste of the meals they prepared.[34]

COOKS IN THE HOUSE There are good reasons to believe that most of the cooking was in fact taking place in the very household where the food was consumed, despite the fact that few passages directly depict home cooking.[35] Hence, in most of the scenes that feature the acquisition or home storage of food, the latter is found in the shape of ingredients (that is, products that will require further transformation before being consumed), such as uncooked meat, including unwashed tripe, and unwashed vegetables.[36]

The scarcity of household cooking scenes may in fact be significant in itself, because it tells us that cooking was not an activity that involved social interaction, even with close friends.[37] It thus comes as no surprise that, when an anecdote tells of the friendship between two major religious figures who would take turns at inviting each other for a meal, the text makes it very clear that the guest would not participate in the host's food preparation.[38]

Thus, centering food preparation at home, rather than buying dishes ready to eat, would assumedly strengthen the importance of the household as a source of social identification. It did so in part by tying an individual's food habits more strongly into one's "family traditions" than to a shared practice in a given category of people. One might contrast this late-medieval practice with the widely shared, class- (rather than family-) based food culture that *esnaf lokantaları*, relatively cheap eateries with standard menus, have created among working- and lower-middle-class men in today's urban Turkey. The family-centric pattern of food preparation also strengthened the social importance of the household by creating extended opportunities for interaction among the people involved in cooking (most likely the women of the house, as we are about to see) at the expense of communications with outsiders.[39] In other words, cooking at home weakened the "socio-" aspect of socioeconomic stratifications.

Sources depict both men and women cooking, although in different circumstances. As I mentioned above, all the "institutional" cooks (employees of the elite, dervishes, and food-related craftsmen) that they mention are male. Males also are the central characters of two different anecdotes depicting individuals preparing delicacies (*ḥalwā'* in one case, cookies in the other) to be offered to religious masters.[40] The only males depicted as cooking a full meal that they are to consume themselves, however, are two high-ranking disciples of Hacı Bektaş Velî who, living in two different cities, regularly invite each other for a meal.[41] But in this case, the way in which the anecdote is told opens the door—and even suggests—that these two individuals were following a celibate lifestyle.

On the other hand, basically all women depicted in the act of cooking appear in a familial context with at least passing reference to some kinship tie (mother, mother-in-law, nanny, and so on).[42] Such contrast between male and female cooks is very sharp and must be at least in part due to the particular bias of sources that overwhelmingly concentrate on male characters. This explains why female characters, more generally, almost systematically appear in their relationship with a male character, whereas a story involving a man may not require the mention of any family tie, male or female. Yet there is every reason to assume that, even if it creates an incomplete picture (the missing parts of which are lost to us), such a contrasted depiction of male and female characters indeed reflects a worldview based on the experience of the authors. Whereas it may seem obvious to identify household cooking in a premodern society as a female task, there is no obvious reason to understand such a division of gender roles as contributing to a hierarchical imbalance between men and women, since the depiction of both high- and low-ranking dervishes cooking appears entirely devoid of any suggestion that this was a lowly or demeaning activity for a man.

COOKING IN THE HOUSE It might be misleading to use, in discussing fourteenth-century central Anatolia, the concept of kitchen as we understand it today—a room devoted to the preparation and, in some cases, to the consumption of food. While the word *maṭbakh* (an Arabic word generally translated as "kitchen") does appear in both Persian- and Turkish-language narrative sources as well as in Arabic-language *waqfiyya*s, these sources usually depict it as an independent architectural structure rather than an area within a multifunctional building. Furthermore, references to it suggest that it was associated with richer households or expanding institutions rather than being a staple of domestic architecture.[43] Even in those cases, this structure might not fit our expectations, as we can tell from a reference to the need for water to be brought there on mule back.[44] In any case, it seems safe to assume that in normal households, food was prepared, rather, in a multifunction room that included, at least in rural homes, a place to make fire.[45]

There were a number of structures or devices intended to hold a fire, only some of which were used in food preparation. It was the case, for example, with the *furn* (sometimes *fırın* or *furūn*), which seems to have been a structure located outdoors rather than inside related buildings.[46] It is probably the same structure that appears on a number of occasions as *tanavvur* or *tanūr*.[47] Whereas written material gives us little to identify its appearance and use, archaeological literature extensively discusses the conical bread oven called in modern Turkish *tandır*, which has been in more or less constant use from prehistoric times to this day. A *tandır* has roughly the shape of an egg with the base cut off flat, and its interior can be accessed through two openings. The first is a flue at ground level to allow oxygen in and take out the ashes. The second opening is a narrow hole at the top through which the baker introduces the dough and sticks it to the oven's inclined inner surface as it is baked into a kind of flat bread. *Tandır*s are frequent occurrences in Anatolian excavations, where they are found both in interior and in outdoor spaces. This, as well as twentieth-century ethnological observations, tells us that they could be used in a communal fashion (rather than belonging to a single household) and that their use indoors for bread baking contributed to heating the house in the winter.[48]

But the shape of *tandırs* is ill-adapted to the preparation of foods other than bread.[49] Furthermore, there are numerous hints that most of the cooking was in fact done by hanging a vessel over a live fire, including a number of passages whose formulation refers to cooking "over" the fire as well as the apparently widespread use of cauldrons.[50] The fact that only one passage refers to a hearth by name (*ocak*)[51] might also be taken as an indication that it was considered as a location, closer to what we would conceptualize as "a place in the house" rather than "an appliance." Whatever the perception may have been, the fact remains that, in medieval archaeological excavations, hearths appear in plentiful numbers, side by side with *tandırs*,[52] which seems to confirm that the two structures had complementary functions (respectively, cooking meals and baking bread).

This does not, however, mean that heating during the winter months was always a by-product of food preparation. Thus, the *bukhārī* seems to have been a contraption exclusively dedicated to heating. Ibn Baṭṭūṭa's claim that these were connected to hollowed columns to let the smoke out of the room, when combined with a reference in the *Manaqib al-ʿArifin* to the addition of a *bukhārī* in an already existing house, suggests that it may have been something closer to an appliance than to an architectural feature.[53]

Anecdotes that refer to food preparation in ovens are generally limited to the baking of bread. The few mentions of dish preparation depict cooking ware set over the fire (but apparently not frying pans, a trace of which I could not find in my sources) or, in some circumstances, roasting pieces of chicken or sheep meat on spits.[54] References to roast meat (*kebab*) and its preparation over a fire appear, interestingly, in extradomestic contexts (military camps, dervish lodges, feasts). It is thus unclear whether a house's *ocak* could be used for that purpose.

Concerning cooking practices, written sources agree that cooking instruments (cauldrons, ladles, trays, and the like) could be fairly valuable, and as such worthy of mention as wedding gifts and objects of plunder.[55] But it is archaeological evidence that holds the potential to tell us the most about cooking techniques. A large amount of cooking ware has already been excavated and published, but, for now, the work of analyzing this material is still largely limited to the single-excavation level and the comparison between individual sites. This constitutes the first phase of a broader endeavor, and there are good reasons to expect significant advances, in the coming years, toward a more comprehensive analysis that would identify region-wide patterns of cooking practice during the Middle Ages.[56]

But all the storage and cooking would be meaningless if they did not lead to the core moment in the food-consumption process, the meal.

THE MEAL ITSELF

As a subject of research, the most obvious characteristic of the meal might be its "ordinary" character. This, paradoxically, prevents sources from depicting it in its most "ordinary" incarnations—the daily meal consumed in middle- and lower-class households. Rather, they most often describe meals that are unusual for one reason or another, leaving the uncritical reader with the bizarre impression that every dinner was a religious celebration hosted by the sultan. Such circumstances, of course, do reflect not the ordinary meals of that period but rather the episodes that the various authors deemed exceptional enough to be worthy of mention.

However, this does not mean that any discussion of the subject should be limited to the exceptional. As will become apparent in this section, a number of methods allow us, at least to some extent, to circumvent the selective silence of sources. For one, a limited amount of information is readily available about the "ordinary meals" of the middle and lower classes. Furthermore, a careful scrutiny of the elite's habits can also offer some hints about how upper-class practices related—in parallel or in contrast—to the habits of other social groups. Finally, it is also possible to get an idea of what was considered a "normal" meal by looking at *how* (rather than merely *whether*) the authors emphasized the unusual character of festive meals.

The Meal as a Concept

Perhaps the most striking feature of meals in my sources is, in fact, their apparent conceptual inexistence. Apart from two occurrences of the Turkish word *yemek* used as a noun, the various authors completely avoid words that could be translated as "meal."[57] Hence, in most passages where we would expect a modern writer to identify the meal as an event ("they sat down for the meal," "after the meal," and so on), they describe, rather, specific actions that we would consider to be parts of the meal (such as "after the eating of the food" [baʿd az tanāvul-i ṭaʿām]; "when they brought the [food/trays]" [chūn khʷān rā biyandākhtand]).[58] The scenes thus described strongly suggest that, as a practice, their meals were similar to what we imagine them to be (the customary practice, several times a day, to temporarily abandon other activities in order to devote oneself to the consumption of cooked foods in the company of a number of other people), yet these authors do not use a separate concept to designate them as a coherent event.[59]

Observing the consumption of food outside of regular mealtimes sharpens the notion that meals indeed took place in a way that would not have been foreign to us. A number of passages contain references to what we would call "snacks," whose consumption is presented differently from the consumption of cooked foods. These "snacks" consist mostly of fresh produce, such as melons (*kharbuza, kavun*)[60] and cucumber (*hiyar*, peeled and cut with a knife),[61] but a few scattered references can also be found to such items as bread rolls or rings (*kulīcha*)[62] and honey (in a garden).[63]

These references to snacks can be contrasted in several ways with other scenes that involve eating. They always mention the consumption of a single type of food, without linking it to any drinking; the food is consumed raw (except for the baking of the bread), with no cooking or other form of processing apart from cutting or peeling; these scenes generally take place outdoors; and the consumption of food appears to be largely spontaneous, prompted by the sudden availability of the product. The co-occurrence of all these aspects, as well as their nearly systematic absence from meal scenes, therefore affords us a term of contrast showing that there indeed were such occasions as regular meals. Conversely, the meal scenes—passages depicting dishes other than snack foods—suggest that a "regular meal" entailed the gathering of a number of people at a predetermined time in order both to drink and to eat a number of different cooked dishes.

Finally, we must consider the symbolic meanings associated with one particular physical object, the *sofra*. Made of flexible material (one *waqfiyya* specifies leather), the *sofra* would be unfolded and put down on the ground to play a part reminiscent of that of a table in modern usage. As a matter of fact, the word *sofra* also serves as a metaphor, just like the word *table*, to refer to the foods served at a meal rather than to the physical object on which they were set. The term occurs only in Turkish sources (which tend to devote more attention to lower social levels than Persian ones), and a strong association seems to have existed between *sofra*s and both lower-class and dervish settings (as opposed to the political elite). This, in turn, might perhaps be taken as indications of the social position of dervishes in late-medieval Anatolian society—closer to the population at large than to the rulers.[64] In any case, while the term *sofra* does not exactly correspond to our concept of meal, its appearance in sources consistently evokes such an event.

Meal Schedules

This brings us to a related question, that of schedule. The relative complexity of this operation that we call "a meal," at least in terms of time required for cooking and number of people involved in its production and consumption, almost necessarily entails that it be held at a more or less regular time of the day. At first glance, the best category of source to document the chronological aspect of this practice is the *waqfiyya*s, since they often include this kind of detail when prescribing the conditions of food distribution to the guests of an endowed institution.[65]

Arabic-language *waqfiyya*s include enough detail for us to see that *khānqāh*s or *zāwiya*s (dervish convents) were to offer, apart from special festivities, two meals a day, respectively designated as *ghadwa* (pl. *ghadawāt*, "morning meal") and *ʿashwa* (pl. *ʿashwāt*, "evening meal").[66] One such reference further identifies this "as is the practice in the *khānqāh*s of Rūm,"[67] whereas another notes that the food given for the morning meal should be lighter (cheese, fruits, olives, and the like) than for the second meal (cooked dishes).[68] Whether the latter prescription was complied with or not in practice, the fact that this claim was implied, and thus assumed to be obvious, in other *waqfiyya*s strongly suggests that medieval Anatolians indeed expected meals consumed at different times of the day to comprise different types of food.

One might argue that the reference to the practice of the *khānqāh*s of Rūm is, at best, representative of a particular type of establishment rather than of the population at large. Furthermore, since these were institutions that would provide food for people staying overnight, one may also argue for the possibility that they did not offer a midday meal, which the guests were expected to find elsewhere.

The five Turkish translations of a passage of the *Qabus-nama* offer an interesting complementary perspective on the issue. The original of this text was written in eleventh-century Persia, more than ten generations before and almost a thousand miles away from the time and place discussed here. Rather than faithful translations, the Turkish texts are better characterized as adaptations produced in fourteenth- and early-fifteenth-century Anatolia. In one passage, the Persian original mentions that great men (*mardum-i muḥtasham*) eat twice a day, first alone and then, after having dealt with their political duties, in the company of their entourage. Four of the five "translations" of the same passage add that the first meal should be consumed in the morning (two specify "at dawn"), even though this schedule was at most (if at all) implied in the Persian original. Furthermore, whereas the original text locates the second meal around the time of the midday prayer (Persian *pīshīn*, Arabic *ẓuhr*, the second of the five daily prayers), three of the five Turkish translations locate it, rather, around the midafternoon prayer (Turkish *ikindi*, Arabic *ʿaṣr*, third of the five daily prayers).[69]

The *Vilayat-nama* also makes a direct reference to this time of the day as the mealtime ("*ʿaṣr* came and they brought food"),[70] as does ʿĀşıkpaşazāde in reference to the first Ottoman ruler, Osman, distributing food to the people ("at the time of *ikindi* they would strike the drums so that the people would come and eat the food").[71] Furthermore, Ibn Baṭṭūṭa mentions a regional ruler offering a daily meal after the *ʿaṣr* and, on another occasion, claims that the *ahi*s receive the wages of their group's members after *ʿaṣr*, and then proceed to buy food that is collectively consumed in their shared dwelling place.[72]

Put together, all of this information thus strongly suggests a widespread practice of consuming two meals a day, the first one shortly after waking up at sunrise, and the second toward midafternoon. Such a meal schedule, incidentally, suggests a time organization where social activity more or less directly followed the availability of daylight, rather than extending long after sunset, as would be more familiar to the readers of this book.

Festive Meals

Festive meals are found in a variety of incarnations and circumstances, from a circumcision feast to the celebration of a military victory and from some highlight of the religious calendar to a bored ruler's routine drinking binge. Among these, feasts taking place at the royal courts are the most visible in sources, yet they often appear under such a thick crust of literary conventions and are so far removed from the daily life of the bulk of the population that I will not try to describe them in detail here.[73] For now, I prefer to dwell on *what* made these meals unusual. References to festive meals often include indications in that respect that can, in turn, help us define regular meals.

The element most consistently associated with festive meals is the presence of sweets, which appear through the mention of particular dishes (rather than as a category, such as "dessert" or "sweets").[74] We notice, for example, "almond sweets" (*shakkar-i bādām*) as an apparently usual occurrence at weddings,[75] as well as *bişi* (probably a type of cookie)[76] and more important *ḥalwāʾ*, whose deep religious significance I will discuss later.[77] *Waqfiyya*s also prescribe supplemental expenses for honey and butter (*samn*) for Fridays and religious celebrations.[78]

Mentions of the quantity of food and the variety of dishes also operate as devices to emphasize the better than usual character of certain meals.[79] More generally, sources sometimes give hints of slightly different procedures or additions that may have added an element of festivity—or even debauchery—to a meal, such as poetry readings, music, and, most important, wine.[80] The one element that almost never appears, however, is mention of the *quality* of particular dishes—there is no reference to some exotic delicacies reserved for the ruling classes or to luxurious foodstuffs that peasants or craftsmen would have borrowed from the elite on special occasions.[81]

The way festive meals are presented can (and should) be explained in part from a literary perspective. Wine, especially, is so heavily laden with poetic and religious symbolism that it would be quite naive to postulate a one-to-one correspondence between the modalities of its appearance in the sources and the modalities of its appearance during actual meals. Yet these sources contain much more than literary motifs, and some of the variations they offer can be taken as reflections of, if not the world in which the authors lived, at least the perception they had of that world.

For this reason, the information presented in the last few paragraphs allows me to make a number of general statements. It seems, for example, that sweet dishes did not appear in regular meals, which, however, included fruits (fresh at harvest time, dried during the rest of the year).[82] Likewise, references to extra amounts served for celebrations suggest that the quantities of food served in a usual meal were generally limited, rather than decided according to one's appetite.[83] Perhaps more important, though, it also suggests that even festive events ("sacred time") would not open temporary doors between social strata by letting the poorer folk taste the usual fare of richer people.[84] There is limited evidence to support this claim, but apparently none to counter it and, together with a number of observations I made in previous chapters, it contributes to a general impression of powerful divisions between the rich and the poor. We can observe these divisions through a number of other practices, though perhaps none clearer than the rules that determine who will serve and who will eat.

Seating and Serving

At first glance, sources discussing meals appear to pay an inordinate degree of attention to seating arrangements. It seems to have been common, at least in elite circles, to hold meals in a room that comprised an elevated platform or bench (*ṣuffa*, not to be confused with the *sofra* discussed above) where the guests would set down carpets (or, in the case of rulers, pillows—

martaba) to sit on. Although texts do not dwell on guests of lesser status, they also seem to imply that the latter sat lower, at ground level.[85] Generally, the places closest to the ruler were the most prestigious; thus, the highest-ranking places at a palace meal would have been (in decreasing hierarchical order) that of the ruler himself (a *takht*), the two *masnads* flanking it, then below the *takht*.[86] There is also a widespread consensus among the sources to depict the partakers in meals of the elite circles as sitting down before the food was brought to them, rather than coming to an already dressed table.[87]

Given the focus of this book on people of the middle and lower social orders, such information may seem of limited interest. Yet to neglect it would fail to take into account a subtle but important element, that is, the sharp contrast between the level of detail that these sources give about seating arrangements among the political elite and their near silence on the issue when it comes to other social groups.[88] Although this contrast is only moderately surprising in the case of the lower classes (one would not expect that people spent much time theorizing on the symbolic load of sitting to the left of a shepherd, or in front of his wife), it is very significant when it comes to religious brotherhoods. After all, modern scholarship always depicts the dining habits of Sufi orders as highly ritualized, with every detail of the ritual built on (or, more probably, rationalized using) volumes of theological considerations and multiple layers of symbolic meaning. Yet it is clear that this detailed organization, as real and observable as it may have been in the nineteenth and twentieth centuries, was the result of a process of ritualization that had not yet come in full swing during the period studied here.[89] In other words, a fourteenth-century dervish would not sit at a particular distance from his shaykh because this was the place associated with the particular stage of discipleship he had reached; he would sit there because the place was free.

More generally, these observations tie into a much broader phenomenon, that is, the low level of institutionalization that religious brotherhoods had reached by the fourteenth century—at least in comparison to the uncritical assumptions of many modern scholars. This is an important issue insofar as the degree of formalization of such social structures has a strongly negative correlation with the importance of the personalities that animated it. It is, in other words, probably a mistake to put too much emphasis on "the Mavlāvī order" or "the Bektaşi order" in fourteenth-century social (and even political) history, and historians should pay more attention to the personal qualities of the various leading individuals in that period. Institution-based conceptualizations have long been, for better or for worse, an Ottomanist's best friend, but adding a strong dose of prosopography might make for a more accurate picture of the fourteenth century.

Sources also concentrate on the political elite when they tell us that the people responsible for cooking the food and those in charge of serving it were two different groups (i.e., that cooks would have no part in service, and servants had nothing to do with cooking).[90] Unlike seating patterns, however, these peculiarities of service among the higher secular classes should not be taken as overly indicative of anything other than financial power, admittedly an important difference between the elite and the rest of the population. Whereas even the poorest of the poor can affix a symbolic load to sitting in particular spots, employing a separate cooking and serving staff was an option available only to a minority of people who had the necessary resources at their disposal. It remains, however, that this minority made the choice of spending part of these resources in a way that strengthened its separation from the rest of the population. Architectural historians expound at length on monumental architecture as conveying a statement of status and power to the population at large ("we are superior to you—and everybody else"), but the comparatively more private courtly meal ceremonials must have conveyed, no doubt among many other messages, a statement of hierarchy for the internal consumption of the elite ("we are superior to them").

One element that seems to have been shared across social layers, however, is that of gender separation. The number of women depicted in eating scenes is fairly limited, but in several cases—involving anything from royal courts to religious communities and middle- or lower-class households—they do interact with men. Two constants seem to characterize all cases within this admittedly limited pool of references: women depicted always act as hosts and never as guests, and although they appear to have freely interacted with their male guests, most of these cases either openly state or carry the suggestion that they did not eat together with men.[91] It is most unfortunate that our sources do not offer feminine perspectives on these occurrences that could let us know, for example, the extent to which meals taken in the female sphere mirrored the more readily observable male sphere.[92] But it is safe to affirm that there was such a thing as a "female sphere" that was separate from the male one and that this separation did not prevent interaction between men and women even when they were from different households.

Furthermore, this can be put in relation with a scene in which an upper-class household's servants clearly eat separately from their masters.[93] This strongly suggests that a significant level of social homogeneity was considered normal—and desirable—among those gathering for a meal.

EATING AND OTHER ACTIVITIES

As I pointed out in an earlier section, the *sofra* played an emblematic role much resembling the one we confer to the "table" today (i.e., evoking food, meals, and even hospitality in general, as in "you are always welcome to my table").[94] But it also marked the beginning and end points of a meal. Thus, sources offer numerous cases (in lower classes and among dervishes) where these moments are designated by expressions such as "setting down the *sofra*" or "picking up the *sofra*," probably reflecting an actual practice that involved the *sofra* as a physical object.[95] Once the *sofra* was set up, a signal was given for people to start eating all at the same time.[96] The *Vilayat-nama* also contains a number of references to pious formulae that are, mostly in peasant settings, uttered just before starting to eat ("bismillah") or, much more commonly, after finishing the meal ("dua ve sena," "Allahu ekber").[97] All of these elements show that, although they may not have entailed ceremonials as complex as those followed at the royal courts, meals held in the lower segments of the social hierarchy also followed a certain number of rituals that distinguished them from the absolutely informal act of consuming food that meals have often become in our contemporary societies.

A few points can also be raised concerning the rules of etiquette. It is clear, for example, that it was normal to eat with one's hands in any type of social setting, even though spoons were also used,[98] and that refusing to eat an elite host's food could be considered an insult.[99] Furthermore, talking during a meal seems to have been very limited, in both courtly settings and religious communities, and real discussion took place, rather, before or after food consumption.[100]

More generally, it does not seem that other activities would normally be held simultaneously with eating. In fact, two mentions of singers are the only references to activities happening at the same time as food consumption, and the formulations suggest that this was limited to the upper reaches of the social hierarchy.[101]

A number of passages, all involving both political grandees and Mavlāvī dervishes, also refer to something called a *samāʿ* that is held just before or just after eating. It is tempting (and perhaps even reasonable) to assume that the word *samāʿ* is used to refer to the now well-known Mavlāvī "whirling dervish" ceremony. Yet I should add that most appearances of this word contain no hint as to its exact meaning, an element that should inspire caution when discussing the earliest stages of development in Mavlāvī practices.[102]

It is clear, in any case, that a number of other activities could be held *after* food was consumed, such as religious discussions or teachings, recitation of poetry, or other forms of social interaction and entertainment.[103]

THE FOOD THEY ATE

The most natural thing one would expect to find in a book that purports to discuss food might be information concerning the dishes that were consumed in the time and place it covers. Yet the fact of the matter is that sources are very quiet on such questions, and the few relevant mentions they contain seldom offer much insight into the late-medieval Anatolian society. Yes, there were such a things as beef stews (said to be very salty); yes, there are references to soup (*abā, shūb*) in literary metaphors; yes, the word *börek* appears once, albeit without any hint that would let us determine whether it refers to the same type of stuffed flaky pastry as it does today.[104] But these individual mentions do not say much on the daily practices, let alone the worldviews, of the people who consumed these foods. The picture, nevertheless, somewhat brightens up when a number of references are put in relation with each other. This section will thus approach the issue in a thematic fashion, starting with the meat.

Meat and Other Dishes

A number of "main dishes" indeed appear in the sources. Rice is one of these, and it appears in a number of contexts where the author very obviously uses it as a literary device to evoke the concept of luxury.[105]

Another dish that occurs now and then—but always with a halo of religious respectability—is *tharīd*, which also appears in a number of hadiths (reports on the deeds and sayings of the founder of Islam). There is no doubt that the latter, describing *tharīd* as a favorite of the prophet Muhammad, largely explains the positive religious connotation that surrounds every occurrence of the word. Yet beyond this religious symbolism, the formulation of the passages in which it occurs strongly suggests that a dish called *tharīd* was indeed made in late-medieval Anatolia, despite the seven centuries, thousands of miles, and enormous cultural gulf that separated it from the founder of Islam.[106] The classical Arabic term *tharīd* refers to a dish of meat and bread in broth, but it is less clear whether this—or any other—recipe was the same that was cooked in fourteenth-century Anatolia.[107] Nevertheless, the sheer presence of *tharīd* here is interesting in itself since it constitutes a rare example of culinary *additions* (as opposed to the limitation brought about by dietary laws) introduced along with the traditions that Muslim religious scholars carried into Anatolia.

As far as meat is concerned, mutton seems to have been the most widely consumed, at all levels of society. As sources of meat, sheep and lambs appear to have been conceptualized separately, and there are some indications (though no clear-cut proof) that lamb was the more desirable of the two.[108]

On the other hand, references to beef are noticeably few in number and completely absent from all descriptions of luxurious meals.[109] This nicely fits a situation where beef production was mainly the result of culling, that is, the slaughter of animals too old to serve other agricultural purposes (plowing, milking, and so on). Such a system, after all, produces less meat and meat of poorer quality than one in which calves are raised specifically for butchery and slaughtered at a tender age.[110]

Fowl was also available, although it presents a particular linguistic problem insofar as the word commonly used to refer to chicken, the Persian *murgh*, can also mean "bird" in a general sense. While sources make it obvious that the consumption of wild birds, ducks, and geese was primarily associated with the upper classes, it is thus rather unclear to what extent this aura of luxury also applied to chicken. One passage does suggest that the cry of a rooster was a common occurrence on a countryside road—hence suggesting that peasants indeed raised chickens.[111] One should also note that the sources I consulted do not contain a single reference to eggs as a form of food, even though there is some archaeological evidence that they were consumed.[112]

As for specific cuts, they seem to have been varied, ranging from tripe to *khuṭāb* (possibly meat cubes), and from fat sheep's tails to ground meat.[113] The broth produced by cooking sheep heads and hooves also frequently appears, largely because of the strong association it had with asceticism. As a matter of fact, it is unclear whether such liquid was sold for a very cheap price or simply given away to the dogs living around the marketplace. In any case, it certainly constituted a "borderline food," the last refuge of those who had no other way to support (or no interest in) their physical well-being.[114] Whatever specific dishes may have been cooked with meat, it is clear that meat was conceptualized as one of the two main elements of a full, hearty meal.[115] The second of these two main elements was, quite simply, bread.

Bread and Baked Goods

It might sound like a cliché to emphasize the central character of bread in feeding a society, yet in the case of fourteenth-century central Anatolia sources support this claim. Incidentally, bread is the only type of food whose preparation is described with some detail, from the milling of the flour to sifting, kneading, letting it rise under a cloth, and baking.[116] In such descriptions, flour is the only ingredient that appears—and it does occur on a number of occasions.[117] While I could find two relatively detailed descriptions of bread baking, neither these nor any other passage mentions leavening agents. This, of course, does not mean that only unleavened bread was produced; in fact, the mention that the unbaked dough was left to sit under a cloth argues, rather, for the use of leaven, assumedly sourdough taken from earlier batches of bread dough.

This absence of leaven from the sources might in itself say something about the relationship that the various authors entertained with the process of bread making. Taking a piece of dough from an earlier batch was a discrete yet essential step in making some types of bread. The combination of a fairly detailed description of the general process, and the absence of this particular step from the description, would suggest that the authors were close observers but never participants in the process of bread making. It is easier to envision such a situation in a context where bread making was a home-based, gender-specific task rather than one altogether limited to a corps of professional bakers (which would provide fewer opportunities to the nonparticipants to witness their work). This thus strengthens the suggestion made earlier that professional bakers would take care of only the last step of bread making, their work limited to baking the dough that their clients brought them.[118] But it also tells us something about what one could call the "visual proximity" that prevailed in this society. Both what I have already stated about home cooking in general and a direct comment to this effect by Ibn Baṭṭūṭa[119] suggest that the production of bread dough was a female activity. That the male authors of these sources could nevertheless witness the process shows that, as set and strict as they may have been, gender roles did not prevent interaction or entail ignorance of other people's conditions and activities. One should, therefore, not assume that a sharp social determinism about *who* one could be entailed equally strict rules about *near whom* one could be, especially in a context of fairly low population density.

Going back to bread itself, there is precious little information about the shape of loaves. In a village setting, the *Vilayat-nama* uses the same word, *tekne*, to designate the vessel that holds both the unbaked dough and the baked bread, but refers to something called a *saç* for the baking phase.[120] Objects identified as baking sheets seem absent from the archaeological literature related to this period, though one should remember that if there were such objects made of metal, it is unlikely that they would have survived in a recognizable shape after several centuries underground.[121]

As I stated in the previous section, bread was considered a central component of a meal—sometimes in combination with meat.[122] It was preferably plentiful,[123] and could serve as a utensil to pick up the food.[124] Furthermore, there are some suggestions that it may have been consumed in sliced form,[125] and, as I mentioned in the previous section, it seems to have been common usage to crumble bread in liquids such as broth or yogurt. Such a practice nicely dovetails with the habit that Ibn Baṭṭūṭa claims to have observed all over Anatolia (but which remains undocumented in other sources) of baking bread only once a week—thus leaving people to eat rather dry bread on most days.[126]

Other scenes depict the consumption of bread along with oil or butter, yogurt, and honey.[127] These ingredients appear as first and foremost intended to make the experience of eating bread more enjoyable. In that sense, they can be taken as proof that taste was a significant part of the experience of eating (which was therefore not a purely mechanical activity with the sustenance of the body as its sole objective) and a strong indication that parallel steps were taken to enhance the flavor of other foodstuffs.

There were variable levels of quality in bread, and the association that one passage makes between "pure bread" (*nān-i pākīza*) and special worldly enjoyments suggests that regular bread commonly contained impurities.[128] There are also references to a number of other baked goods, albeit without much detail. The word *çörek* appears in Turkish sources (clearly made of flour, although it could contain other ingredients such as saffron, oil or butter, and almonds),[129] and the *Manaqib al-ʿArifin* mentions *girda* (which appears to have been a single-serving-size bread roll sold as snack food) on a few occasions.[130]

Dairy Products

Dairy products frequently appear in the sources. The most common of these seems to have been *māst*, a substance that was probably similar to what we today call sour milk or yogurt.[131] It could be eaten with either crushed garlic or honey mixed in and had to be consumed before it became too sour (*tursh*).[132] The way sources present it suggests that it was a perfectly respectable dish, at least respectable enough to be offered to the new conqueror of a city.[133]

Cheese occurs on a number of occasions as well, with one particular passage hinting that *māst* and cheese could be produced in parallel, by the same people.[134] ʿĀşıkpaşazāde mentions cheese among the products that Osman's tribe brought down from the summer pastures, apparently using it as evidence of the early Ottomans' nomadic character that this author so idolizes.[135] In contrast, a passage from the (Persian-language, high-cultured, and sedentary) *Manaqib al-ʿArifin* identifies cheese as the worst possible type of food,[136] and another anecdote depicts a soldier carrying bread and cheese for his own sustenance during a military campaign. If indeed there was such a mental association between cheese and nomadism, the latter anecdote might be taken as a hint about the (lowly and perhaps nomadic) social origins of the troops used in fourteenth-century Anatolia, a question about which sources otherwise leave us in near-complete darkness.[137] Nevertheless, both the reference to the parallel production of cheese and *māst* and a mention of cheese as part of a breakfast in a *zāwiya*[138] should make us wary of too strict an identification between *māst* and sedentarism, on the one hand, and between cheese and nomadism, on the other. Such a clear-cut division, after all, could simply not fit a society where, in all likelihood, a significant part of the countryside population hovered somewhere between the two poles that we call nomadism and sedentarism.[139]

The only references to drinking milk occur in relation to suckling babies.[140] *Māst* and cheese, on the other hand, seem to have made up most if not all the dairy consumption of adults. Many cultural factors may have played a role in the practice of consuming transformed rather than liquid milk, but, at least in the cities, the choice might also be explained in part by transportation practices and technology. The few references available concerning the transportation of liquids (wine or water) suggest that this would have to be done in leather bags or similar containers carried on mule or ox back.[141] The enormous amount of shaking thus involved, combined with the almost inevitable presence of impurities in the containers and the effects of the central Anatolian climate (scorching sun in the summer, freezing temperatures in the winter), would have quite likely meant that, after transportation over even a short distance, milk would have already been partially transformed—and not necessarily for the better. Under such circumstances, it was of course preferable for the producer to effect the transformation into yogurt or cheese in a more controlled setting and only then to carry the final product to the marketplace.

Fruits and Vegetables

Anatolia produced large quantities of fruits in the fourteenth century, as it still does today. Mentioned in the sources are figs, melons (watermelon and honeydew or cantaloupe), apples, pears, peaches, apricots, pomegranates, grapes, plums, and a kind of wild fruit sources call *aluca*, probably also a kind of plum.[142]

Perhaps the most striking aspect of this list is the near absence of berries and wild fruits. This may be explainable in part by the way "foreign sources" (Ibn Baṭṭūṭa and al-ʿUmarī) use fruits to symbolize the wealth of the land,[143] implying that such wealth originates in the agricultural effort exerted in orchards. In fact, al-ʿUmarī sounds genuinely amazed by the one case in which he refers to fruits growing wild, as if reporting that anybody could find and collect freely growing fruits in the region of Germiyan amounted to reporting the existence of a natural wonder.[144] But one should also note that wild berries are notoriously more difficult to collect, transform, and transport than cultivated fruits such as grapes and apricots. One can thus realistically suppose that the severely limited commercial use and value of berries explains why any consumption of wild fruit would not have been deemed worthy of mention. Incidentally, the mention of *aluca* occurs when exceptional circumstances (the failure of a cereal harvest) push a farmer to the apparently equally exceptional measure of collecting and selling wild fruits.[145] The presentation of this anecdote suggests that such a course of action was in itself a strong-enough indication of the gravity of the situation, and thus that commercial exploitation of *aluca* was highly unusual.

This proposition is further strengthened when we look at how nuts appear in the sources. The latter contain a number of references to the fact that walnut and chestnut trees were growing wild around Anatolia,[146] as well as very indirect suggestions (in the form of metaphorical uses) that nuts were regularly consumed.[147] Yet no local source actually contains a direct depiction of somebody eating nuts, a fact that fits very well with the suggestion that goods whose production involved no significant amount of labor before harvest were deemed barely worthy of mention.[148]

As for those fruits that do receive mention, their consumption occurs in two types of settings—apparently the same throughout the social hierarchy. Fresh fruit consumption occurs near the place of production and is prompted by the availability of the produce; fresh fruit played, in other words, the role of a snack food.[149] Dried fruits, on the other hand, were consumed in a rather more "deliberate" manner: stored for long periods, they were then placed in water for a few hours in order to be rehydrated before consumption.[150] It is thus not surprising that they appear as part of full-fledged meals. In either case, however, fruits were clearly seen as playing a complementary role rather than being a central element in a diet, as can be seen from the aforementioned anecdote where a starving man goes to sell the heap of *aluca* he owns in order to buy cereals, rather than consuming the fruits directly.[151]

As for vegetables, they seldom appear in the sources; in fact, Ibn Baṭṭūṭa gives what seems to be an entire meal's menu without including any of them.[152] There are a few mentions of cucumbers,[153] as well as one each for beets and carrots.[154] But otherwise a literal reading of the source material would lead one to think that what we call vegetables were entirely absent from fourteenth-century eating habits. Yet there are references to annual gardens (as opposed to orchards), and the few mentions of vegetables that do occur are worded in a matter-of-fact tone that certainly does not suggest that these were exceptional foods.

Two hypotheses strike me as realistic ways to resolve this apparent paradox. The first is that vegetables would have been integrated in other dishes. As I mentioned earlier, stews seem to have made up a significant part of the menus, and it would be perfectly natural to find root vegetables accompanying stewed meat as part of these, as well as in soups. The second hypothesis, which does not exclude the first, is that the very concept of "fruits" (*mayva, thamar*) was broader for the authors of these sources than it is for us. It may not be insignificant that two of the three scenes mentioning cucumbers present their consumption as taking place outdoors and outside appointed mealtimes, in a way that corresponds quite precisely to the pattern of consumption of fresh fruits as snack food.[155] The latter hypothesis would in fact entail that vegetables are not even absent from the sources, insofar as a number of passages that refer to "fruits" in general would have been understood by their target audience as encompassing what we today would call "vegetables."

Spices and Other Add-ons

Ibn Baṭṭūṭa once complains to his Turkman ruler-host of the absence of "spices and herbs" (*abzār wa khuḍār*) from his meal. If there is any truth to the reaction he describes on the part of his host (who chastises the person in charge for this omission), it would suggest that seasoning was indeed expected, at least when serving a meal to a distinguished guest.[156] And indeed, there is ample evidence that, besides the basic food items—bread, meat, yogurt, fruits, and perhaps vegetables—other ingredients were added to improve the taste of dishes. The range of tastes that the *Gharib-nama* mentions, for example, includes "spicy" and "salty," which almost necessarily entail the addition of seasoning.[157] Yûnus Emre also offers a few passages that leave no doubt that the production process of sugar from sugarcane was widely understood.[158]

It is in most cases impossible to identify the seasoning that was used with any degree of precision, although a few exceptions do exist.[159] One of these is salt, which was apparently so widely used in cooked dishes that its presence was no ground for praise, whereas its absence attracted negative comments.[160] In fact, no passage makes any reference to a dish that would have been *too* salty, although a statement by Hacı Bektaş suggests that the saltiness of beef stew could make its consumption difficult without water to drink.[161]

Saffron appears on a number of occasions, added to *çörek* (small cakes or biscuits) and perhaps to *ḥalwāʾ*, but also to rice.[162] Garlic too seems to have been widely consumed. Although sources sometimes present it in raw form, the formulations they use suggest, rather, that the normal practice was to peel and crush it, then cook it as part of some other dish.[163] It is also clear that people were aware (and not too fond) of the foul breath it causes.[164]

Finally, it seems that edible fats also played a similar role. It is true that, unlike saffron and garlic (and much more than salt), oil and butter play a central role in some cooking techniques. However, given the apparent absence of frying in the context used here (sources contain direct references neither to the technique nor to the required instruments), fatty substances seem to have been used primarily to improve the taste of various dishes.[165] Such a use does explain the allowances that some *waqfiyya*s make for the extra procurement of butter to be served on festive days in a *zāwiya*,[166] as well as the careful removal of the fatty part of a dish as part of an ascetic regimen.[167]

Nonalcoholic Drinks

Although it is clear that nonalcoholic drinks were part of meals (together with or, more probably, after the main dishes), they clearly held a peripheral position, and the various authors do not describe their ingredients in much detail. At the most obvious level, there is no doubt that water was seen as the basic, no-frills drink, the one that ran no risk of passing for luxury.[168] Yet apart from stating that it was preferred cold, sources barely give any detail on its consumption.[169] Considering that, as we are about to see, most other drinks were associated with either children or the upper classes, it is nevertheless reasonable to suspect that water might have been if not the only then at least the most commonly drunk liquid among the urban and rural lower classes.

The word *sharbat* appears with striking regularity, at least in relation to the upper classes, but is never clearly defined. It may in fact have had more than a single definition. On a number of occasions, this word is clearly understood as a form of liquid medication,[170] but in other cases it is equally clearly taken, following its Arabic root (from the verb *to drink*), to refer to any form of drink.[171]

Yet there also seems to have been another, restricted, meaning for the word *sharbat*, closely overlapping that of another word, *julāb*. Although there may have been variations in the recipe, this type of *sharbat* seems to have been made of fruit juice and/or sweeteners (sugar or, for a cheaper version, honey) diluted with water. The few available mentions of fruit juices are indeed formulated in ways suggesting that they would be transformed rather than consumed in their pure, freshly squeezed form,[172] and there are indications that significant attention was given to prevent *sharbat* and *julāb* from being either too concentrated (making it *gulūgīr*, or hard to digest) or not enough (making it tasteless).[173]

Two other drinks occur in sources, milk and *fuqā*ʾ. Most of the references to milk talk of human milk, whose consumption is used both as an indicator of age (i.e., "when he was a suckling baby")[174] and in metaphors for the transmission of knowledge from master to disciple.[175] Combined with a number of direct and indirect references to the milking of sheep and cows as well as to dairy products (but none to adults drinking liquid milk), this suggests that, just like fruit juices, animal milk was exclusively reserved for transformation purposes rather than for direct consumption.[176]

As for *fuqā*ʾ, dictionaries suggest it could be a drink made either of mildly fermented barley or of dried grapes. Because it is listed, along with the *samā*ʿ (assumedly the "whirling dervish" ceremony) and the *ḥammām* (Turkish bath), in a list of the three favorite worldly pleasures for Rūmī, and because it was something that a child could receive from his mother, *fuqā*ʾ probably did not carry the reputation of containing alcohol.[177] Independently from this perception, identifying *fuqā*ʾ as a mildly fermented barley drink would help reconcile the combination of the apparently widespread consumption of *boza* (also a mildly fermented barley drink, still consumed in Turkey and the Balkans) in early Ottoman Bursa with the complete absence of the word *boza* from the sources used for this study, without having to assume a dramatic break in the consumption habits.[178]

The most conspicuous absence from written sources and archaeological discussions is that of hot drinks. It is, of course, bad practice for a historian to use such absences as an explaining factor for the working of a society. But while it would be unwise to claim that the absence of hot drinks was a fundamental characteristic of fourteenth-century Anatolian society, this element should nevertheless be taken into consideration when discussing later social changes such as the rise of coffee consumption, which may therefore have created an entirely new practice of consuming hot drinks.[179]

RELATED CONCEPTS

Questions pertaining to food consumption are by no means limited to meals. A number of other subjects can be approached through the relation they entertain with food. Among these, this final section of the chapter will consider hospitality, taste, health, social identity, and mood-altering substances in more detail.

My intention here is not, of course, to perform an exhaustive investigation of these themes, as each one of them arguably offers enough content to constitute a book of its own. Rather, what I will attempt is, following the general orientation of this project, to describe the points of contact between these subjects and food consumption. I will then use this point of contact not only to investigate the part that food plays in each one of these concepts, but also—and more important—to get a glimpse of how fourteenth-century central Anatolia understood and dealt with this concept.

Giving Food: Hospitality and Charity

As chapter 2, discussing food exchanges, has demonstrated in a number of ways, food was endowed with economic value just like any other good. But both its character as a basic life necessity and the multiple layers of meaning it could carry made it a frequent and unique object of giving. In this section, I will survey two particular circumstances in which food was given, each defined according to the recipients: hospitality, aimed at travelers, and charity, targeted toward the poor.

Hospitality offered to a guest traveler is relatively rare in the sources I used, though Ibn Baṭṭūṭa offers the most salient exception.[180] Insofar as we can trust this traveler's testimony (and fainter hints in other sources suggest that, in this particular case, we should), it seems that serving food was one of the two main components of hospitality, the other being providing a place to stay.[181] As mundane as this statement may seem, it does have two unexpected consequences. First, "offering food" is not the same thing as "sharing food," and there are several references of hosts who send their guests something to eat without inviting them to partake in their own meal.[182] And second, the two components of hospitality could be dissociated from each other, with room provided by one host and board offered by another.[183]

This observation brings us to another aspect of hospitality. Although there is insufficient evidence to determine whether this applied to more than a tiny minority of prestigious guests, there clearly could be cases where offering hospitality conferred prestige upon the hosting party. Ibn Baṭṭūṭa indeed describes a few fairly tense scenes in which various prominent individuals in the town he is visiting (such as *ahi*-led groups and a ruler) compete to invite him, and it seems reasonable to interpret these situations as the crystallization of preexisting tensions or conflicts.[184] This clearly shows that the act of hosting could, at least in some cases, carry enough social (or even political) significance to be worth, literally, fighting for.

Prestige also probably played a role in large-scale meals served to the population at large. A number of such cases appear in the sources, and, in most of them, it is a ruler who thus feeds the population on a day of religious celebration. While these depictions include some references to separate seating for the lower and upper classes, it is impossible to tell whether all groups were served the same food.[185]

Such ostentatious acts of generosity did not attenuate but rather sharpened the hierarchical imbalance between the giver and the recipients of the food on such occasions. A good reason to believe that the actors of this interaction were fully aware of such inequality can be found in the reported practice of generous hosts serving food to the poor with their own hands. In-person food distribution was probably more common as a literary motif than as an actual practice, yet the very fact that this motif appears so often—and always as praise for the individual to whom it refers—betrays its status as an ideal. The quality idealized here is not a concern for equality but rather modesty, and since modesty is the antithesis of a high hierarchical status, serving the poor with one's own hand necessarily alleviated the hierarchical imbalance that the act of giving created in the first place.[186]

The polar opposite of a ruler entertaining a large crowd, both by the magnitude of the event and by the perspective it takes, is the act of begging. Because of their particular biases and concerns, the sources I used contain many references to begging, albeit almost exclusively by dervishes. It is clear that dervishes tended to ask—and receive—charity in the form of food rather than money (though sources offer no hints as to the reasons for such a tendency). A number of references also suggest that the request would take the form of a pious formula, such as "shay᾽ li-l-lah" or "riżā Allāh Ḥaqq içün," and that dervishes would carry whatever they received (usually bread) in a *zanbīl*, a type of basket that the authors of hagiographies very closely associate with the status of dervish.[187]

These scenes, as well as another one involving a reference to the habit that nondervish beggars (*sā'il*) had of going from house to house and singing in return for charity,[188] also offer us one more unexpected insight into the workings of society, insofar as they depict these begging characters as moving through the landscape, both urban and rural. Besides telling us that this phenomenon was common to both the city and the countryside, it also lets us peek into the experience of a low density of population. The beggars of twenty-first-century cities can settle at places that see a particularly high density of traffic and reach several thousand "potential customers" in a day without ever leaving their place.[189] This, however, is not an economically viable option in places where the population density is much lower—be it in today's small towns or anywhere in fourteenth-century central Anatolia. In a broader perspective, this particular example should remind us that social interactions at that time, even in cities, must have had a lot more in common with what we now associate with the countryside. In other words, this was a social landscape where personalities and informal networks held much greater importance than the official, more readily observable institutions and structures on which social historians often concentrate.

Taste and Pleasure in Eating

Fourteenth-century Anatolia did not have a Brillat-Savarin to testify, at length and in detail, about all the particulars of eating pleasures. Yet many references to food clearly show that eating was not a neutral activity—in the manner, say, of walking or breathing. Obvious pleasure was associated with some aspects of food consumption (mostly, though not exclusively, particular tastes), and this section intends to identify these aspects.

Explicit statements about the pleasurable quality of a specific food item or dish ("This coq au vin was excellent!") are almost entirely absent from the sources I used.[190] Rather, the most common form of reference to food quality concerns purity. A number of adjectives used to praise particular foodstuffs and contrasting them with the ordinary fare emphasize their purity (*ṣāfī*, *pākīza*, *khāṣṣ al-khāliṣ*, *muṣaffā*, *torusuz*), suggesting that impurities were indeed common in some food items such as bread and honey.[191] There are also a few references to ingredients that were apparently added with the intent of improving the eating experience by changing the taste, such as oil or fat, as well as saffron and almonds to improve the desirability of cookies.[192]

Rather than making such general statements about given food items, texts often concentrate on particular tastes, which they present in either a clearly positive or a clearly negative light. The *Gharib-nama* thus offers a list of seven "tastes." The list includes *çarb* (fat, making the eater happy and overweight), *şirin* (sweet, increasing intellectual aptitudes, especially when consumed in the morning), *acı* (hot/spicy, causing a certain amount of pain but being good for health), *torşi* (pickled, making the eater's face contort but increasing the appetite), *savug* (cold, whose impact on health disappears when it becomes lukewarm), *ıssı* (hot, necessary for cooked dishes), and *tuzlu* (salty, good for many dishes).[193]

Poetic considerations no doubt played a large part in the selection of terms and the "definitions" that this list offers, and it would be unwise to assume that it provides a comprehensive map of the medieval gustative landscape. Yet many of the "tastes" that are included in this list also appear in other sources, and, despite a less than perfect overlap, the apparent absence of contradiction suggests that the *Gharib-nama*'s list indeed reflects a widely shared perspective.

The first two items on this list, the fatty and the sweet, often appear in a Persian expression ("charb ū shīrīn"). The combination of these two words no doubt acquired the status of a set phrase in the poetic tradition, but the appearance in Turkish prose of a close equivalent, "bal ve yağ" (honey and oil/fat), strongly suggests that it was also present in popular imagination.[194] In all these occurrences, the fatty and the sweet are strongly associated with (worldly) pleasure. The same positive connotations also appear in a variety of circumstances where only one of these two concepts is present, thus strengthening the suggestion that the pleasure associations of the fatty and the sweet were not strictly literary conventions. I have already discussed the positive light in which sweet food items are presented in the case of festive meals, although one should note that such a positive spin also occurs outside of explicitly festive contexts,[195] sometimes emphasized by opposing it to poison.[196] Surprisingly, however, fruits are almost never associated with sweetness, suggesting that they were conceptualized as part of a category altogether different from that of sweets, *ḥalwāʾ* and honey.[197] Fatty foods are likewise clearly associated with pleasure in eating. As I stated earlier in this section, edible fats seem to have been added for the primary (or perhaps even sole) purpose of improving the taste of a dish.

Although the sweet and the fatty are the most common, other "tastes" from the *Gharib-nama*'s list can also be found elsewhere. I already mentioned the pervasive and seemingly purely positive character of "salty" earlier in this section. Hot is the other "taste" that can be found in other sources. Several references make it clear that cooked dishes were considered good only as long as they were warm, losing their desirability as they got cold.[198]

Bad taste in food, interestingly, appears much less frequently than good taste, perhaps because the sources used here are more concerned with praising and inciting than with shaming and warning—and when they do shame and warn, they find more convincing methods than a bad-tasting dish to do so. Yet it does occur in a number of flavors, including the badly prepared (*julāb*, a drink that becomes watery when too diluted and acrid when too concentrated),[199] the too old (*māst*, sour milk that becomes bitter after a while),[200] and the bad side of the otherwise good (garlic, which gives bad breath).[201]

Wine holds a peculiar place with regards to taste, both because it was not expected to taste good and for the moral (or, rather, immoral) weight it carried.[202] Yet this does not mean that the concept of taste was morally neutral for other consumables. As I stated earlier, some tastes, such as fatty and sweet, were closely associated with enjoyment. Given the strong ascetic influence on the religious discourse (or at least its Sufi component), "enjoyment" was to some authors no more than a misplaced interest in physical well-being, to the great prejudice of the spiritual health. This explains why bad taste is associated with devotion and why particularly high religious worth is often exemplified through scenes where the pious character consciously decides to consume less tasty or even downright bad-tasting foods.[203] It is important to point out that such an argumentative device would be used precisely because the religious legitimacy of asceticism was in dispute. The prestige that a great religious master gained by refusing the pleasure of eating good foods had its roots in the contrast this entailed with the behavior of other people who, given access to the same good food, did give in to the temptation. This leaves no doubt that, then as now, food was a very significant source of pleasure. After all, the refusal of small, barely conscious pleasures is no asceticism: nobody would have admired Gandhi for refusing to run his toes through the grass of his lawn.

Disputed notions of spiritual health will hold a large place in the next chapter. But we should first survey the interactions that late-medieval Anatolians identified between food and physical health.

Medicine and Health

The history of medicine is a field unto itself, and for good reason. Today as in the Middle Ages, access to knowledge, both theoretical and practical, on how to cure illnesses and improve health is limited to a minority of people who have undergone advanced training. Study of the topic from a historical perspective likewise requires a thorough knowledge of medical theories and practices that have little in common with those that prevail today—except perhaps their complexity. Trying to describe medicine in fourteenth-century central Anatolia without the proper background knowledge would thus be as fraudulent as the holder of a PhD in history standing up when someone cries out for a doctor to assist a man who just fainted.

But medicine touches the population at large, not just physicians. Hence, without pretending to depict medical theory from the point of view of a specialist group (analyzing, for example, the transmission of Galen's ideas among medical practitioners), it is still possible to discuss the point of view of the nonspecialist population on medical knowledge related to food. This is precisely what this section intends to do.[204]

Before anything else, I should make it clear that knowledge of medicine was associated with knowledge of what we would today call the science of nutrition. This is best illustrated by an episode in which the author, trying to demonstrate a religious master's medical knowledge (*ʿulūm-i ṭibbī*), presents him as he praises the respective health effects of pickled and raw beets.[205]

It may seem surprising at first that sources never label particular food items as "healthy" or "unhealthy."[206] But this would be overlooking something on which they leave no doubt: in fourteenth-century Anatolia, health was conceptualized not as an ideal state that illnesses and discomforts prevent one from reaching, but rather as an equilibrium of the bodily system. This is apparent, among other things, from the use of the word *mizāj* (literally meaning "balance") that was used to refer to health, even in casual formulae (e.g., "How is your balance?" to inquire about one's health).[207] Where such a conception stands in relation to ancient Greek medical traditions is an interesting question but one that falls beyond the scope of this book. After all, people outside the medical profession probably had but a diffuse awareness of the medical theories that formed the core of a physician's expertise.

Among the elements that clearly seeped into the public consciousness, then, is the idea that overcompensating for a health problem was equally bad, as it also breaks the body's balance, a dynamic best exemplified in an anecdote where a man who is prescribed poppy milk as a cure for excessive sleeping ends up finding himself sleep deprived.[208] Overcompensation, in other words, could result from using too much of the appropriate drug or (more important for our purposes) of particular foods.

A relatively large number of food items are indeed associated with particular effects on the body. Insofar as these could attenuate or exacerbate preexisting imbalances, or break the existing balance in the body, each food item could be either "healthy" or "unhealthy," depending on the particular state of the person consuming it. Today's crazes for certain "miracle foods," enjoining unlimited consumption of this or that foodstuff for its high content in antioxidants or omega-3 or whatever may be the fashionable nutrient of the day, would thus have been completely impossible to understand for late-medieval Anatolians.

The principles underlying this association of health effects and given food items are not apparent in the examples that sources offer, though perhaps only because of the relatively limited number of cases available. In fact, only fever offers the beginning of a "handle" to create any form of categorization, as it attracts a number of contraindications (including garlic, *ḥalwāʾ*, almond, meat, and blood).[209] All the other associations between foods and their medical effect, such as the property of raw beets to make eyes "bright," to that of "heavy" (*thaqīl*) foods to increase the risk of abortion, are too isolated to allow for much further discussion.[210]

These properties, however, were not fixed, and there is ample evidence that they were expected to change when a food item underwent transformations such as cooking, preservation through one of several techniques, or even chewing. This expectation is readily observed in a passage presenting raw beets as good for the eyes whereas pickled ones purify the body,[211] and another that, in an obvious parallel to everyday food, describes charmed cereal seeds that must be swallowed without chewing, lest they lose their magical powers of making the eater pregnant.[212]

Descriptions of the body's workings are few, and include some statements that relate to digestion—the primary path of food into health. Sources thus refer to the importance of liquids in digestion,[213] and claim that an empty stomach is more efficient at that function.[214] It is, on the other hand, difficult to determine whether the passage presenting digestion as a process of burning indeed reflects a widespread conception or simply consists in a home-brewed metaphor.[215] It might be relevant to add here that the only apparent medical use of rosewater is nonculinary, as it is sprinkled on people who fainted in order to reanimate them.[216] Conversely, the only two references to vegetarianism strongly associate it with an ascetic lifestyle rather than with any medical concerns.[217] What remains, in any case, is the clear indication that nutrition was seen as an integral part of the workings of human health.

As for physicians, the overwhelming majority of references I could find in the sources put them in relation with the political elite, usually the sultan himself,[218] and there is no doubt that drugs considered to be of the highest quality were very expensive.[219] However, there are reasons to believe that the services of physicians were available, perhaps with less assiduity, to other segments of the population.[220]

An interesting aspect of these depictions is the central place they give to medical drugs, in stark contrast with other medical acts, such as surgery, which are essentially absent from the sources I consulted.[221] To put it bluntly, they suggest that the words *ṭabīb* and *ḥakīm*, although they are generally translated as "medical doctor" or "physician," in fact refer to something akin to a pharmacist, and that medical practice was conceptualized as the art of making drugs. It might be a testament to the complexity of the process involved that these specialists are depicted secluding themselves in their own homes in order to produce these medications, although if there was any attempt at involving the supernatural realm during that process (which we would expect from alchemy), it is nowhere to be found in the sources.[222] It is also clear that the production of these drugs took a significant amount of time, at least several days.[223] The image that thus emerges of the medical profession does not carry the "emergency" associations to which we are accustomed today. In fact, there even are some reasons to suggest that drugs were prepared in advance rather than in reaction to the appearance of particular symptoms.[224] What this entails concerning theoretical knowledge of medicine, however, should probably be left for specialists of medical history to analyze. It is nevertheless possible to notice a widespread assumption that physicians held a large amount of specialized knowledge and a high level of technical expertise.

Sources depict the process of drug making in vague but consistent terms. It generally entails individuals other than the physician himself (sometimes the "customers" themselves) bringing the basic ingredients (sometimes plants, sometimes merely designated as "ingredients") to the physician,[225] who then retreats to his house in order to manipulate (boiling, kneading, and so on)[226] and combine them with liquid or semisolid "bases,"[227] ultimately producing a compound in the form of a liquid or a paste (*maʿjūn*).[228] There is, however, no trace of the process through which the basic ingredients were collected—either from herbalists, from medicinal gardens, or directly from the wild.

Although limited in number, the pool of references to the effects of these medical compounds is fairly consistent and, as I noted earlier, includes no suggestion that they might have been part of the treatment of injuries. These references include the cure of stomach pains and aching eyes, voluntary abortion, and a purgative effect used as a "primer" for fasting.[229]

In any case, we should note that the authors (themselves apparently holding no particular expertise in the field of medicine) do mention the use of medicinal plants, hence strongly suggesting a widespread consciousness of the origin of the active ingredients of the drugs.[230] In these circumstances, it is reasonable to assume that the population at large did hold a certain knowledge of the medical effects of certain plants, yet also held the belief that the physicians' peculiar expertise allowed them to effect some manipulations that could increase the medical potency of these plants. In the absence of other indications, and given the strong association that sources make between the physicians and the political elite, it is thus quite possible that the population at large treated its illnesses with herbal medicine in a way that amounted to a simpler and cheaper version of a more "academic" medical practice.

Ethnic Divisions

Even a casual look at the list of restaurants operating in a typical American city leaves no doubt that culinary traditions are strongly tied to ethnocultural identities. More generally, discussions of food can uncover a host of worldview elements related to ethnic identity, including both positive and negative judgments. For example, Rūmī describes the "people of *Rūm*" (an expression that in this specific case seems to refer to Christian Greeks) as a "people of enjoyment," pointing out that doctors use *fuqāʾ* cups to fool children who refuse medication into thinking that they are about to drink something delicious.[231]

Conversely, another anecdote depicts Rūmī, puzzled by the hiring of Turks to build the walls of a garden, declaring that "the building of the world belongs to the *Rūmīs*, and the destruction of the world is restricted to the Turks."[232] Likewise, another character declares to a Turcoman chieftain who is rising in power that "you came here and you ate what you had not eaten and you wore what you had not worn," therefore suggesting a combination of low esteem for the Turcomans and a clear association between a certain idea of refinement in food and clothing and ethnocultural identity.[233]

Mentions of ethnicity in relation to food also offer us some understanding of the interaction between the two identity layers that were religious and ethnic identifications. It thus seems clear that given ethnic tags (Armenian, Greek, Turkish, and the like) were associated with given religious affiliations.[234] However, the meaning of such ethnic categorization also went beyond mere adherence to a religious creed,[235] and at the very least included differences in languages.[236] It further seems that ethnic identity was experienced more saliently in urban than in rural settings.[237] The languages of the sources I used in writing this book (Persian, Turkish, and Arabic) are strongly identified with Muslim rather than Christian education, and as such carry a built-in bias. Still, they do leave us with a strong impression that ethnic identity was ultimately a less important level of social division than religious identification, the latter being subdivided into ethnic units.[238] I will discuss the meaning that late-medieval Anatolians ascribed to religious identity in further detail in the next chapter. But before doing so, we need to discuss one last very particular category of consumables, mind-altering substances.

Mind-Altering Substances

Food and drinks, as this chapter has made abundantly clear, can have a variety of effects on those who consume them, want to consume them, or are prevented from consuming them. But only a limited subset has direct psychotropic effects. Because some individuals actively seek these effects while others are weary of their consequences on the individual and society, mind-altering substances tend to be set apart from other, "ordinary," foods and drinks. In late-medieval Anatolia, this category essentially comprised two substances: wine and cannabis.[239]

Fourteenth-century sources contain a large number of references to wine, which Islamic law explicitly forbids to Muslims. This, together with a long tradition of literary metaphors, charged wine with an enormous symbolic load, and it would be naive to uncritically accept as fact each and every mention that sources make of it. Yet there is no doubt that, at least in elite circles, drunkenness was sought after and associated with social gatherings, victory celebrations, and music.[240] If we are to accept the inspired justification of some authors, this served the purpose of "transforming grief into joy."[241]

When depicting the consumption of wine, sources strongly suggest that its taste was *not* an important aspect of the product. In fact, it may have been precisely because of wine's perceived bad taste that diluting it with water was the normal practice. Rūmī probably expressed a consensus among fourteenth-century Anatolians when he claimed that "the peculiarity of wine is to make one drunk"—a proposition whose reductive character is bound to horrify any modern-day French nationalist.[242]

It also seems that only red wine was known,[243] and that older wine may have been preferred.[244] Wine bearers (*sāqī*s) do appear, although the number of mentions is very limited in view of the conspicuous place they hold in the pantheon of Persian literary tropes. In fact, this contrast as well as a few other hints suggest that the role of "wine bearer" was, in courtly settings, either taken up by one of the same servants as those in charge of meal service or handed over in an honorary fashion to a younger member of the elite.[245]

Although an anecdote in which a character needs to procure wine depicts him as going to get his pitcher filled in the "Jewish neighborhood,"[246] alcohol consumption also extended to Muslim and nonelite circles. Al-ʿUmarī offers no religion-based qualification when he mentions wine among the three basic commodities (along with jerked meat and oil or fat) that the inhabitants of Anatolia store to live on during the winter.[247] The same author's reference to pomegranate wine suggests that a variety of fermented fruit alcohols may have been available.[248] On the other hand, public scrutiny was obviously a concern: an anecdote depicts a mythologized Baghdad marketplace where (in decreasing order of immorality) drinking, buying wine, and being seen in the company of someone drinking were decidedly unacceptable.[249] Such a concern for public image would have been so prevalent had there been a consensus that only Christians and Jews actually consumed alcohol. In sum, the adjective that best applied to alcohol consumption was not *elite* or *sectarian* but, more probably, *discreet.*

A similar tension between moral disapproval and fairly widespread consumption seems to have prevailed around the consumption of cannabis, the only other mind-altering substance that appears to have been consumed for recreational purposes. Ibn Baṭṭūṭa, in a rare Anatolia-wide generalization, declares the widespread and accepted consumption of hashish to be the only imperfection in the religious practice of the region's inhabitants.[250] He further gives a few examples of rulers or military officers who were common users of the substance.[251]

As with many of Ibn Baṭṭūṭa's claims, this one is to be approached with caution, since at least some of Anatolia's religious elite clearly and strongly disapproved of cannabis consumption. Thus, when a local (Anatolian) source, the *Manaqib al-ʿArifin*, mentions that a Sufi master did not have the habit of consuming cannabis, it does so in a tone that is essentially the same as if it were a defense against slander.[252] This slander, or at least these accusations, was not entirely baseless. In fact, the very same passage includes an admission that the followers of the character in question were regular cannabis users. This suggests that this substance was indeed associated with the dervish crowd. It is conceivable that seeing the substance regularly consumed by a category of people claiming to devote their lives to religion largely lifted, in the eyes of the population at large, the opprobrium that the higher religious authorities would have liked to see attached to cannabis consumption.

Sources refer to this substance as "ḥashīsh." However, Ibn Baṭṭūṭa's description (comparing it to henna powder) suggests that the form in which cannabis was consumed in fact corresponds to what is called "kief" in modern usage, a powdery substance obtained by rubbing the surface of the leaves and flower buds of the marijuana plant. In the absence of smoking, oral ingestion was apparently the only mode of consumption.[253]

There are few references to the effects of cannabis consumption, and these never compare it directly to the effects of wine except by presenting both these substances as means to "escape reality."[254] Yet while some of them present wine as a highbrow product either when using it as a metaphor for Sufi ecstasy or when paying no heed to religious morals, no source sheds a positive light on cannabis. Part of the difference between the social statuses of the two products may have something to do with the costs of production. Wine production requires a dedicated piece of land (at least a few vines to make the process worthwhile), specialized equipment such as a press and containers, and a relatively high degree of attention. It also usually demands several years of growth before the first harvest and a few weeks of fermentation after the first grapes are collected. Furthermore, grapes can be consumed directly, thus creating a competitive market for the acquisition of wine's primary ingredient.[255] By contrast, cannabis probably grew wild in Anatolia,[256] and its transformation into a consumable drug can be effected even on a very small scale, without much specialized equipment. This assumedly resulted in an imbalance in the prices of wine and cannabis, thus making the latter cheaper and associating it with a lower social status.

That being said, other cultural factors—impossible to ascertain based on the relatively limited evidence available here—probably played a part in determining the relative social status of wine and cannabis. A comparison of the consumption patterns and cultural associations of these two products would therefore greatly benefit from the broader perspective of a study on a larger scale.

CONCLUSION

Two striking facts define if not the essence of the fourteenth-century central Anatolians' social experience, at least the essence of the difference between their social experience and ours. The first is a low population density, a social factor that may seem mundane but profoundly shapes the modalities of interaction between people.[257] The second is a set of apparently impassible boundaries between the various levels of the social hierarchy, whose impact might be more readily understandable to us.

Taken together, these two factors create a situation where relationships of inequality had to be very concrete, regularly visible, and constantly reinforced. In a modern setting, this task would largely be undertaken by establishing codes, symbols, and practices common to a category of people, thereby creating a feeling of belonging to a particular segment of society, and by isolating this category of people from the rest of the population. But in a context such as late-medieval Anatolia, where it was almost physically impossible to isolate oneself from people of different status, the reinforcement of social identities and hierarchies had to take place as often *between* the groups as *within* them.

It is precisely the blatant disrespect for such reinforcement mechanisms that is depicted in the anecdote appearing at the beginning of this chapter. That Rūmī and the Armenian butcher Tanyīl would come across each other on the street was almost inevitable. That Tanyīl, member of an obviously much lower social category (perhaps because of his status as a craftsman or as a Christian, perhaps because his profession required that he handle pork, and perhaps for entirely different reasons now lost to us), would bow seven times as a show of reverence was behavior to be expected. But that Rūmī, an accomplished religious scholar and a regular at the sultan's palace, would bow even once in return, however—this was utterly shocking. The author who reports the scene may have seen such a deed as a laudable proof of kindness; it is, after all, the duty of hagiographers to put a praiseful spin on their subject's every action. But for the rest of the population, the blurry majority whose everyday behavior was the standard by which Rūmī's action was deemed exceptional, a Persian-speaking, highly educated religious master bowing back to a mere Armenian butcher was nothing short of a deep stab at the heart of the social order.

(FOUR)

Food and Religion

Because it was a transition moment between the (Christian-ruled) Byzantine and the (Muslim-ruled) Ottoman periods, fourteenth-century Anatolian society is characterized in the scholarship by a fundamental division between Christians and Muslims.[1] As we are about to see, such a view is at best simplistic, and it might in fact be wholly disconnected from the experience of the people discussed here.

In the medieval Muslim world, literacy entailed an at least basic religious education. Furthermore, religion was arguably the single most common subject of intellectual debate. For these reasons, the sources that inform us on various aspects of daily life in late-medieval Anatolia tend to do so through the prism of a religiously educated perspective. This certainly constitutes an obstacle to understanding the point of view of uneducated laypeople, whose religious beliefs and practices may have had little in common with the arcane concerns of the theologians and the lofty inspiration that the literati found in mystical poetry. Yet it is to some extent possible to circumvent these problems by looking at the ways in which food intersects with religious beliefs and practices, precisely because these points of intersection were often of lesser doctrinal importance to the authors who mentioned them. Such details thus create moments of "lowered vigilance," cracks through which unexpected insights about the way ordinary people dealt with the sacred can slip though the lines of an otherwise careful theological discourse.

There are numerous ways in which food intersects with religion, but they can fit in two broad categories: the religious practices that involve food and the religious value given to particular foodstuffs. In this final chapter, I will first discuss food-related rituals with a particular emphasis on fasting and celebrations that were or may have been religious and that involved food. I will then turn my attention to the religious meaning ascribed to specific food items, ending with a detailed discussion of two exceptional cases, *ḥalwā'* and wine.

FASTING

From a political prisoner's hunger strike to Hollywood's slimming fads, from the Muslim fast of Ramadan to a Christian's Lent, fasting—partial or complete—takes many forms and carries a host of meanings. As the conscious choice of eating little or not at all, there is an element of irony in that fasting should be the food-related practice most often appearing in the sources I am using for this study. Ironic, yet easily explainable: the richest of these sources are religious texts, and, at least for part of the late-medieval Anatolian population, fasting was an important religious concept.

Fasting has been the subject of theological debates since the early centuries of Islam, and it may seem risky to study it outside of this intellectual context. But just like medicine, the practices appearing in sources intended for scholarly consumption could also be part of the lives of ordinary people who probably were unaware of these theological debates. Just as I discussed the "general public" incarnations of medical thought among the late-medieval Anatolian population in chapter 3, I thus intend to describe here the image and practice of fasting among those people who did not participate in intellectual debates on the issue.

It is clear that fasting could mean many things to a late-medieval Anatolian mind. More specifically, there seem to have been three relatively distinct popular conceptions of the practice. As we are about to see, although a positive religious connotation may have bound all of these incarnations, it is less than obvious that the population at large actually engaged in fasting to any significant extent.

Among these three incarnations of fasting, the first is the most diffuse and is associated with the religious figures appearing in religious sources. Fasting is frequently mentioned in relation to spiritual retreats called *halvet*, *çile*, or *erbain* and presented as lasting for forty days. However, in passages that present it in this incarnation, fasting tends to play a secondary, almost atmospheric, role in the narration, along with such practices as sacrifice (*qurbān*) and prayer. Its presence helps give a religious color to the scene and underlines the religious credentials of the character, but it could as well be, and sometimes is, completely absent of the narration without any essential change in the praiseful description of the partaker. A good example of such coloristic literary function of fasting can be found in the *Maqalat-i Sayyid*

Harun, where a master in grief retreats to a cell that has been built in the corner of a mosque, where "he would rest his head on a stone and lie on the ground. He would perform the daily prayers with the community, from inside the cell. He spent the rest of his life there. He would eat one iota of food every forty days."[2] Omitting the last sentence would not bring about any fundamental change in the scene depicted.

Furthermore, the positive religious connotation of fasting in such passages does not entail that the population imitated these examples. This becomes clear if we take a closer look at the *Gharib-nama*. As a compendium of spiritual advice intended for popular audiences, this text might be expected to include a large number of references to fasting theory and practice, yet it remains almost entirely silent on the question. When the *Gharib-nama* mentions fasting, it merely points out that the disruption of physical well-being that fasting brings about is a form of struggle against the evils of the *nafs* (the carnal soul in Sufi thought, which is not unlike the Freudian id). These references, however, do not encourage the audience to engage in fasting.[3] Despite being more directly concerned with dispensing explicit spiritual advice than most other sources, it is striking that the *Gharib-nama* also avoids any mention of fasting when it refers to spiritual retreats.[4] Such literary use of fasting is fully congruent with and, I would argue, reflects a society where the positive spiritual associations of supererogatory fasting were widely acknowledged, while its actual practice was not widespread.

The second incarnation of fasting is very close to the first in its association with a special class of religious professionals. This version, however, involved fasting that actually took place on a daily basis, rather than strictly literary or mental representations, and was associated with specific religious groups. The Mavlāvī order of dervishes, following the spiritual example of Rūmī, is the best documented of these groups, and the intensive fasting habits of its members appear to have been an important component of their social identity.

Because I have discussed the practice of fasting among Mavlāvī dervishes at greater length in a separate article,[5] I should limit myself to point out here that fourteenth-century sources depict the Mavlāvī fasting for much shorter, more much "realistic" periods of time (between three days and two weeks) than the religious heroes falling in the first category of fasting cases discussed above (depicted as fasting for several months or even years). Other passages also drop hints that there was some degree of controversy over the intense involvement of the Mavlāvī with fasting. Rather than from any debate on whether fasting was legitimate at all, this controversy probably originated from the fact that, by engaging in extreme fasting, the Mavlāvī were among the few groups to follow the socially marginal, lowbrow religious movement called Qalandariyyah.[6]

The third incarnation of fasting in the fourteenth-century Anatolian context is the form that most readily comes to mind when discussing Islam: the duty for most healthy adult Muslims to fast in daytime during the month of Ramadan. Three observations can be made about the way sources address this question—or, perhaps more accurately, largely avoid it.[7] First, only a limited number of direct references to the month of Ramadan appear, and these tend to be part of theological statements associating this month with piety in general rather than narrative references to the fast.[8] Second, a likewise limited number of references appear to the collective fast-breaking meals (*ifṭār*) that take place every night during that month. These references all come from authors who had especially strong ties with the Islamic scholarly culture, all take place among the political elite, and none explicitly mentions the fast that may have preceded the meal in question during the day. I could in fact not find a single mention, direct or indirect, of people outside the elite fasting during the month of Ramadan.[9] And third, two *waqfiyya*s make special provisions for particular expenses associated with the month of Ramadan, but neither of them includes, among its prescriptions, any change in the number or schedule of meals offered during that month.[10]

This combination of observations suggests that fasting during Ramadan may have been at least primarily a practice of the elite. If this was indeed the case, it may in turn have been part of a larger pattern of uneven distribution of Islamic canonical practices among the nominally Muslim population in late-medieval Anatolia.

OTHER RITUALS

Besides fasting, a number of other food-related religious rituals also occur in the sources, among which animal sacrifice (*qurbān*) is probably the most common. From the way it appears in sources, religious sacrifice seems to have essentially been limited to sheep and oxen. This did not preclude some variations that reflected the generosity of the person offering the sacrifice. This variation is obvious from the number of animals slaughtered: although the "thousand oxen" that a father offers to a saint who performed a miracle may be hyperbolic, it is clear that a large number of animals could be slaughtered together on a given occasion.[11] The choice of animals also mattered, and there are indications that "four-horned sheep" and lambs were seen as higher-quality, more prestigious slaughters than regular sheep.[12]

Accounts vary on who received the meat that resulted from the *qurbān*. Although it is clear that charity and public distribution were the most commonly stated objectives of sacrifice, it is in practice the dervish communities rather than the economic poor that would end up consuming at least a significant proportion of the meat that the ritual produced. If we consider that *waqf* holdings gave dervish communities the status of large landowners (or, more accurately, land administrators) and that, as I stated earlier, livestock could play the part of a savings account for relatively well-to-do peasants,[13] it is probably reasonable to interpret some of the "pious" offerings of animal sacrifices as first and foremost attempts to buy political influence at the local level, a form of "political contribution" from the medieval peasants to their dervish landlords.

The use that sources make of the *qurbān* as a narrative element is not without parallels with the first category of fasting I discussed above, insofar as it often appears to give religious credence and a spiritual color to a character or occasion without playing a central role in a narration. *Qurbān* thus appears in relation to rain prayers,[14] gifts of charity,[15] or requests or thanks for a miraculous favor,[16] or as offerings to a saint or other religious master.[17] This religious character of sacrifice was not a strictly Muslim phenomenon, as can be seen from one of the few explicit references to the religious life of non-Muslims in the *Vilayat-nama*. The scene depicts a *zimmi* (assumedly Christian) village where, in order to celebrate the miracle of a Muslim saint that allows them to harvest wheat when they sow rye and make large bread loaves when they put small lumps of dough in the oven, the villagers perform animal sacrifices and other celebrations every year. Nowhere in the narration is there any suggestion that they converted to Islam along the way.[18]

The *istisqā'* (rain prayer) is another formally Muslim ritual that appears on a number of occasions. References to this ritual, all from the *Manaqib al-'Arifin*, do not describe in detail how it was conducted, but we can gather some general hints from the matter-of-fact tone they take, the variety of detail they contain, and the identity of the characters they include. It therefore seems that when a drought affected agriculture in the region of Konya, it was regular practice for a group of prominent individuals from the local religious and political elite to come out of the city ("onto the plain") in order to perform this votive ritual. Leadership of this group, rather than determined ex officio or befalling a particular member of a given lineage, was bestowed upon a religious scholar (sometimes a member of the Mavlāvī order) selected anew on every occasion—and to be thus selected was considered a great honor.[19] In the absence of further detail, it is difficult to derive much understanding of the broader implications of the rain prayer, but it certainly constitutes a concrete incarnation of the social interconnection between religious and political urban elites.

A number of rituals taking place within dervish communities also involved either some food consumption or a conscious refraining from it. Among the Mavlāvī, the most common is a practice that sources call *samāʿ*. It is tempting to follow the modern usage of this word and simply assume that it refers to what is known, in today's Konyan touristic circles, as the "whirling dervish ceremony." Sources indeed suggest that it was held at frequent but irregular intervals; took place standing up and, as I pointed out earlier on, before meals,[20] without eating or drinking; involved physical activity, dehydration, and even headaches;[21] and excluded gender intermixing.[22] These elements are essentially compatible with an interpretation of the word *samāʿ* in its modern understanding. Yet a number of anecdotes depict an individual (often an outside friend of the Mavlāvī order) "giving" a *samāʿ*, and such a reference to hosting is rather at odds with the practices held in Mavlāvī convents in later centuries.[23] Furthermore, some hints also appear that *samāʿ* may have been a more generic term referring to a category of social interaction and that the modern definition corresponds to only some of the fourteenth-century uses of the term.[24] Whatever may be the case, a systematic, lexically careful study of the question should be performed in order to avoid the risk of letting misleading preconceptions shape our understanding of early Mavlāvī ritual.[25]

Finally, one would expect to find religious ritual around such life events as births, circumcisions, weddings, and funerals, but the few references to these events appear at best tangentially religious. Thus, the religious character of the most detailed account of circumcision ceremonies essentially derives from the fact that a *samāʿ* takes place on the occasion, and that Rūmī keeps a complete fast during the sixteen days that it lasts.[26] In the case of the (more numerous) references to mourning, it is the consumption of *ḥalwāʾ* that, as we will see toward the end of this chapter, creates the most direct link with a religious atmosphere. As for weddings, there are a few references to the feasting they entailed, but these celebrations appear mostly devoid of any sacred contents.[27] Of course, the shariʿa considers marriage as a contract rather than any form of sacrament. Yet the relatively low religious contents of those activities bring up the question of whether there were secular celebrations in late-medieval central Anatolia, which I will address later in this chapter.[28]

RELIGIOUS FESTIVALS AND TIME

Religious festivals, as periodically recurrent social occasions,[29] allow the religious calendar to enter the lives and perceptions of time of ordinary folk. These events can thus offer some interesting insight into the place that a formal organization of time according to the Muslim calendar actually held in public consciousness.

Among these celebrations, it is not a calendar date but rather a day of the week that gathers the most attention in the sources, "Friday night" (i.e., the night between Thursday and Friday). Although it does not systematically appear in association with a particular practice or set of practices, passages that mention Friday night generally entail communal gatherings, in many cases for spiritual exercises, and involve all social classes, from the population of a village to members of the religious and political elite.[30]

Several *waqfiyya*s also prescribe that money should be spent for the salary of Qurʾan reciters, usually to perform on Mondays and Thursdays on the tomb of the endower or members of the latter's family. It is unclear to what extent these prescriptions reflect a popular practice, especially since it is quite possible that the *qadi*s involved in setting up *waqf*s may in fact have used the endowments as instruments to impose a formal religious component upon social gatherings that were otherwise either largely secular or heterodox.[31]

I have discussed fasting during the month of Ramadan in an earlier section, along with the possibility that such fasting may have taken place mostly or exclusively among elite classes. Besides references to this particular month, I should emphasize the extremely limited number of direct references to the religious highlights of the Muslim calendar. For example, I have found only three references to the ʿĪd al-Aḍḥā (also known as ʿĪd al-Kabīr or ʿĪd al-Qurbān, i.e., the Feast of the Sacrifice), which is one of the two main festivals of the Muslim calendar. One reference is strictly used as a chronological marker, with no mention of associated activities, and the other two suggest that some food distribution was the only significant change from the population's regular habits on that day.[32] Ibn Baṭṭūṭa is the only author explicitly referring to the ʿĪd al-Fiṭr (or ʿĪd al-Saghīr), which marks the end of Ramadan. He claims to have witnessed, on that day, a large-scale celebration involving craftsmen of all trades parading in the streets of Lâdik, sacrificing sheep and oxen in cemeteries, distributing the meat along with bread, and attending a feast offered by the local ruler.[33] We can question whether Ibn Baṭṭūṭa's depiction is accurate and, if it is, whether the partakers in this celebration would have understood their activities in the orthodox frame of the canonical

ʿĪd al-Fiṭr, especially given the author's prudish attitude toward heterodoxy and the isolated character of this claim within my source material.

Whatever may be the case, it is striking to see how seldom sources—including texts primarily concerned with spiritual matters—use religious festivals as chronological anchors and, when they do, how much they concentrate on days of the week rather than days of the year. Furthermore, the few depictions of celebration on religious days are exclusively set in urban environments. We should remember that the lunar Muslim calendar is of limited use for agricultural purposes, since it shifts ten days every year in relation to the solar calendar and rhythm of seasons. It would thus stand to reason that, if they were aware of it at all, fourteenth-century Anatolian peasants did not make the Muslim calendar an essential component of their time organization. After all, such integration could not be effected through a mere change of vocabulary or superficial transformation of pre-Islamic habits, but rather entailed a deep reorganization of their mental universe. This hypothesis is strengthened by the apparently widespread awareness of, and compliance with, a seven-day week pattern, which had been present and widespread in Anatolia for centuries before the arrival of Islam.[34]

If this hypothesis is correct, then the Muslim calendar remained at least in large part outside of the daily experience of rural populations during the period discussed here. It is not the only case where late-medieval Anatolian practice would have clashed with orthodox ideals.

Religiosity in Celebrations

Celebrations, which include both regular festivals and feasts that occur on an irregular basis, involved a variable degree of religious contents. In fact, we can set these celebrations on a spectrum ranging from the strictly profane to the strictly pious. Closer to the former end of this spectrum, we find the days of the religious calendar that I discussed in the previous section, as well as the feasts that rich new disciples or their families offered upon their introduction into a religious order.[35]

At the secular and perhaps even impious end of this spectrum, on the other hand, are the many feasting scenes that chronicles present as taking place among the elite. These scenes include frequent references to wine (often formulaic, but also frequently apologetic), leaving no doubt that the political elite could imagine an evening of enjoyment where piety was brushed aside. In fact, the few exceptions to this rule only reinforce the general impression, since they depict (without necessarily condemning it) what many a believer would call a scene of debauchery as a point of contrast with a central character's pious behavior. The possibility of unreligious enjoyment was not limited to the mental landscape of the upper echelons of the population, and some of these scenes actually involve entire army corps. More generally, other passages present feasts that sources implicitly or explicitly associate with impiety, in some cases as examples of behavior to avoid. Perhaps the best example is that of a group of Rūmī's disciples who return from a visit to a political grandee with highly praiseful words for the foods and drinks their host offered, only to be rebuked by their master, who disapproves of their worldly concerns.[36]

In between the religious celebration and the bouts of debauchery, a number of other references come with a religious scent about them, without including any specific element of ritual or doctrine that would allow us to associate it with one particular creed. For example, a mention of the presence of non-Muslims in the funeral procession of Rūmī emphasizes religiosity at the expense of sectarianism.[37] Religious contents vary a great deal in frequency, nature, and level of detail from one of these depictions to the next. However, sources include no clear indication that some events were seen as part of an altogether different category of events (i.e., sacred or profane), and indeed both a celebratory mindset and large amounts of food do bind all of those events.[38]

The question of whether there could be such thing as a secular festival may seem like an anachronistic attempt to slap an utterly modern concept onto a medieval situation. Yet this angle of questioning does yield unexpected insight: if it is difficult to find festivities that are clearly devoid of religiosity, it is comparatively easier to find celebrations whose religious contents show no sign of sectarian identification, as if sectarian identity played a limited role in religious practice. This, in other words, may have been a world in which coexistence with Christians contributed to tone down rather than emphasize the association that uneducated Muslims felt with "canonical" Islam, a possibility that should at the very least make us wary of simplistic assumptions that Anatolia was the theater of a deep social split between Christian and Muslim populations.

Religious Value of Foodstuffs

Looking into the religious values associated with given types of food offers another way to investigate the extent to which the religious "high culture," the theological framework most readily accessible to us through written sources, was actually part of popular worldviews. In this final section, I will first take a general look at the way religious thought created food categories, before concentrating on two types of consumables that both carried a heavy load of religious symbolism, *ḥalwā'* and wine.

FOOD CATEGORIES When sources associate individual food items and religious concerns, they typically do so as part of an exercise in contrast between the evils of giving in to the carnal soul (the *nafs*) and the pious asceticism of Sufis. In the *Manaqib al-ʿArifin* in particular, condemnation of worldly enjoyments is so frequent that we can assume each negatively depicted food item to have been a gourmet delicacy at the time. As I pointed out in an earlier chapter, whatever was fatty and sweet held a large place in this category of "good tasting, and therefore evil," foods.[39] However, the category also included foods whose consumption was associated with circumstances of worldly enjoyment, such as the *nuql* that were consumed along with wine.[40]

On the other hand, there are comparatively few references to foods that are deemed "pious," mostly because opposition to worldly concerns typically appears in the shape of fasting. One exception is barley, which did carry positive associations with pious asceticism stemming from its status of food of lean days.[41] It is difficult to ascertain whether this view was limited to Sufi circles or shared by the population at large.[42] It is clearer, however, that low-quality, popular dislike, or, at the very least, unluxurious status, indeed contributed to give an aura of religious respectability to foodstuffs such as the liquid resulting from cooking sheep heads and hooves, and perhaps the small round bread loaves called *girda*.[43]

Beyond this dichotomy between pious asceticism and carnal instincts, it is clear that sources mention some food items because of the prominent place they held in literary and theological traditions going as far back as the Qur'an itself. Such was the case with *tharīd*,[44] dates,[45] and pomegranates.[46] At a more general level, fruits and, even more commonly, milk often appear as metaphors for theological teaching—the latter not infrequently presented in contrast with the wine of mystical knowledge.[47] These metaphors frequently seem grounded in the experience of the audience. For example, as I stated in an earlier chapter, there are good reasons to believe that adults did not drink fresh, liquid milk, and indeed the metaphorical passages that depict milk drinking specifically refer to breast-feeding.[48]

A few references to the *ḥalāl* (allowed by religious law) and *ḥarām* (forbidden) character of food also occur, although they rarely associate these concepts with specific foodstuffs.[49] Generally, these adjectives appear without any attempt at categorizing food types and are applied to a particular serving ("this plate of rice is *ḥalāl*," to convey that it was acquired through licit means) rather than a type of food (such as "rice is *ḥalāl*" as a general rule).[50] They are also used as nouns in an entirely abstract sense, to refer to a general pattern of behavior that is not limited to dietary habits ("these people eat *ḥarām*," to mean that they behave impiously).[51] The general impression that comes out of these observations, then, is one in which ordinary people, by which I mean those whose occupation did not center on theological study, either seldom or never used the theological, high-cultured categories of *ḥalāl* and *ḥarām* as mental organizers of food categories in their daily lives.

There are surprisingly few passages using particular foodstuffs as a way to mark an association with a particular creed, sect, or other form of religious identity. Perhaps the bluntest case occurs when Ibn Baṭṭūṭa recalls visiting Sinop, on the Black Sea coast, where locals observe him praying in the (Sunni) *malikī* fashion and, noticing the difference with their own (also Sunni) *hanafī* practice, accuse him of following Shiʿi Islam. He then has to kill, skin, cook, and eat a hare (which, he adds, the *rāfiḍī*—i.e., Shiʿis—do not eat) in order to disprove the accusations.[52] Yet if we take into account Ibn Baṭṭūṭa's obsessions of theological purity, his tendency to interpret much of his observations through a scriptural lens, and his outsider's point of view, the surprising element is, rather, that this should be an isolated anecdote in the descriptions of his stay in Anatolia. Even a passing reference to the "Jewish neighborhood" as the place where one could obtain wine, in the *Manaqib al-ʿArifin*, concentrates on the sale and distribution rather than the consumption of the product, in a text where dozens of references to wine never mention (let alone emphasize) an association between wine consumption and the non-Muslims.[53] In fact, the only comparatively well-documented case might be that of pork, or more accurately pigs, since all but one of the mentions I could find refer to the live animal rather than its meat.[54] These mentions do tend to associate the animal with Christians, but one passage suggests that Muslims could hunt wild pigs with bow and arrow, and another rebukes characters who mistreat a wild piglet.[55] Of course, given foods can be associated with given religious groups. But in a heterogeneous social context such as that of late-medieval Anatolia, a context that the historiography consistently depicts as deeply split between Muslims and Christians, it is surprising to see how seldom such a clear-cut division actually appears and how benign the stigma associated with the food of the Other seems to be when such a stigma appears at all.

The surprise is largely defused if we shift the focus of our question from an inquiry on the *existence* of such sectarian identifications to an inquiry on their *importance*. In other words, while sectarian identification of food items probably existed, they may not have constituted a locus of legal or social tensions. The evidence is in fact quite compatible with a situation such as that of the contemporary United States, where associations are widely acknowledged between some foods or dietary practices and particular religious or ideological identities (such as matzo ball soup with Judaism, or vegetarianism with the ecological movement), without such identification creating ironclad markers used to reduce individuals to one such identity and deny outsiders access to these "identity foods" or serving as the pretext for sectarian skirmishes.

This impression is reinforced when we look at some hints of inedible status given to horses, mules, dogs, and perhaps fish.[56] Such dislikes may or may not have been meshed into religious thinking, although it is clear that none of them shares the symbolic weight of wine and pork as antithetical to good Islamic practice. But it is precisely the absence of a religious or identity context to frame them that reinforces the point made in the previous paragraph: such negative associations were part of the background noise and by no means central in the definition of one's socioreligious identity or significant points of contention between members of different groups.

ḤALWĀʾ The word *ḥalwāʾ* occurs on a large number of occasions in the sources I have used for this study. Modern readers have mostly assumed it to refer to one or the other of the sweets designated under the same name in contemporary Turkey—a dryish, mildly sweetened paste generally made of wheat flour, wheat semolina, or crushed sesame seeds (each one designated with an added noun—*un helvası, irmik helvası, tahin helvası*). There are good reasons to believe that, in the fourteenth century, the word likewise covered a relatively wide semantic range. However, it is difficult to ascertain whether the possibilities were limited to a set of predetermined recipes (as with the modern Turkish *helva*), or whether there were a potentially unlimited number of variations within certain parameters (as with the English word *pastry*, for example).[57]

Ḥalwāʾ appears to have been consumed as part of religious celebrations (or, more accurately, occasions that had a religious color about them) in so systematic a fashion that in many instances its very mention becomes a device to emphasize the religious character of a situation, such as when a lonely pious man keeps it warm and ready in case a saint might pass by.[58] Even in those very few cases where the context in which *ḥalwāʾ* appears could a priori be considered unreligious, such as when it is given to children, its consumption either serves as a metaphor for spiritual nourishment or appears as part of the upbringing of a future spiritual master.[59]

Beyond this general air of spirituality, one activity is closely associated with *ḥalwā'*: mourning. Although it remains unclear whether *ḥalwā'* would systematically be distributed at every funeral, such distribution would at least take place in those cases where the deceased was an esteemed individual, seven days after the passing away as well as during the commemoration held forty days after the death.[60] Indeed, one anecdote depicts the daughter of Rūmī cooking *ḥalwā'* that an unidentified third party then distributes to the disciples in order to honor a devout cat that gave up on life after the religious master passed away. The part that *ḥalwā'* plays in this narration could be interpreted as a way to emphasize the higher than ordinary standing entailed by having *ḥalwā'* distributed on one's behalf after one's death.[61] It might be relevant to note that it is a common practice, in today's Turkey, for the family of the deceased to offer *ḥalwā'* to their visitors during the funeral wake. Although there is every reason to assume that this tradition is a direct continuation of the medieval practice discussed here, the latter might have been limited to the upper classes, as upper-class social norms often trickle down to the rest of the population.[62]

One final observation before closing this section: the ceremonial or sacred character that sources ascribe to *ḥalwā'* seems to be strictly limited to its consumption. The production phase appears in comparatively few passages, and the sources I have used never depict it in a ceremonial way. In fact, the few extant references to cooking *ḥalwā'* concentrate on the distribution that follows it and the generosity that it entails.[63] This might be related to the fact that *ḥalwā'* could be either produced as part of a professional activity (thus allowing customers to buy it ready-made) or homemade.[64] The product itself was therefore, at least in a significant number of cases, the only common element in the two phases, the people taking part in production not necessarily being involved in consumption.[65] This would indeed seem to reinforce the suggestion I made on several occasions in the previous chapters, of a society where groups living side by side indeed limited the contacts between one another.

WINE As I pointed out at the beginning of this chapter, literacy and religious education were almost systematically associated with each other in the period discussed here. It is therefore rather unsurprising that among all the foods and drinks appearing in the sources I have used, wine—so explicitly banned by Islam—carries the clearest religious significance. But this significance, as we are about to see, blurs our understanding of how alcohol was perceived (and, a fortiori, consumed) outside of the religiously trained elite.

Wine, the only alcoholic drink observable in these sources,[66] commonly appears as a metaphor for mystical knowledge. By no means limited to late-medieval Anatolia, such a metaphorical usage carried both a reference to the ecstatic, irrational state of "Sufi intoxication" and a built-in opposition with milk, itself symbolizing the comparatively innocuous and more mainstream legal (shariʿa) theological knowledge.[67] Those conservative authorities who rejected Sufism as unorthodox would have accepted that metaphor, albeit understanding it in a negative light. Beyond references to Sufism, a limited number of passages also condemn alcohol consumption as something negative by Muslim standards, associating it either with non-Muslims[68] or with impious Muslims.[69] Still, in most of these cases the rebuke appears as bookish arguments rather than depictions of real-life scenes.[70]

Yet "real life" is the main realm of interest of this book, and it seems obvious that alcohol consumption was, at the very least, widespread within the politicomilitary elite. This is particularly obvious from *Bazm u Razm* and the *Dustur-nama*, two sources whose perspective is not as heavily religious as others. Most of the references they contain to alcohol present it in a reluctantly neutral or even cautiously positive fashion, often including drunkenness in poetic lists of celebrated worldly pleasures.[71]

As far as the civilian population at large is concerned, however, relevant passages are hard to come by. Perhaps the most explicit author in this respect is al-ʿUmarī, who includes "wines" (*khumūr*) as one of the three food items that Anatolians stockpile before locking themselves inside their houses for the winter (the other two being jerked meat, *qadīd*, and oil or butter, *adhān*).[72] The same author also marvels at the production near Denizli of pomegranate wine that, his informant tells him, is higher in alcohol content and produced in larger quantity than grape wine.[73] Another, fainter, hint appears when ʿĀrif Chalabī (the spiritual master of the author of the *Manaqib al-ʿArifin*) dismisses drinking wine as the stuff of those who are "hamrang-i mardum" (of a similar nature or disposition as [assumedly ordinary] men).[74] Likewise, the characterization that the *Gharib-nama* twice makes of wine in heaven (calling it "wine, but good and legal" [hamr, ve likin hoş helâl]) suggests that both the experience of drinking bad wine and a certain guilt or shame for indulging in it existed among the popular audiences of that text.[75] I could not, however, find any form of lament over a widespread habit of drunkenness in the population, something that could have been expected among the religious authors, at the very least from the holier-than-thou observations of Ibn Baṭṭūṭa.[76] Why no such lament? A look into the way that the sources describe the consequences of alcohol consumption does bring up a possible explanation.

There are, as I stated earlier, very few *direct* references to the immoral and religiously illegal character of wine drinking, but a very large number of *indirect* references (such as the "like wine, but good and legal" line I mentioned above).[77] It thus seems clear that alcohol's immorality and illegality were obvious to all. A limited number of passages also sketch the physiological effects, such as knowledge and intellect going away and, in a more lyrical interpretation, "heads becoming light, wind falling in the mustaches and the candle of felicity being consumed."[78] More interesting is a different, more practical, set of consequences, centering on the inability to assume one's military assignments,[79] to defend oneself against assassination,[80] and to carry out one's political duties.[81]

It is relatively safe to assume that the daily experience of late-medieval Anatolian peasants did not require them to lead an army, tend to the affairs of the state, or dodge assassination attempts by political rivals. Such depictions of the ill effects of drunkenness were obviously meant to edify the members of the elite, and sources that were targeted at more popular audiences (such as the *Gharib-nama* and the *Vilayat-nama*) do not seem to include any serious advice aimed at reducing the consumption of alcohol. Drinking wine, in other words, very much seems to have been concentrated at the top of the social ladder.

The reason for such an uneven distribution of the practice is anything but obvious, yet both the observation that Ibn Baṭṭūṭa makes on the widespread use of *ḥashīsh* and the comparison between cannabis and wine I presented in chapter 3 suggest a possible explanation: wine may simply have been too expensive for the masses, limitations in economic power rendering any discussion of popular alcohol consumption outside the elite irrelevant for the various authors. Assuming that, in the general population, the economic means of Christians were equal or inferior to those of Muslims, the lower classes as a whole would thus have been equally affected by this economic constraint on alcohol consumption, irrespective of sectarian affiliation. In other words, if this hypothesis is correct, then there were only limited opportunities for wine drinking to arise as a visible contrast between the Christians and Muslims in late-medieval Anatolia.

CONCLUSION

There is no question that both Christians and Muslims lived in late-medieval Anatolia. It is, however, much less obvious that a social divide along these sectarian lines was deemed extremely significant for those it involved. In fact, sources tend to present sectarian conflicts as more common between Muslim sects than between Muslims and non-Muslims.

A historical process of prime importance in this respect is the long-term conversion of the Anatolian population from Christianity to Islam. The extreme paucity of data on the mechanics of this transformation makes an empirical study all but impossible. Yet it is clear that it took place, if only from the fact that the proportion of Muslims in central Anatolia rose from none, in the eleventh century, to a majority a few centuries later.

We should remember that the entire life span of any of the people I discuss here could cover but a tiny fraction of this centuries-long process. In their subjective experience, this historical trend would consequently have seemed much more static than it appears to us in hindsight. In other words, the "intermediary steps" of the Islamization of Anatolia had a much heavier bearing on their perspective than any difference between the starting and the final moment of this transformation.

The outcome of my investigation in this chapter strongly suggests that there indeed were such intermediary steps in the spread of Islam among the population of Anatolia. The way in which the Muslim calendar was integrated in daily life is a prime example: The widespread Muslim practice of celebrating on Monday and Thursday nights, based on a seven-day week already present in Byzantine Anatolia, appears to have been fully integrated in the religious practice. On the other hand, particular festivals based on the Muslim lunar calendar that is ill-adapted to agricultural conditions do not seem to have held an important place in the lives of peasants. There is no doubt that "orthodox" Islam (the Islam of the Qurʾan, of the Sunna, and of the five pillars) was a central component of life in courtly circles and at the top of the social ladder, in Anatolia as much as anywhere else in the Muslim world at that period. Yet only a select few components of this canonical set of beliefs and rituals seem to have become part of the daily experience in the lower layers of society.

The sources I have used seldom present religious affiliation as an identity marker. This, of course, does not mean that religion (as a source of identity, as a set of practices, and as a way to interpret the world) was unimportant. But if we combine two elements—the constantly reinforced stratification between the upper and lower echelons of the social ladder and the still limited penetration of "high Islam" in the population at large—then it would stand to reason that the texture of daily life in late-medieval Anatolia did not in fact entail much by way of tensions or conflicts between people defining themselves as Muslims and people defining themselves as Christians.

Conclusion

From this broad survey of the food-related practices in fourteenth-century central Anatolia, a few general observations emerge, a few societal characteristics that we find incarnated in many aspects of daily life. Most striking perhaps are the social inequalities, pervasive and constantly reinforced. Sources leave us with a strong impression that everyone knew the place assigned to them in the hierarchy, and although it is difficult to estimate how often lower-class people tried to challenge the social order, it is very clear that such challenges were by no means seen as benign, amusing missteps.

The stability of this strict social hierarchy was very much strengthened by forceful limitations on the interactions between members of different social groups and between genders. A corollary to such a crystallized and segmented social makeup is that the affairs of the state were the exclusive domain of a very small group of people sitting at the very top of the social ladder. This elite sought to exclude the rest of the population not only from the political decision-making process but also, to the extent it was possible, from its outcomes. The presence of such a sharply defined vertical division of society may very well have toned down the significance of another type of social division that scholars have up to now (wrongly, I argue) assumed to have been central to fourteenth-century central Anatolia, the confessional division between Muslims and Christians.

The above statements may seem a rather anticlimactic way to end this book. Some of them feel generic; some correspond to what a nonspecialist reader would have expected in the first place. To present the issue bluntly, it begs the question: did I really spend all those years digging up evidence that late-medieval Anatolia was not an egalitarian democracy?

But to present a conclusion in such a way, to try summarizing all my findings in a few key sentences, runs in direct opposition to one of the primary objectives of this book: to reconstruct the texture, the subjective experience, of daily life in fourteenth-century central Anatolia. Rendering any texture necessarily entails paying more attention to little details and concrete incarnations than to the "big picture." In other words, what this book should have achieved is not merely to state that a steep social hierarchy existed (in this society just like in many other societies throughout history), but rather to identify, by using food's unique status as a "total social fact," the specific gestures, practices, and ideas that led everyone to settle in a given place within that hierarchy—all elements that were unique to this particular society.

Short of a two-hundred-page conclusion repeating every piece of evidence from the previous chapters, short of trying to summarize the unsummarizable, then, a better way for me to use the last few pages of this book is probably to try to evaluate the extent to which I achieved this objective—and to what extent it is possible to reach it in the first place. And the best way to do so is to compare it with a gold standard: literature.

But before going any further, I should add one word of warning: the next few pages may seem, at first, to be little more than a catalog of this book's shortcomings. They are not. Throughout the previous chapters, I have tried to present the results of my research not only in positive statements, but also by defining them negatively—often using statements beginning with the expression "as opposed to." This format, I believe, renders information in a much crisper form and lessens the likelihood of misunderstanding. This conclusion is thus an application of the same principle on a much broader scale. It is, after all, difficult to fully appreciate the value of a dimly lit zone of knowledge until we become aware of the expanse of darkness from which it was conquered.

LITERATURE

Of all forms of expression, from the scholarly to the artistic, literature is perhaps the one that can most fully convey the subjective experience of one individual to another. The work of writers of talent manages to seamlessly integrate the intellectual and emotional components of their characters' perspectives, the cumulative weight of their life experiences and sudden changes in mindset, the effect of external stimuli and the flow of consciousness, the constant chatter inside one's mind, and the slip of the tongue at an emotionally loaded moment of a conversation. But of course, this requires a thorough understanding (and therefore knowledge) of the characters' subjective experience: had it not been for the incomplete availability of data (and for the stylistic dictates of academic historiography), this book would consequently have best fulfilled its ultimate objective of exposing late-medieval central Anatolian worldviews and subjective experiences by taking the shape of literary fiction, either as a historical novel or as a series of short stories. Among the many reasons that kept this from happening, one stands out: an incomplete knowledge of the period I discuss.

And it is precisely through this shortcoming that the comparison with literature does offer a fruitful angle not only to evaluate the degree to which this book reached its objective, but also to further discuss the particular aspects of daily life and worldviews that primary sources allow or prevent us from understanding.

One preliminary observation: in order to be of any use in understanding worldviews in late-medieval central Anatolia, the story told in this hypothetical novel would need to fall within the realm of the "possible" for the period. The narration, in fact, should probably try to stay as much as possible within the limits of what was considered "normal" at the time and to make any straying from these limits obvious for the reader.[1]

Perhaps most striking, given what we have grown to expect in storytelling, is that our knowledge of the experience of late-medieval Anatolians is particularly deficient in its visual component. There is no way, for example, to determine the colors of clothing, the appearance of the food served, or the shape of the houses that a traveler would see as he arrived in a central Anatolian town. Archaeology does offer some hope for improvement in this respect, but the data remain far from available. Ironically, although several years of research on daily life may seem like an ideal preparation for a consulting role on the set of a historical film set in fourteenth-century Anatolia, what I gained from it, rather, is an acute awareness of how speculative the guidance is that I would be able to give.

Because of this shortcoming, the most ill-adapted literary style in which to set such a story would probably be detail-oriented nineteenth-century realism. In order to make the fullest use of the information available without being too directly hindered by the limitations in our knowledge, the text should concentrate, rather, on the actions and social interactions of the central character at the expense of his moods and limit the references to material culture to those objects that play a central part in the narrative. It should come as no surprise that such a barebones style closely resembles the general tendencies of medieval narratives—the very sources used for this study in the first place.

The reader may have noticed that I used the pronoun *his* in reference to the central character. It is difficult to imagine the potential novel discussed here centering on a woman, as there is simply not enough information available on the experience of women in late-medieval Anatolia to get much further than wild speculation. The few hints that we do have in fact *increase* rather than attenuate this problem, since they suggest that there existed fairly separate gender realms at all levels of society, and thus that it would be ill-advised to simply extrapolate on the basis of what we know about men.

INTERACTION AND COMMUNICATION

The narrative elements that relate to communication are probably those that are the easiest to document based on primary sources. But even in this particular respect, the picture one can paint of fourteenth-century central Anatolia contains sharply contrasting zones of light and obscurity.

We do have, for example, fairly reliable hints as to the situations where people of different social backgrounds would find themselves near each other, in many cases actively trying to limit their interactions. In some circumstances, such as when members of the elite enjoyed themselves in gardens, it is clear that they preferred to avoid the presence of gardeners, and, in upper-class households, masters and servants would eat separately. On the other hand, some circumstances required active interactions. Hence, tax collectors and representatives of *waqfs* went to the peasants to collect a share of the harvest, long-distance traders probably visited villages, and a mix of locals and out-of-towners congregated in urban markets.

That being said, a story presenting the main character as having anything more than very limited interactions with people outside his immediate social circle would probably misrepresent the period. Communication with people higher up or much lower in the social ladder (and, perhaps, with the other gender) was probably very limited by our standards. One would expect that when they did occur, such encounters would entail a heavy dose of ritualized reinforcements of the social order, though the nature of such "rituals" remains very much obscure.

Our knowledge of interactions within a social group is likewise plagued with holes. I investigated popular festivities, for example, in my discussion of the relationship between food and religion and could come up with a few general observations, such as the apparent commonplace character of communal gatherings on what we would call Thursday evenings. A more exhaustive research (that is, one not limited to food-related passages) could probably expand the base of our knowledge two- or threefold, shedding light on such issues as who participated in such happenings or where they took place. It could also potentially bring up some hints to help us relate these festivities to traditions observable in other eras, from ancient Greek literature to twentieth-century anthropology. Yet any scene depicting fourteenth-century central Anatolian peasants gathered on a freezing winter evening would necessarily contain a large proportion of speculation.

This brings up the more general absence of information on colloquial language. It is probably safe to assume that, at least at the beginning of the period covered here, Persian speakers tended to stand higher in the social hierarchy than Turkish speakers and that there was at least a general association between a linguistic and a religious identity (the Greek language and Christianity, for example). We even have a few echoes of the expressions that may have been used in spoken language, suggesting, for example, the use of Arabic formulae by Turkish-speaking beggars. However, venturing beyond these observations would involve guesswork, becoming all the more problematic given that language seems difficult to avoid in a piece of literary fiction set in a multilingual environment where the choice of language carried social implications. In a passage of the *Manaqib al-ʿArifin*, for example, an upper-class man is depicted as using the Greek language to address his servant. While the very mention of this detail (which to the modern reader plays no obvious part in the narrative) strongly suggests it was meaningful to the narrator, the nature of the implied message seems impossible for us to determine.[2]

Still, these shortcomings are only those that take place at the verbal level, which by its nature can easily be committed to paper. Even more problematic is the issue of nonverbal communication; any depiction of gestures made in the course of a conversation would constitute absolutely unwarranted speculation. The application of physical anthropology to archaeological findings may bring some general notion of the physical posture of people.[3] But the tilt of the head, the cocking of a finger—all those small, discrete gestures that determine whether a verbal expression of humble salutation is in fact an acrid mixture of spite and irony are gone, and gone forever.

THE SUBJECTIVE EXPERIENCE

It is one of the great strengths of literature that it can offer a representation of the subjective experience (the mood, the biases, the obsessions, and countless other modalities) through style without ever making explicit mention of it, in a fashion that closely resembles the experience itself. This, the filter through which an object is seen (rather than the object itself or the beholder's relationship with it), might be the province that suffers the most from the shortcomings of a historiographical approach, at least as far as a poorly documented period such as the late Middle Ages in central Anatolia is concerned.

It is, for example, impossible to tell the degree of pain and hardship that was considered normal to endure. At first glance, this may seem relatively unimportant for the reader who has no hope or intention of "experiencing" the fourteenth century in anything more than a metaphorical way. Yet this ignorance threatens all our estimates of, say, the amounts of food and firewood destitute people would consume or of the possibility for a population to live without a particular type of medical treatment. The seminal work of Piero Camporesi has opened up the discussion on the radical implications of such a variable, but I do not believe, as he does, that we can safely estimate the levels of subjective symptoms that were endured.[4]

The normative statements appearing in some sources afford us a significant amount of information concerning personality traits and qualities that were considered ideal and laudable. Just like physical resistance, piety and modesty would, for example, tend to attract positive responses in late-medieval Anatolia. It is even possible to detect a certain degree of association between given social backgrounds and given preferred qualities; modesty was thus probably more often praised within the religious elite than among peasants. What we do not know, however, is the extent to which the perspective on the relative value of these qualities would vary from one person to the next within a given group. In other words, the degree of individuality involved in the process of defining what is "a good person" is essentially inaccessible to us.

A potentially more important, though also more readily identifiable, component of the subjective experience that escapes us is time perception. Available information on this issue remains superficial. One of the few exceptions, Ibn Baṭṭūṭa's description of a local ruler's daily routine, appears precisely because the traveler found it unusual.[5] Likewise, we certainly know that peasants plowed and harvested and tended their cows, yet it is essentially impossible to determine how many hours they spent on any given task on a daily basis and how much time they devoted to leisure (i.e., noneconomically productive) activities. Perhaps even more important, we have no way of understanding the extent to which they saw the future as "organizable" in a planned schedule and how they perceived time passing.[6] Still, it would certainly be ridiculous for the hypothetical novel suggested here to present characters dividing their days in terms of modern-style, precisely measurable hours.

Yet another zone of darkness is the question of motivations, that is, what drove an individual to act in a certain way. The problem here is not limited to identifying these motivations, but also encompasses determining the hierarchy of possible motivating factors, the range of possible variations between individuals within a group, and the map of social acceptability that allowed or prevented an individual from expressing his or her motivations publicly. In other words, we lack the necessary knowledge not only to determine whether it was possible, say, for a man to engage in violence for financial gain, but also to estimate how common this would have been and how much the surrounding society expected this man to be up front about the importance of the money—or, rather, to hide his greed under claims of other, more noble-sounding, pursuits. Our ignorance on this point would seriously weaken the historical accuracy of a novel set in the fourteenth century, given the importance of the "whys" and the "becauses" for the genre. Furthermore, the issue of what was admissible and what had to be hidden is a question that has been largely ignored in the debate surrounding the motivations of the *gazi* volunteers that helped the early Ottoman expansion.

But perhaps the most important problem, because we tend to pay so little attention to it, is that of what we would call "ignorance." There is, of course, a significant body of knowledge available to us that was entirely absent from the lives of late-medieval central Anatolians—and that obviously explains why direct references to cancer or soil nutrients never appear in the sources I surveyed for this study. Yet we should be wary of conceptualizing knowledge as the simple result of an accumulation, and this for two reasons. At the more superficial level, it is structurally closed to the possibility that late-medieval Anatolians may have had access to elements of information that escape us. The second and more serious reason to be dissatisfied with a simplistic representation of ignorance is precisely that it misrepresents the way countless bits of knowledge are woven into each other to create an internally consistent conception of the world. This is not the place for a lengthy discussion of how some of the principles of Thomas Kuhn's *Structure of Scientific Revolutions* can be applied to realms far beyond scientific thought. But even without expounding detailed theories of knowledge, one can note that no individual knows everything and that any worldview necessarily has to accommodate areas of ignorance (or else run the risk of turning into a debilitating mental condition). The shapes taken by this accommodation, ranging from superstitions to scientific theories and from absence of interest to appeals to *Wikipedia*, are defining components of any worldview, and ignoring them prevents our understanding of said worldview.

From a strictly literary point of view, it is, of course, a challenging-enough task to represent a character's perspective accurately when that perspective is entirely foreign to the modern reader. Literary strategies used to circumvent the problem may have a tedious effect (lengthy explanations breaking the narrative flow, for example), or even obscure the period discussed more than expose it (for example, by presenting "being incapable of imagining the Internet" as fundamental to a character's way of thinking). The task becomes a maddening one when the author cannot even ascertain the character's perspective to begin with.[7] This brings me to my final comment on the limitations of this research—and of all historiography concerning the Middle Ages.

EPILOGUE: OF FOOD, LOVE, AND EXPERIENCE

For the first two years of the research that ultimately led to this book, I lived in the neighborhood of Kadıköy, on the Asian shore of Istanbul. This is also the place where Barış Manço, who appeared at the beginning in my introduction as the author and singer of the reggae "Domates Biber Patlıcan," was born and spent a good part of his life.

In the course of those two years, I developed a deep love (and, in the view of many friends, an irritating apologist's bent) for this neighborhood. Besides the salty smell coming from the Marmara Sea, the cool and youthful atmosphere, the used bookshops, and the old houses, one of my fondest memories of Kadıköy rests in the cries of the open-air sellers, many of them carting in fresh produce daily from the faraway suburbs of the city. I could also witness the slow but steady trend toward a relatively new practice, that of abandoning specialized shops in order to buy all of one's food supply in the convenient one-stop-shopping facility that is the supermarket. This is one of the incarnations of modernization, in today's Turkey as in many other places around the world, one that sees practicality justify what many a "foodie" would consider a declaration of war on quality food.

Many decades, even centuries, from now, historians might come across the text of Barış Manço's song "Domates Biber Patlıcan." More interested in knowledge than in feelings, as historians often are, they may leave aside the love story and use the song to investigate a number of issues about social and economic life in the society whence it originates, 1980s Istanbul. They may talk about periurban gardening and the social interconnections it created between rich and poor neighborhoods. They may discuss public health laws inspired by the European Union and how these concretely affected the food culture in all layers of society. They may talk about the peculiar place that eggplant plays in Turkish cuisine and about the gender roles audiences would have cast upon lyrics that are nowhere explicitly heterosexual.

But one element will be missing from their analysis, as it is missing from this study, an intrinsic limitation of all scholarship on medieval history that sets historians apart from most novelists. This final asterisk that all medievalists should add to even their most compelling conclusions is, simply, an admission that they did not themselves experience the period they describe.

And experience matters. I imagine these future historians struggling with "Domates Biber Patlıcan" as a historical source. I imagine them coming up with a host of accurate and creative conclusions about 1980s Turkish society. And I suspect they will miss out on one very crucial point, one lesson I learned at Çiya, a restaurant of Kadıköy that has turned its menu into a study of sorts in Turkish food culture: when properly prepared, *domates tatlısı* (candied tomatoes), *biber dolma* (stuffed peppers), and—my personal favorite—*patlıcan salatası* (puréed eggplant) *can* be so good as to outshine any declaration of love.

(APPENDIX)

Sources

The primary sources I have used include the bulk of the original narrative material produced in fourteenth-century Anatolia. During the first part of my research, I combed through each one of them in order to identify the relevant passages. As will be seen below, the nature, frequency, and importance of such passages vary widely from one literary genre to another and from one source to the next. The narrative sources I have used fall into three broad categories: hagiographies and other religious texts, chronicles and epics, and travelogues and other texts. To this, one should add two more groups of sources: approximately forty endowment deeds (*waqfiyyas*), closer in form to archival documents than to narrative texts, as well as a significant body of archaeological reports.

HAGIOGRAPHIES AND RELIGIOUS TEXTS

While diversity may be the master word as far as the source material for this study is concerned, religious texts and especially hagiographies were no doubt the single most important type of source for my purposes. That this type of source contains a higher concentration of relevant data per page is due to many factors, particularly the format in which they are written.

Unlike modern biographies, where the general narrative gives way to specific scenes and dialogue only to illustrate a given event or personality trait in greater detail, hagiographies composed in medieval Anatolia are essentially collections of anecdotes, mostly centered on the performance of miracles or other pious deeds by a Muslim saintly figure. Because these anecdotes are used as arguments to demonstrate the sanctity of the main character (rather than as the building blocks in a general depiction of his life), they are often presented in a loose chronological order and framed by few if any generalizing narrative statements (such as "he lived there for the next five years" or "he had a good relationship with his neighbors"). These comments apply to a variable degree to the various hagiographies, but most are best described as argumentative texts seeking to prove a master's sainthood, rather than descriptive ones giving an account of his life. This anecdotal structure makes hagiographies immensely useful for my purposes, because they impose the presence of "trivial" elements in the text: a philosopher can explain an Aristotelian principle in "the sublunary world," but a saint who miraculously makes fruits grow in the middle of the winter has to do so in an orchard.

It is, of course, a general characteristic of medieval literature to provide little if any descriptions, and anybody hoping to find Flaubertian flourishes about the landscape visible from the kitchen window or the texture of a character's skin in the *Manaqib al-ʿArifin* is bound to be disappointed. Yet the harvest is quite rich if one measures it by medieval standards. Because hagiographies *have* to mention some narrative "props" to allow their main character to perform miracles, and because the primary objective of the text is to convey the miracle as a believable event, these "props" have to appear realistic to the intended audience, people often living in the same or similar settings as the actors of the anecdotes, and only shortly afterward. It is consequently possible to find in these sources much detail about the practice of meals, garden production, religiously inspired dietary practices, and the like. Furthermore, reporting miracles requires witnesses, and these witnesses often make passing (but, for the purposes of this study, crucially important) comments about their social interactions along the way.

Besides those hagiographies, this section also contains works of religious advice by two authors, ʿĀşıkpaşa and Yûnus Emre. Both wrote in verse, which puts them in a tricky category of source material for this study. The literary landscape of late-medieval Anatolia was clearly dominated by a Persian canon developed over the previous three hundred years. As a matter of fact, one of the major contributors to this canon, Mavlānā Jalāl al-Dīn Rūmī, had lived most of his life in the region. By the fourteenth century, Persian poetry was governed by a set of rules and motifs so rigid as to make it a culture of its own, leaving little opportunity or encouragement for individual authors to express in their writing the unique circumstances in which they lived. To put it differently, any work of Persian poetry produced in fourteenth-century Anatolia should be understood as part of a literary tradition rather than of a particular cultural context. This association makes it effectively impossible to identify those passages that could reflect the daily experiences of its particular author. It is for this reason that I have stayed away from poetic works in Persian, including the works of Rūmī himself, and of his son Sultān Valad.

On the other hand, fourteenth-century Anatolia saw a small group of authors adopt Turkish, previously only spoken and mostly by lower-class individuals, for their writings. Since it is impossible to mechanistically transfer versification rules and set phrases to a new language, the process of adaptation opened opportunities to express conditions peculiar to the Anatolian context and, to some extent, limited the influence of culturally foreign elements appearing under the guise of literary conventions (or at least made them easier to spot for this reader). It is for this reason that religious poetic works in Turkish, by ʿĀşıkpaşa and Yûnus Emre, can appear in this section.

Manaqib al-ʿArifin

The *Manaqib al-ʿArifin*[1] is the work of Shams al-Dīn Aḥmad al-Aflākī al-ʿĀrifī (ca. 1290–1360), who was a personal disciple of the grandson of the famed Sufi poet and originator of the Mavlāvī order (whirling dervishes) Jalāl al-Dīn Rūmī, also known as Mavlānā (1207–1273). Aflākī composed this Persian-language text, his only known work, in two stages: after a first redaction in the late 1310s, Aflākī revised and supplemented his text around 1353, producing the version we know today.

The *Manaqib* is a collection of biographical anecdotes concerning the "founding fathers" of the *Mavlāvī* order: Rūmī himself, of course (the section about him covers more than half of the work as a whole), but also his father and spiritual masters, as well as successors down to Aflākī's own time. These biographical sketches are made up of anecdotes introduced by expressions attributing them to specified or unspecified transmitters (or simply mentioning "it is reported that . . .") and arranged in a loose, partly chronological, and partly thematic order. It contains a very limited number of narrative transitions, especially at the beginning and end of chapters.

The *Manaqib* might be the most geographically specific of all my narrative sources. Although it begins in Balkh (whence Rūmī migrated to Anatolia in his youth) and contains a few episodes set outside Anatolia (most notably in Damascus), the overwhelming majority of anecdotes take place in Konya, the dwelling place of the author. From a social point of view, most interactions it depicts involve members of the Mavlāvī circles as well as educated religious characters and members of the ruling elite in a city that was, for most of the period the text covers, the political center of Anatolia, therefore offering a "view from the top" of the social landscape. The perspective is, of course, very religious, with a constant underlying effort to demonstrate the theological legitimacy of Rūmī's teachings and practices and, through it, a suggestion that this legitimacy was indeed contested at times. The intended audience is never directly specified, but one can assume that it is at least in large part composed of later generations of Mavlāvī dervishes who may have heard of but not met the main characters.

As far as this study is concerned, relevant information abounds in the *Manaqib al-ʿArifin*. For example, since fasting was among the central pious practices of its main characters, it is discussed at length and in ways that allow exploring both its theoretical justification and its practical aspects. Likewise, Aflākī offers many descriptions of gardens, serving as the setting of a large number of anecdotes, and of food-related crafts. The *Manaqib al-ʿArifin* first and foremost offers the perspective of urban dwellers, and although it is relatively quiet on cereal farming and animal husbandry, it does offer a lot of information on food consumption and food as a mediator of social relations.

Risala-yi Sipahsalar

The *Risala-yi Sipahsalar*[2] is closely related to the *Manaqib al-ʿArifin*, as it covers the same topic in more or less the same way (biographical sketch of the early Mavlāvīs through a series of anecdotes) and also uses the Persian language. It is, in fact, generally considered to be the main source of the *Manaqib*, with which it shares many anecdotes, although neither text directly mentions the other.

This is not the place for an in-depth discussion of the relationship between these two sources, yet this generally accepted assumption that the *Manaqib* borrowed from the *Risala* should in my opinion be seriously reconsidered. The *Risala* is a much shorter text,[3] the (numerous) anecdotes that appear in both texts sometimes contain supplemental detail in the *Manaqib*,[4] and the *Risala* has a much stronger topic-based, argumentative structure (whereas the *Manaqib al-ʿArifin* is generally organized along more chronological lines).[5] As a matter of fact, if one was to produce a shortened version of the *Manaqib*, the result would very much resemble the *Risala*, whereas it is hard to understand what intellectual process could have brought an author to write the *Manaqib* by drawing from the *Risala*.

For the purposes of this study, the *Risala* covers more or less the same ground as the *Manaqib al-ʿArifin*, albeit on a much smaller scale. Such a situation, however, does not make either source redundant, since the variations between them can be of significance, if only by showing which elements could change and which couldn't between texts intended for similar audiences.

Vilayat-nama-yi Haji Baktash Vali

The *Vilayat-nama* is also a hagiographical source, although in many ways it stands as the polar opposite of the *Manaqib al-ʿArifin*. This Turkish-language text is based on an oral narrative composed of anecdotes that presumably took shape shortly after the death of its main character (ca. 1270). In the introduction to his edition of the *Vilayat-nama*, Gölpınarlı shows that the written prose version was probably produced between 1481 and 1501.[6]

The *Vilayat-nama* centers on the life of Hacı Bektaş Velî, a popular holy figure and patron saint of the Alevi-Bektaşi tradition. It begins with his family origins in Khorasan (today's northeastern Iran) and goes on to discuss his migration to a central Anatolian village, his rise to fame as the head of a thriving dervish community up until his death, and, in a short section, his immediate successors. In contrast to the "beads on a string" style of the *Manaqib al-ʿArifin* or the *Risala-yi Sipahsalar*, the narrative structure of the *Vilayat-nama* is rather smoothly integrated, although the text does include a limited number of independent anecdotes. It also incorporates sometimes lengthy passages devoted to other major religious figures who were contemporaries or near contemporaries of Hacı Bektaş Velî. Changes in tone and focus (sometimes the only narrative link to the main text is a short conclusion where the "guest hero" comes to pay homage to the main character) strongly suggest that these passages were pasted in from other sources in order to enhance the religious status of Hacı Bektaş Velî and strengthen his place in the preexisting hagiographical landscape of Anatolian Muslims.

Whereas the *Manaqib al-ʿArifin* is clearly an urban source, the *Vilayat-nama* is essentially rural. With a few exceptions, the bulk of the action takes place in or around villages, allowing for comparatively vivid depictions of agricultural practices. Closer in tone to fairy tales and legends than to highbrow theological debates, it is also obviously intended for a less educated, lower-class audience. In a context where written texts, by definition the work of educated individuals, were an elite phenomenon, the *Vilayat-nama* does offer unique insight into the lifestyles of the poor and nonfamous, covering anything from household management to peasant religious practices and from animal husbandry to gender relations.

Maqalat-i Sayyid Harun

Just like the *Vilayat-nama*, the *Maqalat-i Sayyid Harun* is a Turkish-language hagiography based on an earlier oral tradition. This 1554–1555 work by ʿAbd al-Karīm b. Shaykh Mūsā, however, also draws from Persian sources and carries a strong scholarly flavor.[7]

The *Maqalat* tells the story of a saint, Sayyid Hārūn, who came from Khorasan to Anatolia in the first quarter of the fourteenth century. It does so in a single flowing narrative, devoting a significant amount of attention to the settlement, under Sayyid Hārūn's leadership, of the city of Seydişehir in southwestern central Anatolia.

Unfortunately, both the brevity of the text (about thirty pages in the manuscript) and its frequent recourse to literary motifs conspire to make this source a rather poor one as far as food and daily life are concerned. A few passages are nevertheless relevant, if only for a discussion of the religious and symbolic value of given foodstuffs.

Karamat-i Akhi Avran

The origins of the *Karamat-i Akhi Avran* are unclear; although the author of this work in Turkish-language verse claims be the poet Gulşehrī (d. after 1317), it may very well be an impersonation used to profit from the latter's fame at the time.[8] The *Karamat-i Akhi Avran* praises the religious merits of Ahi Evren, a historical character who was to become a major figure in the religious lore of Anatolia and beyond, most notably as the patron saint to the tanners' guild. Many factors limit the use I could make of the *Karamat* in this study: not only is this a short text (thirteen pages in the Taeschner edition)[9] in verse, but it also relies heavily on the conventions and motifs of Persian poetry and contains a limited number of usable anecdotes.

The *Karamat* does, however, contain a few interesting passages, such as cases where given food items are used in a metaphorical way, as well as some food-related Turkish-language expressions that may reflect food-related ideas and practices current at the time (as opposed to a purely conventional linguistic use). It is also possible that some of the allegorical scenes it depicts (Ahi Evren serving *ḥalwāʾ* in heaven, for example) may to some extent reflect actual practices that would have been known to the intended audience of the text.

Manaqib al-Qudsiyya fi Manasib al-Unsiyya

The *Manaqib al-Qudsiyya fi Manasib al-Unsiyya* is another source in verse praising a semifictional historical figure, in this case Baba Ilyās-i Khorāsānī, one of the leaders of the Babaʾī revolt against Seljuk rule over Anatolia in 1240. It is the work of Elvan Çelebi (d. after 1358), himself the great-grandson of his main character, son of ʿĀşıkpaşa (author of the *Gharib-nama*, discussed below), and grandfather of the famed Ottoman chronicler ʿĀşıkpaşazāde (discussed later in this appendix).

Most of the text describes the salient moments of the life of Baba Ilyās, preceded by a section (partially lost) on his spiritual master, Dede Garkın, and followed by some discussion of his children, most notably Mukhliṣ Pāshā (father of the author). The flourishes in style, however, and the somewhat "mythological" overall tone combine to limit the presence of those concrete details that make the *Manaqib al-ʿArifin* and the *Vilayat-nama* such precious sources.

Still, the *Manaqib al-Qudsiyya* offers some significant data concerning religious norms relating to food, as well as quite a few food-themed metaphors that, with a thorough analysis, can provide some information on more concrete aspects of food consumption.[10]

Gharib-nama

The last two works in this section stand apart from the other texts in this set of religious works. Rather than a hagiography, the *Gharib-nama* is a book of spiritual advice, written in verse. One of the first original compositions in Anatolian Turkish (1330), this is the work of ʿĀşıkpaşa (1272–1332), a member of the prestigious central Anatolian family of scholars that included the authors of two other sources discussed in this appendix, Elvan Çelebi and ʿĀşıkpaşazāde.[11]

As a book of advice, the *Gharib-nama* does not describe the life of a given spiritual master but, rather, is organized in ten chapters, each one offering lists of a given number of items that offer spiritual guidance. For example, chapter 9 contains a list of the nine elements necessary in order for a mill to perform its duty (from a millstone to the water that gives it motion), which is then used as a metaphor for the spiritual order of the universe.[12]

From the down-to-earth flavor of the examples and metaphors it uses, it is clear that the *Gharib-nama* was meant to be read by (or, perhaps more accurately, *to*) people of relatively modest sociocultural levels. This characteristic would normally indicate a fairly high level of reliability of the daily-life elements appearing in the text. However, both the peculiar constraints of the verse format (where a word that fits the meter better may be substituted for another that would have been more common in daily usage) and the fact that these daily-life elements appear mostly as metaphors for a religious discourse (rather than as part of narrations meant to carry a high degree of realism to its audience) contribute to mitigate the usefulness of this source. A highly critical reading of this text can nevertheless offer significant insight into the worldviews of the *Gharib-nama*'s intended audience.

Divan and Risalah al-Nushiyyah

Yûnus Emre (ca. 1240–ca. 1320), who probably lived his whole life in central Anatolia, is widely considered to be the godfather of Anatolian Turkish as a literary language. He owes this distinction to two works in Turkish-language verse, the *Divan* and *Risalah al-Nushiyyah*). Just like the *Gharib-nama*, these two texts are best seen as spiritual advice and do not contain significant hagiographical contents.[13]

Yûnus's choice of language makes him particularly relevant to this study, and this for two reasons. For one, the use of Turkish imposes some limitations on adopting Persian literary motifs, if only because the translation in some cases reduces their linguistic attractiveness (by eliminating conventional puns or alliterations, for example). This, in turn, makes some passages more likely to reflect local tradition than literary conventions. Second, Turkish was the language of the poor and the uneducated, and it seems reasonable to assume that at least those of his passages that appear less formulaic would indeed have been meant to resonate with the daily experiences of a popular audience.

Unfortunately for the purposes of this book, the poetic works of Yûnus Emre do contain a very large amount of motifs imported from Persian, though among them the more reliable passages are relatively easy to identify. Their contribution to the data used for this study is therefore modest, residing in a few glimpses of worldviews that appear here and there and cover anything from perceptions of fowl as food to attitudes toward sweets.

CHRONICLES

Early Ottoman studies are still, to this day, dominated by political history. It thus comes as no surprise that the best-known, most studied sources for the period are chronicles. It would be foolish to consider, as used to be the case, chronicles as "general histories" or (even worse) "histories of everything" for a given time and place. Their scope can in fact be likened to that of hagiographies in the sense that they tend to concentrate on an individual or a series of individuals (usually a ruling lineage), with the scope of the "story" broadening to include the context and consequences of these characters' actions in a given perspective (religious in the case of hagiographies, political and military for chronicles). These different perspectives are directly reflected in their respective contents. This in turn also means that the relevant data are, from both a qualitative and a quantitative point of view, very different in hagiographies and chronicles.

Ruling families, as modest as their dominion can be, are by definition part of an elite whose worldviews and lifestyles are different from those of the population at large. As reporters following them, chroniclers are thus unlikely to offer us the same scenes of daily life that are so common in the *Vilayat-nama* and the *Manaqib al-'Arifin*. They tend, however, to pay much attention to the army and the state institutions, providing us along the way with significant insights into how their actions may have involved the population at large. To put it differently, they often speak of food as a point of contact between the rulers and the ruled.

In researching this book, I have used five texts that can be gathered in the category of chronicles, even though two of them are perhaps better described as pieces of epic poetry.

Iskandar-nama (Ahmedī)

Although the bulk of the *Iskandar-nama*, a versified Turkish-language work, is devoted to the adventures of Alexander the Great, its final section constitutes the oldest extant Ottoman history.[14] It is the work of Ahmedī (ca. 1334–1413), a poet originally living at the court of the Germiyan, a rival polity that was integrated into the Ottoman realm through marriage alliances in the late fourteenth century. It is during this process that Ahmedī himself crossed over to the Ottoman court.

The Ottoman section of Ahmedī's *Iskandar-nama* retains over its short length (334 lines) the heroic tone that is appropriate for an Alexander romance. It emphasizes the piety of the first Ottoman leaders and their troops, which it illustrates with the latter's numerous feats in defeating the forces of the infidel. This, to be sure, leaves little space for such mundane concerns as agriculture and meals, and indeed Ahmedī's is a relatively marginal entry in this list of sources. It does nevertheless contain a few mentions of food in relation to religious norms and values.

Tavarikh-i Al-i ʿUthman (ʿĀşıkpaşazāde)

ʿĀşıkpaşazāde's *Tavarikh-i Al-i ʿUthman* (Histories of the family of Osman), as its title indicates, tells the history of the Ottoman house, from its rise to power at the turn of the fourteenth century to the beginning of the rule of Bayezid II (r. 1481–1512).[15] Many consider this Turkish prose text as the most important source concerning the beginnings of the Ottoman state because, although written approximately seventy years after Ahmedī's *Iskandar-nama*, it partly relies on the (now lost) earlier tradition of Yahşi Fakıh, son of the imam of the second Ottoman ruler, Orhan (d. 1362), and therefore conveys an insider's perspective to some key aspects of the early Ottoman period.

The author, ʿĀşıkpaşazāde (1400–after 1484), is no stranger to this list of sources, as he was the great-grandson of ʿĀşıkpaşa and grandson of Elvan Çelebi (respectively, authors of the *Gharib-nama* and of the *Manaqib al-Qudsiyya fi Manasib al-Unsiyya*, both discussed in the previous section). More important than his family tree, however, is the ideological bent of this author, whose vision idealized the beginnings of the Ottoman adventure as one where a pious *gazi* ideology was not contaminated with later additions such as wealth accumulation and "orthodox" theologians.[16]

This ideological stance is important because it colors the way that this source should be read for the purposes of this book, that is, as an idealized world where everything was simple and pure. ʿĀşıkpaşazāde's critical attitude toward his contemporaries, on the other hand, offers us unexpected insights into the mindsets of the time. For example, he denounces wealth accumulation by his contemporaries by telling us that the first sultan Osman owned only a few items at the time of his death (possibly including a saltbox and a set of spoons). It may not be wise to assume that he accurately depicts the actual situation of this historical character. The passage does, however, point to the idea that people had of the typical possessions of a modest Turkish chieftain, a piece of information that is in fact much more valuable than a mere discrete statement concerning a particular individual.[17]

As can be seen from these examples, the bulk of the relevant information in ʿĀşıkpaşazāde's text concerns, more or less directly, the ruling family. It does, however, also contain some passages dealing with the animal husbandry practices of the seminomadic early Ottomans, as well as pious charity, state policies on food production, and the impact of armies on agriculture.

Bazm u Razm

If ʿĀşıkpaşazāde dreamed of humble beginnings, the glorious achievements are of much greater interest to the author of the Persian-language *Bazm u Razm*, ʿAzīz b. Ardashīr Astarābādī. As he writes at the beginning of his chronicle, Astarābādī was a man of letters who had to flee Baghdad before Timur's conquest. In 1394 he came to the service of the *qadi* Burhān al-Dīn Aḥmad (d. 1398), a regional ruler of central Anatolia and self-appointed successor to the Ilkhanid power in the region.

Rather than a chronicle, *Bazm u Razm* is perhaps best characterized as the political biography of Burhān al-Dīn, whom it follows from his birth to a family of jurists to his rise to power and beyond. This source thus concentrates on central Anatolia, unlike the other sources in this subsection that are mostly concerned with the western end of the peninsula.[18]

Given its title (Banquet and battle), one could have expected a high concentration of relevant information in this source. Unfortunately, when it comes to the numerous feasting scenes, the author so systematically uses formulaic expressions and literary flourishes that it becomes extremely difficult to extract any information regarding the actual use of food and drinks at the court. Despite this extremely ornate style, which prevails throughout the text, *Bazm u Razm* can still be of some use here, particularly in relation to army logistics and its effect on the food-production systems, as well as, to the extent that they are not entirely bound to poetic conventions, some views on wine consumption.

Musamarat al-Akhbar (Aqsarāyī)

Karīm al-Dīn Maḥmūd b. Muḥammad al-Aqsarāyī's Persian-language *Musamarat al-Akhbar* is the earliest of all chronicles surveyed here (dated 1323). The text is divided into four sections, the (very short) first three discussing, respectively, various calendars, the history of the Islamic world down to the Abbasids, and the Great Seljuq. The fourth section, which makes up about 80 percent of the volume, is devoted to events surrounding Anatolian politics from the middle of the thirteenth to the beginning of the fourteenth centuries—a period that roughly corresponds to the best estimates of the author's lifetime. Most of the contents appear to be based on his firsthand observations as a high-ranking bureaucrat for the Anatolian Seljuq and (mostly) the Ilkhanid rulers of Anatolia.[19]

Compared to the other works presented in this section, the *Musamara al-Akhbar* might be the closest to offering a purely "political" perspective (as opposed to biographical or epic), paying more attention to processes and events than to individual characters. In keeping with his professional background, the author is especially keen on administrative and, by extension, military matters. On the other hand, the text offers very little by way of details of daily life; it does not even include the motif-laden, overly literary depictions of banquets that one finds in *Bazm u Razm*. Apart from a few literary expressions involving food items, it is of relatively little value for the purposes of this study.

Dustur-nama

If *Bazm u Razm* is closer to a biography than to a chronicle, the Turkish-language *Dustur-nama* should perhaps be put in an altogether different category, that of epic poetry. Committed to paper in 1465 by an otherwise unknown poet of the Ottoman court named Enverī, it is probably based—just like the *Vilayat-nama*—on a century-old oral tradition.[20]

The second part of the text,[21] being the one used here, follows the military feats of the historical character Umūr Pāshā, son of the lord of Aydın,[22] who lived in the first half of the fourteenth century. Written in verse, the text is remarkably free of the literary motifs and conventional metaphors that often make it difficult or even impossible to gather information on practical elements such as food and daily life in works such as *Bazm u Razm*.

This makes the *Dustur-nama* a very rich source as far as feasts and their sociopolitical implications are concerned. It also contains relevant passages concerning military logistics and the impact of military action on food production. All of these, however, should be taken with a grain of salt, considering that the action takes place around the Aegean Sea, a region whose cultural traditions at the time may have been quite different from those of central Anatolia. It is thus best seen as a complement to geographically more relevant sources, able to give further detail once the existence of a given phenomenon can be ascertained for central Anatolia as well.

OTHER NARRATIVE SOURCES

In addition to those already mentioned, three other narrative sources were of particular use in this research project. Though very different from each other, they all have in common an outsider's point of view on late-medieval Anatolia.

Tuhfat al-Nuzzar fi Ghara'ib al-Amsar wa 'Aja'ib al-Asfar (Ibn Baṭṭūṭa)

The *Tuhfat* (*Travels of Ibn Baṭṭūṭa* (1304–1368 or 1377) is probably the best-known travelogue from the medieval Muslim world. In the course of his travels around most of what was at the time the known world, Ibn Baṭṭūṭa visited the major Anatolian cities ca. 1330–1332, making his Arabic-language testimony directly relevant for the purposes of this study and the only travelogue used here.[23]

Travelogues are often seen as perfect sources for the study of daily life due to the outsider status of their authors. Such a status gives them a point of view that often, as is the case with Ibn Baṭṭūṭa, leads them to describe elements that the people living in the visited culture would have considered too mundane to deserve mention. This is especially true when it comes to regional peculiarities such as the crops grown only in a specific locale or cultural practices associated with a given region.

On the other hand, this outsider's point of view deprives Ibn Baṭṭūṭa from an insider's knowledge and understanding of what he describes. Combined with his strong religious views (a very "by the book" Sunni outlook) and some memory lapses (the *Tuhfat* was written down about twenty-five years after his visit to Anatolia), it puts strong limitations on the reliability of his text. It may, for example, be dangerous to trust him blindly when he discusses fasting during the month of Ramadan, considering that other sources are unnaturally quiet on the subject.[24]

Ibn Baṭṭūṭa nevertheless provides useful information, most notably concerning the urban and rural landscapes, the hospitality practices of various circles, and regionally specific crops.

Masalik al-Absar fi Mamalik al-Amsar (al-ʿUmarī)

The *Masalik al-Absar*, written by the Mamluk civil servant Ibn Faḍl Allāh al-ʿUmarī (1301–1349), is a lengthy encyclopedic work that contains a geographical section pertaining to Anatolia.[25] Al-ʿUmarī, based in Damascus, relied on two informants to provide him with information on the region, which he apparently never visited himself. As far as the section on Anatolia is concerned, this source gives the strong impression of being written for merchants, since it concentrates on the variations of prices and currencies as well as weights and measures from one city to the next. It also mentions a few regional productions.

Although this book does not concentrate much on economic history, the data found in the *Masalik al-Absar* profitably complement other sources, notably in uncovering the regional units and trade networks that shared monetary as well as systems of weights and measures. Al-ʿUmarī's references to the agricultural production of given regions can also be of some use, although a few passages are so thick with literary flourishes that they actually become difficult to interpret with any degree of confidence.

Qabus-nama Translations

The *Qabus-nama* is one of the most famous pieces of advice literature in Middle Eastern history. Written in Persian by the ruler of Gīlān (northern Iran) Kay Kāʾūs b. Iskandār in 1082–1083, it has little if anything to do with fourteenth-century Anatolia. Translations of this text do, however, hold a significant place in the history of the written Anatolian Turkish language. Strictly oral up to that point, this language began to be used in the fourteenth century in a small number of original works (e.g., ʿĀşıkpaşa's *Gharib-nama*) as well as many translations from Arabic and (especially) Persian. This early translation movement included no fewer than five different Turkish versions of the *Qabus-nama*.

It would have been a tedious and relatively unproductive task for someone with little training in philology to perform an in-depth, exhaustive comparison of these five translations (not to mention the problem of access, since the manuscripts are scattered around the world). Fortunately, the editor of one of these translations, Eleazar Birnbaum, had the good idea of including, as an example, all five translations as well as the original Persian of a chapter on the very relevant topic of table etiquette and traditions.[26]

As the reader may have guessed, there are significant variations in contents both between these translations and the original and among the various translations. These variations provide us with valuable insights in three main respects. First, they inform us on the food-related vocabulary. For example, when the original Persian refers to the *khʷānsālār* (a Persian word that can mean "maître d'hôtel" or "food taster"), one of the Turkish translations replaces it with *çaşnī-gīr* (another Persian word, literally meaning "food taster"), suggesting that the latter was indeed a word of common oral use at the early Ottoman court.

A second type of information that can be gathered here concerns changes in the etiquette and table manners between the time of the original composition and that of the translations. For example, one of the translations adds an apparently original passage stressing the importance of offering salt to one's guests and never asking for the latter's leftover food. Such a variation in the discourse on etiquette can reasonably be assumed to reflect local practices.

The third category is made up of hints concerning the limits of the discourse on food (what could and could not be said). On two occasions, differences between the original Persian and the Turkish translations strongly hint at the possibility that criticizing pious people's extreme fasting was not as acceptable in fourteenth-century Anatolia as it had been three centuries earlier in northern Iran. As Birnbaum points out,[27] the translators may have made some mistakes simply because they misread or did not understand the original Persian. Still, the very fact that the translator would not have picked up these mistakes would be quite telling and will thus be considered as well.

WAQFIYYAS

The Documents

Waqfiyyas fall in an altogether different category from the sources mentioned up to this point because, although they do not emanate from any state institution,[28] they are much closer in form to archival documents than to narrative texts.

Essentially, a *waqfiyya* is the document that legally frames a *waqf*, or pious endowment. A private individual establishes such an endowment by donating some of his or her property in order to provide revenues that will fund social or religious services to the community (from the upkeep of a mosque to the living expenses for the students of a madrasa). The revenue-producing property is, from that point on, "untouchable" either by the person who donated it (no longer the legal owner) or by the state (no longer allowed to collect taxes on it). Although the motivation to establish a *waqf* ostensibly revolved around piety and social benevolence, it is worth noting that the *waqfiyyas* generally include a provision that puts aside a significant part of the revenues to serve as the salary of the manager (*mutawallī*) of this "charity," a position more often than not occupied by the endowers themselves or their descendants, or both.[29] In other words, the alienation of private property that came with the establishment of a *waqf* did not necessarily deprive the former owner of that property's revenues.

*Waqfiyya*s follow a rather standard structure. They begin with a series of pious formulae explaining that the endower established the foundation after realizing that this world is but a place of passage, unimportant in view of the afterlife. It then goes on to describe the revenue-producing property of the *waqf*, most often agricultural holdings of various sorts but also shops put out for rent, salt mines, or others. This description can be extremely detailed, and in many cases goes as far as listing every geographical boundary that surrounds a given village, field, or building.[30] This is then followed by a description of the services for which the revenues are to be used, which can in theory include anything from the protection of books to the building of hospitals. However, the great majority of the *waqf*s in the period I study were established for the benefit of *zāwiyas*, institutions that are best described as dervish convents, usually providing food and lodging to visitors.[31] This description of the services to be provided includes a widely variable degree of detail: whereas some *waqfiyya*s simply mention that "the revenues are to be used for the benefit of the *zāwiya* located in *X*," many include detailed provisions on how the money should be spent, ranging from the salaries of each one of the institution's employees to the types of foods that should be served on regular days and religious celebrations. A series of standard legal provisions then follows, intended to protect the integrity of the endowment and cursing the one who may be tempted to tamper with it. The document ends with a date as well as, very often, a list of witnesses.

Because these institutions were in theory perpetual (or, more accurately, valid until the Day of Judgment) and finding their legitimacy in the shariʿa rather than in the authority of any given state, the documents supporting them had to be preserved in perpetuity as well and were therefore recopied when their physical support became too damaged.[32] For this reason, the approximately thirty-five *waqfiyya*s used in this study are much later copies of the original documents.[33]

Thirty-five may seem to be a relatively limited number, when historians of the later Ottoman Empire have access to thousands if not millions of archival documents. Yet for an early period such as the fourteenth century, it is such a high number that one can only wonder why historians who seem so comfortable invoking the lack of sources have paid them so little attention.

Having said that, the use of *waqfiyya*s is certainly not without its particular problems. For one, the language they use, Arabic, was by no means a widely spoken language in the land it describes. There is, therefore, a distinct possibility that slightly different features designated by different words in the locally spoken languages may have been lumped together under a single Arabic designation, consequently leaving us with a simplified or distorted picture of the landscape features to which it refers. Conversely, the documents also use Turkish and, less frequently, Persian and Greek words, chiefly as proper place-names, although it is often difficult to determine the extent to which these place-names were descriptive or conventional (i.e., whether a place named *pınar* [spring] would necessarily be a spring or could in fact be a village named after a spring).

But, perhaps most important, the "revenue-producing property" that a *waqfiyya* describes is just that: property that deserves mention by virtue of its providing revenue for the *waqf*. This means that the selection of bordering elements derives from a concern for preserving the integrity of the endowed property, and thus may not reflect the way in which the landscape was experienced by those inhabiting it. Furthermore, the geographical features that could not provide revenues appear only when they constitute one such "useful bordering landmark," therefore limiting the extent to which these documents can actually be used in an extensive description of the landscape. It also means that, even in the case of endowed property, uses that are not associated with the production of revenue (gardens as places of entertainment, for example) are left aside, giving us a slanted view of these elements.

Analysis of the Waqfiyyas

In late-medieval Anatolian historiography, *waqfiyya*s have typically been used for political (or even dynastic) history, because they offer an attractive combination of grandees' names, genealogical data, and fairly reliable dates.[34] Slightly more adventurous historians have also consulted them when researching *zāwiya*s and *imaret*s (service-giving institutions often funded by *waqf*s), albeit with a strong tendency to take at face value the prescriptions that *waqfiyya*s contain on how the endowment's revenues should be spent.[35] To my knowledge, however, barely any use has been made of the descriptive section of these documents (concerning the revenue-producing property), despite a context that suggests a high degree of reliability.[36] The near absence of studies whose topic (i.e., agriculture or, with a few exceptions, urbanism) would call for this type of data goes a long way toward explaining such a lack of interest, although the Arabic language used by nearly all early Anatolian *waqfiyya*s may also have deterred some researchers.[37]

I did analyze these documents by submitting them to the same type of textual analysis I used for the narrative sources. As one may have expected, the relatively standardized format of *waqfiyya*s does make them comparatively poor sources in this respect. Nevertheless, details can be found here and there that provide interesting information on such diverse topics as food and religious celebrations, ownership of food-producing infrastructures, the equipment required in the working of a farm or a mill, and even, in one case, a list of fountain locations.

Yet much more interesting, I believe, is a second, more statistically minded, approach to *waqfiyya*s. I have used such an approach for two main purposes. I first tried to estimate the economic status of cooks in *zāwiyas*. As I stated earlier, several of the documents discussed here prescribe the salaries to be given to the employees of a charitable institution, including in some cases the cooks (*ṭabbākh*). There are too many variations in currency rates to compute an overall average of cook salaries, not to mention the annual cereal grants (using a number of different weight units) that frequently supplemented the salary in money. Yet, assuming internal consistency within each document, I have calculated the relation between salaries of various employees in each institution (e.g., cook in relation to imam, imam in relation to sweeper, sweeper in relation to cook, and so forth) and compared these ratios across the *waqfiyyas*. The results of this analysis can be found in chapter 2.

Even more central to this study is the second form of statistical analysis, pertaining to the rural landscape. The documents discussed here contain more than three hundred items of revenue-producing property, of which more than two-thirds are given a basic location indication of variable precision (ranging from "in the province of *X*" to "near building *X* in neighborhood of *Y* of city *Z*"). Furthermore, no fewer than eighty-five of these items are accompanied by a list of features bordering them, as a way to ensure the legal integrity of the endowed property.[38] The elements used to delineate the endowed property comprise both natural and human geographical features. In some cases, those bordering elements are of the same nature as some of the endowed property. A garden can, for example, be bordered by a road, a river, another garden, and a cereal field.[39] As I stated earlier, the "revenue-producing property" section of a *waqfiyya* includes a large number of agricultural properties, such as fields and gardens. I have hence been able to compare the frequency, for each type of property, of the presence of neighboring elements of various types in order to derive extensive information about the rural landscape (for example, what kind of people would own what kind of property and where it would be located). I have primarily used the results of this analysis in chapter 1.

These approaches are far from exhausting the potential of *waqfiyyas* as historical sources, but they do serve two main purposes. First, such documents can serve as independent checks on my narrative sources. Second, they constitute a form of experiment through which this book intends to contribute to the methodology of late-medieval and early Ottoman historiography.

ARCHAEOLOGICAL LITERATURE

Besides written sources, the usual fodder of the historian, this study also relies on archaeological material. Anatolia, because it was part of the heartland of classical Greece, has a long archaeological tradition that includes perhaps the most famous (or infamous) excavation of the nineteenth century, Schliemann's work on Troy. Archaeology of the medieval period is a more recent phenomenon. In the early days of modern archaeology, scholars would quickly get rid of the upper (including medieval) layers of whichever site they were excavating, anxious to reach "the good stuff"—artifacts from the ancient and prehistorical periods. This pattern no longer holds true, and thanks to the evolution of archaeological practice, a large body of evidence from the medieval period has now been properly excavated and cataloged. Hydroelectric projects such as the building of the Keban Dam in the 1970s further led to a wave of rescue excavations that dramatically expanded the scholarship on artifacts from the Middle Ages.[40]

But even more than written sources, excavated material requires expert analysis to yield any reliable meaning. The field of medieval Anatolian archaeology is growing but still fairly small, at least in comparison to the mountain of evidence currently sleeping in university vaults around Turkey. My own expertise in archaeology was built on a few weeks of excavation work followed by extensive reading in secondary literature over the years and the occasional guidance of archaeologists.[41] I can therefore understand and, to some extent, evaluate the evidence that the archaeologists present to support their conclusions. However, I do not have the competence to draw conclusions directly from the primary material—for example, extrapolating on cooking techniques on the basis of the shape of a pot. The reader should therefore feel confident that claims that this book makes using archaeology are, indeed, those of specialists and not only my own.

Despite this caveat, the body of knowledge that this book has drawn from archaeology remains significant on some key issues. Pottery pieces and animal bones are by far the two most commonly excavated types of artifacts. Pottery was the primary material used in cooking ware and tableware, therefore providing an array of data that contribute to discussions ranging from cooking to food-storage techniques, not to mention cultural and commercial interactions with neighboring regions (when pots are found far away from their production site). Because bones can contain information about the animals' sex and age at death (and, in some cases, slaughtering techniques), zooarchaeological analysis yields extensive knowledge not only about which animals were raised, but the purpose of their exploitation.[42] Besides these two main types of excavated material, seeds and pollen can be collected from excavation soil that tells us a lot about agricultural plant production, and architectural remains allow for some insight into the physical layout of the space in which late-medieval Anatolians were living.

All of this information has great significance for this book, not only because it complements the topics covered in written sources, but also, and more important, because it constitutes an entirely independent body of evidence that is subject to an entirely different set of biases and limitations. Any conclusion for which textual and archaeological data confirm each other, therefore, most likely entails a degree of reliability that textual sources alone can very seldom provide.

Notes

INTRODUCTION

1. On a more pop-cultural note, the sociocultural landscape described in this book corresponds, to a very large extent, to the life circumstances of famed Sufi master and poet Rūmī, designated with only slight exaggeration as the best-selling poet in the United States. Franklin Lewis, *Rumi Past and Present, East and West*, 1.

2. For a detailed discussion of the climate of Anatolia and of its evolution over time, see Warren J. Eastwood et al., "Integrating Palaeoecological and Archaeo-historical Records: Land Use and Landscape Change in Cappadocia (Central Turkey) since Late Antiquity," 51.

3. Elizabeth Zachariadou, in "Notes sur la population de l'Asie Mineure au XIVe siècle," offers insightful observations on the demographic balance between Christians and Muslims, but these remain impressionistic and provide no numbers, even tentative, except when discussing military forces. Of more immediate relevance is the work of Speros Vryonis (*The Decline of Medieval Hellenism in Asia Minor and the Process of Islamization from the Eleventh through the Fifteenth Century*, 25–30), which offers a critical discussion of demographic issues that mostly concentrates on the period that immediately precedes Seljuk rule (ten and eleventh centuries), but incorporates evidence for later periods as well. The figures I offer here derive from his conclusions, but give a greater relative weight to the later figures.

4. There are much fewer data available on the size of villages. However, a passage from the *Vilayat-nama* emphasizing the tiny size of a village by mentioning its having only seven houses gives us an idea of the mental image medieval Anatolians may have had of "a very small town." It might also be taken as a suggestion that peasant houses standing isolated in the countryside and hamlets comprising only two or three houses would have been at most very unusual, if they existed at all (VN 56a). For further discussion of the size of villages, farms, and everything in between, see p. 31.

5. Archaeological analysis of pollen contained in the sediment layers of a central Anatolian lake makes it clear that the political instability of the period discussed here had a

direct (negative) impact on agricultural production and, therefore, on the daily lives of the people who engaged in it. See Eastwood et al., "Integrating Palaeoecological and Archaeohistorical Records," 54, 58.

6. A number of monographs are devoted to individual *beyliks*, each one of them typically concentrating on the rather arduous task of establishing a political chronology for one of these states. The best examples include Paul Wittek, *Das Fürstentum Mentesche: Studie zur Geschichte Westkleinasiens im 13.–15. Jh*; Himmet Akın, *Aydın Oğulları tarihi hakkında bir araştırma*; Mustafa Çetin Varlık, *Germiyan-oğulları tarihi (1300–1429)*; Elizabeth Zachariadou, *Trade and Crusade: Venetian Crete and the Emirates of Menteshe and Aydin (1300–1415)*; and Elizabeth Zachariadou, ed., *The Ottoman Emirate (1300–1389)*. In addition, İsmail Hakkı Uzunçarşılı produced a single-volume collection of studies on the same model, purporting to cover the "entire history" (i.e., political chronology) of each known *beylik*, accompanied by very general sketches of economic, intellectual, cultural, and social history: *Anadolu beylikleri ve Akkoyunlu, Karakoyunlu devletleri.*

7. The main contributions to the "*gazi* debate" include, in chronological order: Paul Wittek, *The Rise of the Ottoman Empire*; Rudi Paul Lindner, *Nomads and Ottomans in Medieval Anatolia*; Cemal Kafadar, *Between Two Worlds: The Construction of the Ottoman State*; and Heath W. Lowry, *The Nature of the Early Ottoman State.*

8. Vryonis, *Decline of Medieval Hellenism in Asia Minor*. The usefulness of this ambitious and thoroughly researched study is unfortunately limited by the strongly ideological lens through which the author forces his entire depiction of the process, which he presents as nothing short of a tragedy.

9. Mehmed Fuad Köprülü, *Türk edebiyatı'nda ilk mutasavvıflar*; Abdülbâki Gölpınarlı, *Mevlânâ'dan sonra Mevlevîlik*; Ahmet Yaşar Ocak, *La révolte de Baba Resul; ou, la formation de l'hétérodoxie musulmane en Anatolie au XIIIe siècle*; Ahmet T. Karamustafa, *God's Unruly Friends: Dervish Groups in the Islamic Later Middle Period, 1200–1550*; Irène Mélikoff, *Hadji Bektach: Un mythe et ses avatars; Genèse et évolution du soufisme populaire en Turquie*; Dimitri Korobeinikov, "Orthodox Communities in Eastern Anatolia in the Thirteenth and Fourteenth Centuries," pts. 1 and 2.

10. Franz Taeschner, "Beiträge zur Geschichte der Achis in Anatolien (14.–15. Jht.) auf Grund neur Quellen"; Claude Cahen, "Sur les traces des premiers Akhis."

11. Lindner, *Nomads and Ottomans.*

12. Most of these integrate social elements into studies methodologically centered on architectural history. Among those paying the most direct attention to a social perspective are the works of Ethel Sara Wolper (*Cities and Saints: Sufism and the Transformation of Urban Space in Medieval Anatolia*) and Zeynep Yürekli-Gökay ("Legend and Architecture in the Ottoman Empire: The Shrines of Seyyid Gazi and Haci Bektaş").

The important study of the interactions between economy and politics in the Aegean during the fourteenth century by Elizabeth Zachariadou (*Trade and Crusade*), although it concentrates on a region located just outside the western limits of this study's geographical scope, also intersects to a significant extent with the social history of Anatolia as a whole.

13. Speros Vryonis, "The Muslim Family in 13th–14th Century Anatolia as Reflected in the Writings of the Mawlawi Dervish Eflaki." One might be tempted to point out a number of studies on peasant life during the transition into Ottoman rule, in particular those by Heath Lowry, but these are all concentrated on areas lying outside central Anatolia, be it the Aegean Islands, the Balkans, or the eastern Black Sea coast, and mostly take a state-centric perspective. See, for example, Anthony Bryer and Heath Lowry, eds., *Continuity and Change in Late Byzantine and Early Ottoman Society.*

14. For a more thorough discussion of *waqfiyya*s and archaeology, see, respectively, p. 142ff and p. 145ff.

15. Günay Kut, "13. yüzyıla ait bir yemek kitabı." To assume that the seventy-seven recipes appearing in Shirvānī's translation but not in the original Arabic should be the work of Shirvānī himself (or even the product of the Ottoman era at all) is a good educated guess, although Kut herself notes that they are integrated in a seamless way into the work. One should thus be careful in not overstating the already limited extent to which this is an "Ottoman work."

16. On medieval Middle Eastern cookbooks, see the surveys of the source material by Maxime Rodinson ("Recherches sur les documents arabes relatifs à la cuisine"), Lilia Zaouali (*Medieval Cuisine of the Islamic World: A Concise History with 174 Recipes*, 8–16), David Waines ("Prolegomena to the Study of Cooking in Abbasid Times: A Circuitous Bibliographical Essay"), and, most recently, Paulina B. Lewicka (*Food and Foodways of the Medieval Cairenes: Aspects of Life in an Islamic Metropolis of the Eastern Mediterranean*, 27–39). At least two of these cookbooks have been translated into English. See Nawal Nasrallah, trans., *Annals of the Caliph's Kitchens: Ibn Sayyār al-Warrāq's Tenth-Century Baghdadi Cookbook*, esp. 22–24, as well as A. J. Arbery, "A Baghdad Cookery-Book." The latter is the text that the Ottoman Shirvānī translated in the fifteenth century and was the object of a second English translation, by Charles Perry, as *A Baghdad Cookery Book: The Book of Dishes.*

17. Iraj Afshar, *Kar-nama ve Maddat al-Haya: Matn-i Du Risala dar Ashpazi az Davra-yi Safavi: ʿAsr-i Saltanat-i Shah Ismaʿil-i Avval ve Shah ʿAbbas-i Avval.*

18. See the annotated list by Turgut Kut in *Açıklamalı Yemek Kitapları Bibliyografyası: Eski Harflı Yazma ve Basma Eserler.*

19. Furthermore, most of these treatises date from the fifteenth century and remain unpublished to this day, thus making them difficult to access. See, for example, the *Muntakhab al-Shifa'* by Jalāl al-Dīn Khiḍr b. ʿAlī al-Khaṭṭāb al-Qunawī, who is better known as Ḥājī Pāshā (Zafer Önler, ed., *Celālüddin Hızır [Hacı Paşa]: Müntahab-ı Şifā. Cilt 1: Giriş, Metin*), dating from the late fourteenth and early fifteenth centuries; same author, "Shifa al-Askam wa Dawa al-Alam" (unpublished), dated 1381; "Kitab Adwiya-yi Mufrada" by Ishāq b. Murād, dated 1390 (unpublished); the "Yadigar" of ʿAlī Çelebi Ibn Sharīf, dating from the fourteenth or, more probably, fifteenth century (unpublished); and the *Haza'in al-Saʿadat* by Ashraf b. Muḥammad (Bedi N. Şehsuvaroğlu, ed., *Eşref Bin Muhammed: Hazā'inü's-Saʿādāt*), dating from ca. 1460. I should acknowledge here Sara Nur Yıldız (personal communication) for pointing out most items on this list.

That being said, I nevertheless tried to look into popular interpretations of medical theories in a way that, I hope, largely circumvents the problems identified here. See below, p. 96ff.

20. For subsequent periods, archives do provide much material concerning food. For example, later Ottoman archives contain accounting documents for the palace kitchens that indeed offer quite impressive detail on what was eaten when, prices of foodstuffs, and the like. Yet shifting the scope of this book to a later time frame because of the availability of these documents would also have entailed a change of topic, since the customs and manners of the Ottoman court are only marginally related to the issue discussed here. This is a research project about the population at large, and as detailed as data on sultanic banquets can be, they refer to something that would have been completely invisible (and largely irrelevant) for the bulk of the population.

21. Maqrīzī, *Ighathat al-Umma bi-Kashf al-Ghumma.*

22. Muṣṭafā ʿÂlī's *Mawaʾid al-Nefaʾis fī Qawaʾid al-Majalis.*

23. MA 3/567.

24. For more on *ḥalwāʾ*, see p. 116ff below.

25. MA 9/9.

26. The word *audience* is clearly a better one than *readership* in these circumstances, given that many of these texts were most likely read *to* (rather than read *by*) their target audience.

27. MA 3/33.

28. The main dictionaries I have used for this study are, for Turkish, *A Turkish and English Lexicon* by James W. Redhouse and *Tarama Sözlüğü*; for Persian, *A Comprehensive Persian-English Dictionary* by F. Steingass; and, for Arabic, *A Dictionary of Modern Written Arabic* by Hans Wehr and *Arabic-English Lexicon* by Edward Lane.

I should also point out that some of the terms appearing in Old Anatolian Turkish, Persian, and even (in much fewer cases) Arabic are still in use in modern Turkish. It would, however, be careless to simply assume, as some scholars have done, that identical vocabulary entails identical objects or practices designated. For example, the word *bardak* refers, in modern Turkish, to a (water) glass, but usage in sources clearly entails that the same word must have referred to a larger container, akin to a water pitcher (VN 165b).

29. I address the question of vocabulary much more directly in two forthcoming articles, one on terms designating gardens and the other on kitchenware and cooking ware. The reader can also find excellent examples of "semantic quests" by Lucie Bolens ("Le haricot vert en Andalousie et en Méditerranée médiévales [phaseolus, dolichos, lubia, judia]") and Françoise Aubaile-Sallenave ("Al-Khishk: The Past and Present of a Complex Culinary Practice").

30. These short and conventional metaphors, which I excluded, should be understood as opposed to literal uses as well as to lengthy, original metaphors that the reader is expected to visualize in full (such as when the *Gharib-nama* compares the various parts of a mill to the spiritual order of the universe), both of which I have retained for analysis.

31. AE 1/4.

32. IB 259–260, 278, 281, 286, 292, 307, 312, 323–324.

33. IB 265, 266 (two instances), 271, 281, 284, 286, 292, 307, 312, 317–318.

34. IB 271, 284, 286, 307, 312, 317–318.

CHAPTER ONE

1. MA 4/101.

2. "Ṣanʿat-i bāghbānī" (MA 6/22).

3. See, for example, Scott Redford, "The Just Landscape in Medieval Anatolia," 317.

4. See, for example, MA 6/7.

5. MA 3/328.

6. It may, for example, have been in contrast to this stark social divide that Aflākī, in order to emphasize the kindness of Rūmī, depicts him bowing back to an Armenian butcher who had bowed before him (MA 3/67).

7. MA 8/50; MQ 1703. Sources indeed associate *būstāns*, *bāghs*, and sown fields with human work, opposing them to land left wild (see, for example, IN 268–270).

8. VN 43b; MA 6/22; GN 1:82a.

9. *Waqfiyyas* include references to a number of urban shops designated as "baqqāl" (WQ14, WQ21, WQ33), which could refer to a greengrocer, but also, as Lane indicates, to "a seller of dry fruits" or even "a seller of eatables of various kinds, and particularly of dried and salted provisions, cheese, &c." In narrative sources, however, none of the several references to food buying in markets includes produce, and conversely every example of acquisition of produce takes place in a garden (MA 3/457; GN 1:36a–37b; VN 43b). The implications of this trade in terms of traffic between the city and its outskirts were pointed out to me by Cemal Kafadar (personal communication).

10. VN 122a. See also MA 3/301 and YER 407.

11. AU 325.

12. Redford, "Just Landscape in Medieval Anatolia," 318.

13. This should perhaps be related to the presence of *bostancıs* (literally "gardeners") rather than, say, sweepers or bricklayers among the palace guards for the Ottoman sultan in later centuries.

Kaplan (*Les hommes et la terre à Byzance du VIe au XIe siècle*, 36), using both textual and pictorial evidence, suggests that protecting fruit trees against birds was a major concern for gardeners in the Byzantine period. I have not come across any mention of avian depredation in the sources I have used, though here again the absence might be explained by the fact that guarding against birds does not entail interacting with other human beings.

14. VN 123b. Of course, there is a strong legendary component to the character, and it is quite likely that this passage does not correspond to a factually accurate life story. Yet I would argue that the most important aspect here is that such a career change was deemed plausible enough by the authors to be presentable to their audience. A passage in

the *Gharib-nama* also hints at the practice of gardening by people who had other occupations at earlier states in life (GN 1:65b).

15. For other, nongardening, cases, see, for example, BR 285 and APZ 159.

16. See, for example, MA 3/592 and VN 122a.

17. See MA 6/7, which incidentally refers to the interaction between the garden's owner and "his gardener" (*bāghbān-i khūd*).

18. This is, once again, the story of Ahi Evren (VN 122a). This character was widely known, and nothing in his lore appears to identify him as a slave, even at earlier stages of his life. Had the status of a gardener been associated with slaves in the popular view, this would have implied a major change in the character, an original touch that would in turn have required some justification in the text suggesting it. The very fame of the character, in other words, is a further argument against an essential association between gardening and slavery.

19. There is, in the *waqfiyya*s I have used here, one exception to this rule (WQ8), where a garden (*junayna*) is endowed along with "those living in it," *al-masākīn fīhā* (who, since endowed property had to be owned in freehold, could not have been other than slaves). I also found another, more explicit, case, located in Bursa (that is, outside of the geographical scope of this book: Ankara Vakıflar Genel Müdürlüğü, *Defter* no. 734, *sayfa* 108, *sıra* no. 120, dated 796/1394). These two cases show that it was indeed possible to endow the slaves working in a garden. On the other hand, the redactors of *waqfiyya*s obviously went to great pains in order to include every piece and aspect of the property they record, since these were legal documents. It is therefore rather unlikely that the inclusion of slaves would be implied in those *waqfiyya*s that do not explicitly mention them.

One could argue that slaves were simply not endowed along with the gardens in which they worked. Yet considering the strong tendency of endowers to retain a significant part of the endowed property's revenues (through their position as managers, or *mutawallī*), their benevolence had obvious limits. It is thus unlikely that someone owning both a garden and the slave(s) working on it would systematically retain ownership of the slaves themselves (and hence their living expenses) while they endowed the means through which slaves brought in wealth (i.e., garden revenues).

None of this, to be fair, precludes the possibility that slaves belonging to somebody other than the garden's owner may have been employed in the garden for a salary. In such a case, however, their status would have been in many respects similar to that of a nonslave employee—in their relationship with the owner, of course, but also and perhaps more important in the extensive independence they had in their professional activities. In other words, whether they legally belonged to another person or not, the position of gardeners was in any case very different from the tightly controlled and repressed plantation workers of nineteenth-century America, from whom our image of slavery mostly originates. For a detailed look at slaves as wage workers in a not-so-distant context, see Iklil Oya Selçuk, "State and Society in the Marketplace: A Study of Late Fifteenth-Century Bursa," 188ff.

20. For example, see BR 207.

21. See, for example, WQ20, which, if we make the rather safe guess that most pieces

of land designated as *milk* (real estate) and surrounding a garden are indeed also gardens, may include references to a *khayyāṭ* (tailor), a *baqqāl* (see p. 174n below), and a *bāzār-bāshī* (market superintendent) among the garden owners.

22. See MA 3/245 and 4/43 as well as WQ1; other cases of female ownership of real estate in *waqfiyyas* include WQ25 (land) and WQ28 (villages). Insofar as the grammatically gender-neutral Turkish and Persian primary sources allow us to judge, however, they do not seem to include any case of female gardeners.

23. Most references to garden ownership in the *Manaqib al-ʿArifin* refer to the same individual, Ḥusām al-Dīn Çelebi (3/21, 3/56, 3/79, 3/121, 3/378, 3/542, 3/556, 6/5, 6/7, 6/22, 7/14, 8/12), but there are also other cases: MA 2/3, 3/592, 4/43, 6/25, 9/7; RS 93; SH 19b; IB 265.

24. "Kimde varsa bağ ve çift ve sim ve zer / Laceram her gün gönül anı düzer" (GN 2:166/3). See also DN 86. Furthermore, the frequent references that Ibn Baṭṭūṭa makes to *bustāns* occur in such a way that they seem to be primarily used as a metaphor to praise a city rather than a careful description of its visual appearance. See IB 259–260, 265, 266, 276, 278, 281, 283, 286, 287, 292, 294, 295–296, 297, 312, 317–318, 323–324, 349.

25. MA 4/21. Given the way that Aflākī compares this garden to Paradise (*kih Būstān-i Fardūs munāẓara mī kard*), this is clearly not an attempt to use a formula akin to "he gave up on even the smallest things."

26. VN 110a. Furthermore, approximately 35 percent of the roads and 50 percent of waterways used as delineating elements in *waqfiyyas* appear as bordering cereal fields, as opposed to, respectively, 20 percent and 5 percent for gardens. This suggests that easily accessible, easily irrigable land was used for cereal cultivation more often than for gardening, despite the fact that gardens provide much higher revenues than cereal fields for the same surface area.

27. This is proven by the sheer inclusion of numerous gardens as revenue-producing property in *waqfs*. See also MA 3/592 and Redford, "Just Landscape in Medieval Anatolia," 323.

28. The first example is İznik, where Ibn Baṭṭūṭa claims that each inhabitant enjoys their own garden within the walls of the city (IB 323–324). Although some Ottoman chroniclers make formulaic references to the large population of the city (possibly in comparison to the other early conquests), it is probably safer to follow the claims of Clive Foss (*Nicaea: A Byzantine Capital and Its Praises*, 84–85), for whom the city had indeed decreased in population during the century or two preceding its conquest by the Ottomans. For a digest of all references to the conquest of İznik in Ottoman chronicles, see Halil İnalcık, "Osmān Ghāzī's Siege of Nicaea and the Battle of Bapheus," in *Ottoman Emirate*, edited by Zachariadou, 77–98.

Another example, this time given by ʿĀşıkpaşazāde, is that of newly conquered Istanbul in the middle of the following century, where a similar situation seems to have prevailed (APZ 124). I should, however, mention the unique case of the owner of a *bāghcha* whose status, although it cannot be determined with any degree of precision, seems to have been lower than that of a grandee (RS 90–91).

29. See, for example, IB 259–260, 281; as well as AU 375. Elizabeth Zachariadou (*Trade and Crusade*, 59) also notes a clause referring to the export of dried vegetables from western Anatolia in trade agreements with Venice dated from the fourteenth century.

30. As opposed to, for example, sheep's milk (AU 310), on which see below, page 163.

31. As Eastwood et al. put it, "Precipitation values for much of central Turkey lie just above the limits for extensive dry farming, where the crop plant (mainly cereals) taps into moisture preserved in the soil from winter precipitation and grows to maturity and [is] harvested during the early summer. In Cappadocia, particularly in areas some distance away from stream courses, moisture stress would have been of particular importance given the permeable nature of the free-draining volcanic-derived soil" ("Integrating Palaeoecological and Archaeo-historical Records," 51). In other words, irrigation was all but necessary for the more water-intensive garden cultures. That late-medieval Anatolians understood it as such seems clear from a line of Yûnus Emre, who states, "Wherever there is a *dūlāb* [water wheel], gardens occur" (YER 97:2).

32. The garden culture that this reflects clearly followed central Anatolian elite practices. See Scott Redford (*Landscape and the State in Medieval Anatolia: Seljuk Gardens and Pavilions of Alanya, Turkey*), 41 and passim; and Redford, "Just Landscape in Medieval Anatolia," 322. Likewise, as part of a story from "olden times," the *Gharıb-nama* mentions a king establishing a grandiose garden (*ulu bir bağçe*); the location selected for its establishment is a "well-watered plain" (*sular akar bir sahra* [GN 1:80b]), which betrays the same type of concern for water availability.

33. IB 287 and 292. See also YER 97:3.

34. WQ6, WQ8, WQ20. The exception can be found in WQ14.

35. There is at least one such case, where the document indicates that an endowed garden receives its water "from the garden of a *zāwiya*," which appears to be across the road that forms one of its borders (WQ17).

36. GN 2:121a; MA 3/460, 8/34. The only hint that waterwheels indeed were powered by the stream itself rather than human or animal (and thus intermittent) force is the word *nawāʿir* (plural of *nāʿūrah*), used by Ibn Baṭṭūṭa (IB 287, 292). This word usually refers to the instrument called in English "noria," a much more efficient but also much more complicated and costly device (in which the wheel is powered by the very stream from which it takes its water) than the human- or animal-powered machine that Arabic sources call the *saqiyya*. One *waqfiyya* entry does use the latter word (WQ8), but *saqiyya* may also refer to an irrigation ditch and probably does in this case, since a waterway lends itself much better than a water-raising device to being used as a border. Redford (*Landscape and the State*, 84), observing the same term used on several occasions in a thirteenth-century *waqfiyya*, also translates the word *saqiyya* as "irrigation ditch." For more detail about these and other water-raising devices, see Donald Hill, *A History of Engineering in Classical and Medieval Times*, 127–154. For that section, Hill made extensive use of the wonderfully confusing *Roman and Islamic Water-Lifting Wheels* by Thorkild Schioler.

37. An irrigation scheme serving a large number of gardens existed around the city of

Konya both before (early thirteenth century) and well after (seventeenth and eighteenth centuries) the period studied here. See Redford, *Landscape and the State*, 61–62.

Without going back to the simplistic classical argument according to which the Mongol invasions ended the development of the Muslim world by destroying the irrigation schemes in Iraq, it remains that both the technical challenges and the division of water between the beneficiaries make the organization and management of a shared irrigation scheme a natural source of communal tensions that must be mitigated at the political level, no matter how large or small the area it covers. There is thus no doubt that there were frequent interactions both between the gardeners working in neighboring gardens (mostly over practical issues such as repairs) and between the latter's owners (probably over more abstract notions of rights, duties, and privileges).

38. MA 3/460 and 8/34 further indicate that these were permanent structures, which would remain in place during the winter (despite the waters freezing) and the spring (despite the river's flow rising). These conditions no doubt damaged the equipment, in turn indicating that repairs and readjustments would be necessary on a regular basis. Although there is no direct information on this subject, it would thus seem likely that knowledge about the technology used for water raising was relatively widespread, rather than limited to specialist "engineers" or technicians.

39. That cereal agriculture was conceptualized as distinct from garden agriculture can be seen not only through the nomenclature found in *waqfiyya*s (on which see p. 31), but also in literary expressions (the contrast between *ḥubūbāt* and *nabāt*, literally "cereals" and "plants" [GN 2:57a]) and through mentions of the two as separate sources of revenue (MA 3/592).

40. On the metaphorical meaning associated with fruit, see p. 88ff.

41. I have tried to avoid using later sources as much as possible, including the relatively plentiful pool of Ottoman cadastral surveys (*tapu tahrir defterleri*), on which historians interested in cereal production in post-Byzantine Anatolia tend to rely most heavily. The elements that are the most likely to have changed with the Ottoman conquest (that is, fiscal and administrative practices) are those that occupy the central space in the relevant Ottoman documentation. The absence of these and other types of administrative documents, however, also means that no discussion of crop yields is possible here.

42. GN 1:178a; APZ 64; DN 102. Archaeological evidence (studies of pollen deposits in lake sediment as well as floatation samples) overwhelmingly supports the suggestion that these were the two most widely cultivated cereals, at least from slightly before to slightly after the period studied here. See, for example, Andrew Fairbairn, Catherine Longford, and Bronwyn Griffin, "Archaeobotany at Kaman-Kalehöyük 2006," 151–152; Naomi F. Miller, "Patterns of Agriculture and Land Use at Medieval Gritille," 234, 250; and Eastwood et al., "Integrating Palaeoecological and Archaeo-historical Records," esp. 53–55.

Ibn Baṭṭūṭa also refers to the two cereals as a duet when he says that he was offered the wheat and barley revenues of a village, in this case using the Arabic conjunction (*qamḥ wa shaʿīr* [IB 344]). This adds credence to the hypothesis that these were indeed the two basic cereal productions and not simply a set expression in Turkish that may have survived beyond the reality it describes. Amy Singer (personal communication) pointed out that, in Ottoman cadastral surveys (*tapu tahrir defterleri*) pertaining to southern Syria, the word used for wheat is *ḥinṭa*. However, *qamḥ* is attested as meaning wheat grain, and Ibn Baṭṭūṭa's choice of vocabulary probably reflects his not being acquainted with the tradition that later entered the Ottoman administrative lexicon.

Sources are mostly silent about crop-raising techniques and practices; however, both a passage in the *Vilayat-nama* (VN 61a) and the common expression "wheat and barley" suggest that they were raised alongside each other. There is in any case no hint in sources that wheat farmers and barley farmers would have formed two different groups.

43. Either in reference to the Muslim tradition (according to which the "forbidden fruit" in the Garden of Eden was indeed a grain of wheat [MA 3/481; SH 28a–b; YED 57:8, 191:6]), or in what appears to be a truncated use of the Persian expression "to show wheat and sell barley" (*gandum namāyī jū furūsh*), meaning to have ulterior motives (MA 9/7).

44. Cappadocia: VN 61a. Konya: APZ 64 and MA 3/524.

45. AU 310; IB 344.

46. DN 118; QN 24; MA 2/12; MQ 350, 408; APZ 64 (implicitly, through an association with straw rather than wheat; one manuscript adds a specific mention of its use as horse feed). It is worth noting that barley was also, in all likelihood, the main ingredient in the fermented drink called *fuqāʾ* (on which see p. 91ff). However, both the absence of direct references to the production process of *fuqāʾ* in the sources and the obviously limited amounts of grain required to provide a person with barley drink in relation to that needed to feed a horse suggest that this kind of use was a relatively marginal factor in price determination for barley.

47. "And as for the medium price, a *mudd* of wheat is fifteen *dirhams*. Likewise [for] barley, or a little less than it" ("Wa ammā al-siʿr al-mutawassiṭ fa-mudd al-qamḥ khamsa ʿashar dirham, wa kadhalika al-shaʿīr, aw dūnuhu bi-qalīl" [AU 331]).

48. Miller, "Patterns of Agriculture and Land Use," 250.

49. This mental association between barley and hard times, conflated with the religious symbolism of the color green, is probably what is reflected in an anecdote of the *Vilayat-nama* in which a *timar beg* is jailed in a cell whose limestone walls are known to make the inmates blind, only to be saved by staring at the green barley he grew in a handful of soil (VN 54b).

50. MA 2/5, 3/9, 4/41, 3/487. Other anecdotes mention barley in relation to extreme poverty rather than asceticism (MA 3/219, 3/557). Half of these (3/219, 3/487, 3/557) refer directly or indirectly to hadiths (MA 3/487, for example, is a fairly accurate retelling of a hadith that can be found in Bukharī, vol. 7, bk. 65, no. 325: "The Prophet never ate his full of barley bread"). Yet even a casual look at other hadiths that mention barley makes it obvious that this cereal was not systematically associated with poverty or asceticism in early Islam. In other words, it was not a religious convention that prevailed from the beginning of Islam down to late-medieval Konya, but rather a locally held opinion for which Rūmī finds support in selected hadiths. Kaplan (*Les hommes et la terre à Byzance*, 28) sug-

gests a similar status for the Byzantine period—which can hardly be ascribed to a purely Islamic influence. Kaplan's suggestion nicely meshes with the continuity that Eastwood et al. ("Integrating Palaeoecological and Archaeo-historical Records," 54) documents in land use from mid-Byzantine to Ottoman times.

The *Risala-yi Sipahsalar*, whose origins closely parallel the *Manaqib al-ʿArifin*, contains another reference that also goes toward showing the low status of barley bread (RS 38). The *Divan* of Yûnus Emre, a completely independent source, contains yet another (YED 140:4).

51. The apparent exception, as we are about to see, might be the city of Niksar, about fifty miles south of the Black Sea coast, to the north of Sivas and Tokat. In the fifteenth century, Ottoman archives also document rice production in the region of Hamid (around the lakes located at some distance west of Konya) and that of Beypazarı (about fifty kilometers west of Ankara), two regions that receive significantly more rainfall than the core area covered by this book. However, these documents include no indication that, unlike in some other locations, these productions started as early as the fourteenth century. Al-ʿUmarī also mentions a village in the province of Germiyan (near Kütahya) that produced only rice, presumably pointing it out because of its unusual character (AU 330).

Considering that rice cultivation was undergoing a process of geographical expansion throughout this period, it is thus quite likely that rice production outside of the coastal areas during the period I study was extremely limited and concentrated in a handful of locations on the transitional ground between the valleys of the Aegean coast and the Anatolian Plateau itself. For more detail on this topic, see Nicoara Beldiceanu and Irène Beldiceanu-Steinherr, "Riziculture dans l'empire ottoman (XIVe–XVe siècle)," esp. 12–15.

52. I will discuss the specifics of rice consumption in further detail in chapter 3. References to rice consumption can be found in various sources. See, for example, IB 348; AE 9/97; MA 3/101, 3/254; and WQ21 (two instances). Ibn Baṭṭūṭa also claims that he was offered rice when he visited the ruler of Aydın near Birgi, inland from the Aegean coast (IB 300).

These associations stand in stark contrast with the situation that seems to have prevailed in such regions as Iraq, during earlier centuries, where rice (and most notably rice bread) was deemed a lowly type of food (on this subject, see Marius Canard, "Le riz dans le Proche Orient aux premiers siècles de l'Islam"). I have found no trace of rice bread or flour in my own sources.

53. The labor-intensive character of this production may also have played a role in its price. See Halil İnalcık, "Rice Cultivation and the Çeltükci-Reʿâyâ System in the Ottoman Empire." On carts and transportation of cereals, see p. 47ff.

54. RS 126.

55. WQ8 (three instances in two items), WQ31. The two *waqfiyyas* are both located in Niksar, but are set fifty years apart and the endowers do not seem related to each other. I should also note that, although it does not appear in the Beldiceanu and Beldiceanu-Steinherr article mentioned above (see note 51), it is possible that rice production may have taken place at that time in Niksar, which is located only a short distance across the mountains from the rice-producing empire of Trebizond. For what it is worth, a travel-

ogue dating from a half millennium later (and otherwise including very few mentions of rice) indeed points out that it was "cultivated extensively in the plain" of Niksar (James Brant, "Journey through a part of Armenia and Asia Minor, in the Year 1835").

56. I wish to acknowledge Dr. Reiko Yamada for pointing out the necessity and intricacies of rice milling.

57. All three appear in WQ8. There is no indication of either rural or urban setting for the fourth (WQ31).

58. VN 45b, 61a. Mark Nesbitt ("Grains," 51) mentions the practice (still common in Anatolia) of planting a mixture of wheat and rye. Although this may very well have been the case in the period I discuss here, it remains clear from textual evidence that rye could also be planted by itself. Archaeological evidence suggests that rye gained in popularity in later centuries and was indeed intermixed with other cereals. See Fairbairn, Longford, and Griffin, "Archaeobotany at Kaman-Kalehöyük," 152, 154; and Eastwood et al., "Integrating Palaeoecological and Archaeo-historical Records," 54.

59. VN 34a is a story set in the haze of the early days of Hacı Bektaş Velî in Khorasan (today's northeastern Iran), whereas DN 102 mentions millet as transported in carts, along with barley and wheat, somewhere in Thrace. Archaeological evidence shows that millet was indeed present in the twelfth and thirteenth centuries at the Avşan Kale site, slightly outside the eastern boundary of the area discussed here. The authors add, however, that "too few grains of millet were recovered from the . . . Medieval samples to make any definite statements about its cultivation" (Mark Nesbitt and G. D. Summers, "Some Recent Discoveries of Millet [*Panicum miliaceum L.* and *Setaria italica (L.) P. Beauv.*] at Excavations in Turkey and Iran"). Analysis of the evidence from Gritille, in southeastern Anatolia, reaches similar conclusions. See Miller, "Patterns of Agriculture and Land Use," 234.

60. VN 61a.

61. On harvests, see p. 33ff.

62. Complex, that is, in comparison to a binary single-crop cultivation-fallow cycle. For archaeological evidence from southeastern Anatolia, see Miller, "Patterns of Agriculture and Land Use," 236, 251.

63. VN 64a.

64. In other words, it is difficult to determine the exact place of this culture on the spectrum that goes from the gathering of wild plants to tightly controlled cultures such as hothouse hydroponics. Archaeological evidence, in any case, strongly supports the suggestion that vetch was harvested and stored (Miller, "Patterns of Agriculture and Land Use," 236, 238, 242, 245). See also Fairbairn, Longford, and Griffin, "Archaeobotany at Kaman-Kalehöyük," 152.

65. Anybody who has ever had to carry hay bales can testify that even a low level of humidity can add a tremendous amount of weight in comparison to the same volume of the dry product.

66. VN 43b.

67. For general information about the history and geography of oats, see Nesbitt, "Grains," 50.

68. In this respect, the argument developed above concerning the status of gardeners

as employees rather than slaves (see p. 151n) is equally valid here. I was able to find one case of what appears to be an endowed farmer (*zarrāʿ*) in my *waqfiyya*s (WQ21), just as I found two cases of endowed gardeners.

The *Vilayat-nama* mentions one individual by the name of "Açak" who was "on the farm of Hacı Bektaş Velî," assumedly referring to land endowed to the religious community. The passage concentrates on describing his kindness toward oxen and remains silent about his status as a worker. Even though his obviously non-Muslim name opens up the possibility that he may have been a slave, there is no particular reason to put forward such a hypothesis. After all, the main objective of this text (VN) is to convey the (at least formally) Muslim religious legitimacy of a central character whose name (Bektaş) is not Muslim.

At least two passages, while fairly ambiguous, suggest that dervishes themselves could be involved in agricultural work: VN 64a and YED 140:4.

69. For example, the responsibility to graze buffaloes would normally be a task that was collectively supported (the villagers sharing the costs of hiring an employee to carry it out), without, however, forgetting which animal belonged to which individual (VN 56a).

70. A minority of cases also use words that are best translated as "farms," such as *mazraʿa*. I will come back to these shortly.

71. WQ8 and WQ21 contain both "villages" and "land."

72. Generally, the properties surrounding endowed land (be it "land" too or simply designated as "property," *milk*) are associated with an individual's name. Such designations sometimes reflect a high status ("the *waqf* belonging to Amīr Atabeg," for example, in WQ14), but are in many cases limited to a single name that rather suggests a man (all of them being masculine names) of little or no stature, presumably the very person cultivating the plot in question (such as "Khiḍr" and "Wafā," both in WQ4).

In the minority of cases where "land" is associated with a place-name, the formulation is generally along the lines of "land located in the place called X" (*al-arḍ al-kāʾin fī mawḍiʿ al-musammāʾ X*), whereas name identification for villages is much more direct, such as "the village named X" (*al-qariya al-musammāʾ X*).

73. Quite tellingly, one notable exception to this rule is a village whose bordering elements are designated as "the land of" other villages (WQ6; a similar expression is also used in WQ14, but this time in reference to the borders of a piece of land rather than to those of a village). There is also one case of a village that is explicitly endowed along with the land that surrounds it (WQ7).

It would, however, be excessive to assume on this basis that other endowed villages did not likewise comprise their respective surrounding fields since such logic would lead to the absurd conclusion that villages bordered by other villages would form nothing short of an urban network with no cultivated space between them.

74. See, for example, WQ8 and WQ25, both bordered by cemeteries.

75. In the same way, that is, that Ottoman tax registers record taxes not only on cereals, but also on such productions as garden produce, sheep, and other, less important, ones (honey, nuts, and the like). Concerning the fiscal implications of such differences, see p. 56.

76. As anybody who was ever provided by their employer with equipment of lesser quality than that of their colleagues can testify, the inequalities discussed here do not have to be inscribed in legal ownership to affect the participants.

77. WQ22 and WQ29, both located in the region of Konya. Furthermore, all five revenue-producing elements in WQ34 (around Afyon Karahisar), designated with an illegible word, might also be of the same nature.

78. AU 335–356. A few centuries later, Ottoman administration used the term *mazraʿa* in reference to tracts of land detached from villages, often formerly populated places going in and out of production on the basis of need (see Leslie Peirce, *Morality Tales: Law and Gender in the Ottoman Court of Aintab*, 34, 52). Although the definition seems to be compatible with the one suggested here, we should be careful about projecting the specifics of its meaning to a period when legal and administrative practices were neither set nor homogenous, even by the fluid Ottoman standards.

Furthermore, *Bazm u Razm* uses the word *ḍiyāʿ* on two occasions: one tells of a political grandee who, having fallen from grace, retreats to his "estate" (*ḍaʿyat*) outside of the city of Kayseri, whereas the other refers to the same individual's "properties and estates" (*amlāk va ḍiyā*) in the vicinity of Konya (respectively, BR 95 and 97).

Vincent Lagardère, discussing medieval Spain, suggests a similar understanding of *ḍiyāʾ* as a single independent agricultural unit of a smaller size than actual villages ("Structures agraires et perception de l'espace à travers les recueils de consultations juridiques [XIe–XVe siècles]," esp. 147–150).

79. See, for example, the episode (VN 65a) in which grain to be milled is referred to as *ekin*, a collective noun that, both later in the same source (VN 118a) and, much more explicitly, in another text (GN 1:189b), is used to refer to "planting material" (i.e., seeds). The same passage from the *Garib-nama* designates individual seeds as *tuhm ü dane*.

The *Gharib-nama* (a text that peasants may have regularly heard) also points out the six elements necessary for plants to grow: someone to plant the seeds, the seeds themselves, soil, water, sun, and God's will (GN 1:189). It is difficult to determine the extent to which these would be part of a general knowledge shared among peasants. What is clear, however, is that everyone knew that some seeds would grow while others would not (see YED 388:3 and YER 323).

80. Sources make explicit connection between droughts, agricultural scarcity, and prices rising (VN 30a, 117a; AU 310; GN 2:56b; MA 3/466, 3/592, 6/8, 7/11).

81. Waterways constitute 18 percent of all the bordering elements given for endowed cereal fields. Cereal fields for which delineation is provided are surrounded, on average, by approximately four bordering elements.

82. One *waqfiyya* mentions one field bordered by a *khandaq* (irrigation ditch) and another by a *saqiyya* (WQ8). Concerning *saqiyyas*, see p. 154.

The benefits of manual irrigation for cereal fields obviously vary with the type of terrain, but may be significant even if applied once or twice a year. For an archaeologist's view on an early-twentieth-century Anatolian example, see Gordon Hillmann, "Agricultural Resources and Settlement in the Aşvan Region" and "Agricultural Productivity and Past Population Potential at Aşvan." See also my discussion of irrigation of gardens, p. 26.

83. Quite tellingly, these are among the few Turkish words to appear in Arabic-language *waqfiyyas* of that period, thus suggesting a generalized popular use of that word (which, in the document, is preceded by the expression "which they call in Turkish . . ." [yaqālu lihā bi-l-Turkī jiftlik] [WQ21]). This *waqfiyya*, furthermore, confirms the appropriate nature of the nomenclature, since the endowed property includes "two buffalo oxen" (*al-baqirayn al-jamusayn*).

84. See GN 2:150b; VN 90a; and MA 4/53. These references do not include any hint as to whether the instrument used was indeed a plow (a technologically more advanced device, with an asymmetrical blade that turns over wide slices of soil) or the more primitive ard (a straight, spike-like blade that simply digs a narrow trench). Archaeological evidence is of no great help here, since the metal from which these blades are usually made is unlikely to have survived in a recognizable form. On the difference between ard and plow, see Georges Duby, *Rural Economy and Country Life in the Medieval West*, 18.

85. The word *çiftlik* is still the most commonly used to refer to a farm in modern Turkish, no matter the number of tractors used to exploit the land.

86. Once again, absence of direct references can by no means be taken as the proof of anything, although one could indeed have expected to see oxen used to pull threshing sledges, for example. This in turn suggests that oxen were idle for a significant part of the year, explaining the hiring of a cattle drover (*sığırtmac*) who would bring these animals to graze at times when they were not used (VN 54a).

Kaplan (*Les hommes et la terre à Byzance*, 50–52, 86) makes the rather puzzling opposite suggestion that, in Byzantine times, oxen may have been exclusively used for threshing, and never for plowing. It is, of course, reasonable to imagine that the use of animals in threshing may have indeed been practiced without making its way into the sources I used. It is, however, rather more difficult to believe that the transition from Byzantine to Turko-Muslim rule, largely taking place through the immigration of sheepherding pastoralists from central Asia, would have led to the introduction of oxen-powered plowing as a new technique in the region. It seems more reasonable to imagine that oxen-drawn plowing expanded in late-Byzantine times, and, indeed, modest archaeological evidence does suggest an increase of cattle population in the centuries preceding the arrival of the Seljuks in Anatolia (see Derya Silibolatlaz, "Animal Bone Studies on Byzantine City of the Amorium [*sic*]," 55).

87. On horses, see p. 39ff.

88. APZ 39; VN 61a. This should be contrasted with other activities such as plowing, garden work, and fodder collection (VN 64a–b), which appear to have primarily been solitary tasks.

89. A passage in some manuscripts of ʿĀşıkpaşazāde's chronicle (and omitted in others) shows that he expected his readers to find normal that people would stay overnight in the fields, albeit only at the time of harvest (APZ 39).

I should also note that the very use of collective plurals prevents us from determining who exactly (in terms of gender, social status, age, and so on) were "the people" attending the process and, conversely, who would stay in the village.

90. This impression is strengthened by the observations of Jacques Bordaz who notes,

observing "traditional" techniques in central Anatolia in the early 1960s: "Each farmer brings his harvest to his own section of a communal threshing area on the outskirts of the village—an area chosen for its proper exposure to the wind, an essential in winnowing" ("The Threshing Sledge," 28). A similar observation was made in an ethnoarchaeological study of the region surrounding the Aşvan excavation in the early 1970s (Gerald Hall, Sam McBride, and Alwyn Riddell, "Architectural Study," 245).

91. See VN 61a; MA 3/524; GN 1:218a–b; and APZ 64. VN 61a specifies that the scene it describes "was their habit," thus strongly suggesting a practice that changed between the moment the story is said to have taken place (thirteenth century) and the time when the text was written down (ca. 1500). The nature of the change to which this refers is not clear, but it might primarily revolve around tax-collecting practices rather than the threshing and winnowing techniques themselves.

APZ 64 mentions that barley and wheat are kept on the *meydan* (public place), within the city walls of besieged Konya.

GN 1:218a–b uses the word *düken*, which may in theory refer to any kind of threshing instrument. However, the most common use of the word and the formulation of the passage in which it is used both suggest a sledge, rather than any kind of flailing or beating instrument or the use of oxen treading directly on the crops: "Altına aldı düken sürdi yire" (The *düken* took [the wheat] under and drove it to the ground). In various historical contexts, threshing sledges are usually pulled by animals (including in Byzantium: see Anthony Bryer, "The Means of Agricultural Production: Muscles and Tools," 109–110; and in Anatolia down to the 1960s: Bordaz, "The Threshing Sledge"), although human force has also been used in some instances. The same passage also mentions a sickle, in Turkish *orağ*, although without any further detail that may give its mention anything more than a lexical value.

Two other passages, although overall less reliable (the first, VN 34a, is set in Iran in "olden times," whereas the other, VN 83a, describes a phantasmagoric underwater scene), also convey the impression of grain being gathered to be winnowed near habitation quarters.

92. In a metaphorical expression of the value attributed to cereal harvests, Yûnus Emre states that "those who die young are like the harvest of Heaven" ("Yigid iken ölenlere gök ekini biçmiş gibi" [YED 388:4]).

93. Used as fodder or litter for animals or even for prisoners. APZ 64, 97; MA 3/408; VN 117a; IB 334; QN 24.

94. APZ 102; BR 110; IB 344; VN 48a. The concept of "ownership," in this case, should be taken in its legal sense, that is, with regards to the real estate's monetary value and the ability to change its legal status—for example, by turning it into a *waqf.*

95. In a case-study article ("The Tekke of Hacı Bektaş: Social Position and Economic Activities"), Suraiya Faroqhi attempts to "show how the *dergāh* or central monastery of the Bektashi order of dervishes related, economically, to its social environment" (183). Although the author superbly manages to bring together a wide variety of sources into a comprehensive picture of the *dergāh* as an institution (and of its relation to state institu-

tions), she makes no serious attempt at examining the situation from the point of view of the peasants themselves.

96. MA 6/2.

97. VN 90a. This anecdote, however, pertains to the beginnings of the Bektaşi order and may very well reflect the more or less spontaneous development of an endowment that was later formalized as a properly legal *waqf*.

98. "Bazı halk [Seyyid Hārūn]'s didi ki, Sultanum mescidlerün medreseleründür, bu yirler senün vakfündür. Bu yirlere bir mikdar icâre tayın olsa n'ola didiler. Sultan didi ki, haşa, bağışladum gelüp ev yapana. Amma ziraat olınan yirlere bir mıkdar [icâre] tayın câizdür didi. Bunda ahvāl çokdur" (my translation). SH 20b. I should acknowledge Professor Amy Singer's precious help in my attempt at deciphering this passage.

99. For example, it is indeed rather unlikely that an individual of any standing would have been designated merely by an *ism* (given name) such as "Sinān" (WQ26), "Masʿūd" (WQ17), or ʿAbd Allāh (WQ13) in a legal document.

100. AU 310. It was so generalized, he claims, that "in the spring, [milk] is not among the things that are sold and bought, for there is almost no one in Anatolia who does not have sheep to milk, so there is no need to sell it or to buy it." Although this is a good indication of the very widespread ownership of sheep, it should not be taken literally, since the same author (but relying on another informant) later on points out that milk in Anatolia is "very cheap," which implies that it indeed could be bought and sold (AU 331).

The *Vilayat-nama* further contains indications that there were both two-horned and four-horned sheep, the latter apparently being rarer and more expensive (VN 100b and 112b).

101. As the discussion in the appendix makes abundantly clear, internal evidence from various sources points toward a fairly wide range of target audiences, from soldiers (*Dustur-nama*) to peasants (*Vilayat-nama*) to the nobility (translations of the *Qabus-nama*). None of the extant sources, however, seems to have been targeted toward a nomadic or seminomadic audience.

102. VN 77a; MQ 250.

103. Respectively, VN 42a and MA 3/497.

104. Hitomi Hongo, "Patterns of Animal Husbandry, Environment, and Ethnicity in Central Anatolia in the Ottoman Empire Period: Faunal Remains from the Islamic Layers at Kaman-Kalehoyuk," 288; Hitomi Hongo, "Patterns of Animal Husbandry in Central Anatolia from the Second Millennium BC through the Middle Ages: Faunal Remains from Kaman-Kalehoyuk, Turkey," 129; Sebastian Payne, "Kill-Off Patterns in Sheep and Goats: The Mandibles from Asvan Kale," 301.

105. AU 310; MA 3/49. A number of factors might make reproduction more likely at certain times of the year: day length and latitude, genetic variations, seasonal changes in diet, and, of course, human intervention that keeps rams and ewes apart. One should also note that, while Anatolia's harsh winters are a challenge unto themselves, it is summer that brings about the highest likelihood of disease for lambs. See Richard Redding, "Decision Making in Subsistence Herding of Sheep and Goat in the Middle East," 81–94.

The same author (168–169) also points out that, for the kind of sheep breeds that probably populated Anatolia in the Middle Ages, the period during which they would be milked (which is slightly shorter than lactation) tends to range between three and four months.

106. I will discuss the issue of seasonal availability of food products, from the consumer's point of view, in chapter 3.

107. This argument is inspired by the methods developed by archaeologists for the determination of culling patterns through a statistical analysis of faunal remains. For an excellent example of the application of such an analysis, including clear explanations of the principles and methods it involves, see Gil J. Stein, "Medieval Pastoral Production Systems at Gritille."

Concerning the ritual slaughter (*qurbān*), see p. 108ff. Butchers would perform "secular" slaughter (i.e., for primarily commercial purposes) all year long, apparently near the selling places in the market (MA 3/486, 3/497). Considering the limited means of meat preservation, it indeed made sense to limit as much as possible the time and distance between the live animal (the freshest form of meat) and the table. Sheep were exported to very distant regions ("Syria, Diyarbakır, Iraq and Iran" [AU 310]), surely in no small part because, unlike cereal (the export of which does not seem to have happened from central Anatolia), they could carry themselves to their destinations rather than requiring costly means of transportation.

See also DN 95; VN 85a, 159b; and WQ21 (two references to mutton consumption).

108. Wool production can be inferred from mentions of productions that require it, such as that of felt caps (VN 106b). This absence from sources could perhaps be interpreted as a sign that, like horticultural work in a vegetable garden and unlike cereal harvest, shearing the sheep would involve a very small number of people (or even be a solitary activity), and thus entail relatively limited social interaction. This activity did not, after all, involve the same urgency as cereal harvest (during which the product has to be reaped and at least partially processed within a few days). Archaeological evidence supports the suggestion of both meat and wool production. See Hongo, "Patterns of Animal Husbandry, Environment and Ethnicity," 288; Hongo, "Patterns of Animal Husbandry in Central Anatolia," 129; and Payne, "Kill-Off Patterns in Sheep and Goats," 301.

109. As opposed, that is, to the connotation of inherent luxury that would have been attached to an animal, as seems to have been the case for horses (on which see p. 39).

110. The relative price of sheep and cattle can be inferred from a passage in the *Vilayat-nama* (VN 159b), which gives a 1:10 ratio for the cattle and sheep to be slaughtered at a religious man's funeral. This should by no means be taken as direct proof of their precise value, but nevertheless offers an order of magnitude (i.e., a head of cattle was several times more expensive than a head of sheep).

Zooarchaeological evidence from Kaman-Kalehöyük indeed reveals culling strategies that are congruent with the upkeep of relatively small herds (Hongo, "Patterns of Animal Husbandry, Environment, and Ethnicity," 288; Hongo, "Patterns of Animal Husbandry in Central Anatolia," 129).

111. Several passages from *Bazm u Razm* refer to Turkmens in negative terms (see, for example, BR 234), though none links them to sheepherding as clearly as VN 100b.

112. Concerning upper-class ownership of sheep, see, for example, MA 3/165; APZ 29; and VN 112. See also WQ14, which includes the only case of sheep (in this case a flock of 250 head) endowed in one of the *waqfiyya*s I used. VN 51b is a rare case of villagers explicitly described as full owners of sheep (as well as, for that matter, oxen). However, it is worth mentioning that this particular passage refers to a couple that, although directly involved in agriculture, probably formed a (very) local elite, since the husband was the son of a scholar to whom, the text claims, the Seljuk sultan had "given" the village in which they lived and worked.

For an extended discussion of the Ottoman state's attitude toward the nomad (which does not, however, include the possibility I suggest here of nomadic pastoralists being seen as economic rivals), see Lindner, *Nomads and Ottomans.* I should also thank Scott Redford (personal communication) for pointing out the shortcomings of an earlier version of this argument.

113. Although written sources do not differentiate between cattle and water buffalo, Hongo ("Patterns of Animal Husbandry in Central Anatolia," 65–66) points out that only the former appear in prehistorical layers and that water buffaloes may have become popular in the region sometime during the Middle Ages.

114. VN 90a, 146a; GN 1:150b/3; MA 4/53; WQ20. That plowing was not an easy task, even with the help of a pair of oxen, is well expressed in a passage of the *Vilayat-nama* (VN 90a), where a man known for his kindness becomes so irritated as to resort to violence against one of his animals.

Interestingly, pathological bones excavated in Kaman-Kalehöyük directly confirm the use of cattle and water buffaloes for traction purposes (Hongo, "Patterns of Animal Husbandry, Environment, and Ethnicity," 299).

115. Concerning the part that oxen played in plowing, see p. 38. On their use as pack animals, see APZ 3 and VN 118a, as well as p. 47.

116. VN 56a–b. This episode refers to the population of a village that, because it is too small to be able to afford such a hire, gives the task to the villagers in rotation, thus hinting at the otherwise generalized practice of hiring ox drovers. Although it makes no direct reference to cows and calves, both the clearly specified presence of bulls and the mention, in another passage, of cows and calves remaining near the village during the day suggest that the animals thus led were only the males. A parallel practice is attested from legal documents for the Byzantine period (Kaplan, *Les hommes et la terre*, 195–196).

The *Vilayat-nama* (the best Turkish-language source for agriculture) uses both the word *öküz* and the word *sığır*. The former is used whenever the animal appears—even indirectly—as a source of power, whereas the word *sığır* occurs in more general references, further hinting at the generalized use of male animals for traction power (see, for example, the way both words appear in VN 56a–b). That the only use of bulls or oxen was their traction power is best expressed by another passage in this source, where a farmer intends to slaughter an *öküz* that has become too old to pull his plow (VN 146a). Sources give no hint as to whether males were castrated, though the taming requirements to use them as a source of power would suggest that they were.

117. VN 52b. This episode is, incidentally, one of the few cases of women interact-

ing with farm animals, as cows are being watched over by a female servant hired by their female owner. This particular case includes no hint as to its typicality and is far from sufficient to make any claim of generalization. Furthermore, the "coincidence" of male peasants interacting with male animals and female peasants interacting with females might be rooted in (even oral) literary patterns or symbolic references. Still, if there was indeed such a pattern of symbolic functions, it is not very far-fetched to suggest that it could have participated in organizing actual daily life activities. In other words, this cross-species gender division pattern might be, rather than a reflection of the actual practice, a reflection of the cultural assumption that organized the actual practice.

In any case, kill-off patterns extrapolated from faunal remains indeed support the idea that, along with obtaining traction power for plowing, the production of milk (and, to a lesser extent, meat) was the objective in bovine husbandry. On this subject, see Herman Buitenhuis, "Preliminary Report on the Faunal Remains of Hayaz Höyük from the 1979–1983 Season," 66; Hongo, "Patterns of Animal Husbandry in Central Anatolia," 127; and Stein, "Medieval Pastoral Production Systems," 205–208. A passage in the *Gharib-nama* ("İlla ol avret kim anun udi yok / Eyle bil-kim bir inekdür südi yok" [But this woman who has no shame, know that she is a cow with no milk] [GN 2:171b/4]) indeed strongly suggests that a cow that did not give milk was considered nothing more than a useless burden.

118. See, for example, MA 3/89, 3/581; VN 72a, 90b, 146a; and YED 407:10. As in the case of sheep, I will come back to the religious slaughter of cows (*qurbān*) in my discussion of food and religion.

119. See VN 90b, 146a. Furthermore, two anecdotes from two different sources (which do not seem to be variations on the same story [VN 146a; MA 3/89]) display saintly figures "freeing" a cow or ox that then disappears in the wild. This may indeed reflect a potentially common phenomenon of improperly restrained animals breaking away and thus being lost to their owners.

120. See especially VN 56a–b.

121. As, indeed, is the case in VN 52, where a relatively well-off couple of peasants hire a servant (designated in the text both as *hizmetkar* and as *cariye*) to look after their cows.

122. Even though the bones of these three closely related animals are difficult to tell apart, in all three cases archaeological evidence indeed confirms that they were a marginal presence in the life of peasants. See Hongo, "Patterns of Animal Husbandry in Central Anatolia," 71–74, tables 5.25–5.26; as well as László Bartosiewicz, "Animal Remains from the Excavations of Horum Höyük, Southeast Anatolia, Turkey," 152, 154.

What feed equines are given to eat is seldom specifically mentioned, but the use of words such as *ʿalīq* (BR 163, 238) and *qaḍīm* (BR 238) as well as contextual evidence and agronomic knowledge suggest a mix of green fodder and barley.

Furthermore, Ibn Baṭṭūṭa's complaint that he could not find food for horses in a meadow shows that horses could not be left to graze for themselves, as was the case for sheep. This passage, however, might be a rhetorical instrument to give a negative image of the band of Turkmens who, he claims, owned the meadow (IB 315). Ibn Baṭṭūṭa also suggests that there would often be places to shelter horses (*marbaṭ*) in the *zāwiyas* where he usually alighted (IB 333), though it may not have been the normal practice for the hosts to provide them with bedding straw (IB 334) or even fodder (IB 295–296). See also MA 4/101.

123. See in particular this line from the *Gharib-nama*: "Kimisi atdur kim ol binmek-içün" (Some [animals] are horses, which are to [be] mount[ed] [GN 1:178b]).

Horse-feeding requirements had an impact on military tactics, not only because feeding the horses created prolonged (yet obviously necessary) idle time, but also because it was a moment during which an army would be especially vulnerable to attacks (all the more so when preparing to settle for a few days, which required soldiers to scatter in the surroundings to gather the feed [BR 238–239]). It would also affect military strategy, insofar as the animals had to be put to rest after a military season (DN 104). For other references to horses in military contexts, see, for example, DN 102; MA 3/16; and RS 18.

124. "Meydanın sakka[sı]" (VN 147a). One episode from Ibn Baṭṭūṭa's travelogue also suggests that horsehides could be sold. However, every passage that could have hinted at the consumption of horse or mule meat (either when depicting a greedy man trying to gain as much profit from a dead horse as possible or when mentioning the value of these animals in relation to meat-producing ones) conspicuously avoids doing so, thus suggesting that it was not consumed by human beings, or at least not publicly. See GN 2:89a/3–6; IB 336; and MA 3/581.

125. It is worth noting that, when depicting them as riding animals, sources tend to associate horses with political figures and mules with religious ones, although the extent to which this reflects practice (as opposed to literary conventions) remains unclear.

A passage from the *Gharib-nama* notes that "it is the horse and the mule that are the *begs* of all animals" (at katırdur cümle hayvanun begi [GN 1:178b/3]). Other references emphasize the high prices of these animals. Two independent accounts mention with obvious awe that a high-quality horse could be sold for as much as a thousand *dīnārs* (MA 5/11; AU 314), and in another passage the sale of a single mule by a dervish brotherhood fetches enough money to provide for a large feast (*ʿurs* [MA 3/581]). Furthermore, another account mentions a man specializing in the rearing of horses, which he sells to grandees (*akābir* [MA 3/16]). This tendency to concentrate on the sale and acquisition of horses and mules (as well as frequent references to their high value) is, in itself, a strong indication that they were seen as objects of luxury.

126. It was a specialty of some regions (Germiyan and Kastamonu [AU 314, 330]) and some people (a professional horse trader [MA 3/16]).

Lindner devotes a chapter of his *Nomads and Ottomans in Medieval Anatolia* (75–103) to a large nomadic tribe living in areas ranging from the Taurus Mountains to the north of the Tuz Gölü, the Horse Drovers (At Çeken, Asb Kashān), which he studies primarily through sixteenth-century sources (cadastral surveys, *kānūnnāmes*, and a few references in narrative sources). As Lindner himself points out, the name tag "Horse Drover" as well as the "horse tax" they paid (which was in fact a poll tax on the human population) survived much longer than the actual practice of horse husbandry in that group, and probably had all but disappeared by the beginning of the sixteenth century (84). Although I have found few references to horse husbandry, it seems reasonable to follow Lindner's claim that the group had been involved in this activity in earlier centuries, including in the period studied here.

That nomads were (or at least could be) in charge of raising and selling horses indeed strengthens the impression that cereal-cultivating peasants did not have close and regular contact with horses. That being said, the geographical distribution of this tribe indeed suggests that the two populations did encounter each other on occasion. For more on nomad-sedentary interactions, see p. 42ff.

127. Thus, the metal findings of the archaeological excavation at Korucutepe include both horse-related and military equipment, namely, three horseshoes and a spur, as well as an arrowhead, a dagger, and what appears to be a Mongol spearhead (Maurits N. van Loon, "The Other Medieval Objects," 255–257).

128. Hongo, "Patterns of Animal Husbandry in Central Anatolia," 68, 131, 145; Hongo, "Patterns of Animal Husbandry, Environment, and Ethnicity," 288, 302–303; Maurits N. van Loon, conclusion to *Korucutepe: Final Report on the Excavations of the Universities of Chicago, California (Los Angeles), and Amsterdam in the Keban Reservoir, Eastern Anatolia, 1968–1970*, 277; J. Boessneck and A. von den Driesch, "The Animal Bones from Korucutepe Near Elâzığ, Eastern Anatolia: Finds from the 1968–1969 Excavation," 218–219; Silibolatlaz, "Animal Bone Studies," 55, 75. There are no direct depictions of individuals consuming pork, although one anecdote presents a "good Muslim" who has promised to do whatever his wife orders and who is ordered to eat pork. He is delivered from his promise in extremis after a religious man intercedes (thus hinting at the abomination that it would have entailed [MA 3/380]). Such general absence of pork might be the result of some combination of three factors: the limited number of sources that contain direct references to specific foods, the extremely limited space held by Christians in these sources, and the actual absence of (at least overt) pork consumption.

129. VN 76a, 126b; APZ 42.

130. VN 76a.

131. An interesting exception is Gritille, where pork appears to have remained the most widely consumed meat in the twelfth and thirteenth centuries. It seems reasonable to assume that this particular site, unlike most others that have been excavated in Anatolia, retained a primarily or even exclusively Christian population long after the Turkish invasions. See Stein, "Medieval Pastoral Production Systems," 193–197.

132. As I pointed out above, this practice is attested in written sources (see APZ 42 and VN 126b). See also Hongo, "Patterns of Animal Husbandry in Central Anatolia," 84; and Hongo, "Patterns of Animal Husbandry, Environment, and Ethnicity," 293.

133. MA 3/592, 4/101, 7/4, 9/8.

134. Hongo, "Patterns of Animal Husbandry in Central Anatolia," 81–82; Hongo, "Patterns of Animal Husbandry, Environment, and Ethnicity," 283, 299.

135. GN 2:3a/8; DN 95; YED 319:5; MA 3/254; RS 100–101. The latter two both tell

the same story, most likely relying on the same source. YED 166:2 and 407:10 suggest farm-based production, as opposed to hunting, for geese. There seems to be limited presence of wild bird bones among the material excavated from medieval layers, at least in comparison to earlier periods (bronze age and before). Hongo, "Patterns of Animal Husbandry in Central Anatolia," 87–90.

136. See, for example, MA 2/12.

137. AU 310.

138. Incidentally, this scene takes place slightly outside of the geographical scope of this book (APZ 12).

Archaeological evidence is difficult to use as far as goats are concerned, because most of their bones are difficult or impossible to distinguish from those of sheep. Still, it is worth noting that goats tend to be more resistant than sheep to tough ecological conditions and were prevalent at Gritille, the same site that retained pork consumption into the medieval period. On this subject, see Stein, "Medieval Pastoral Production Systems," 197–205; and Payne, "Kill-Off Patterns in Sheep and Goats."

139. See especially VN 90a, as well as VN 85b and DN 116. The nature of such animal housings is unclear, although, as Scott Redford pointed out to me (personal communication), the archaeological record suggests the possible presence of stables under some houses, as well as animal pens that were either built as dedicated structures or through the reuse (or parallel use) of architectural works intended for other purposes, such as military fortifications. However, among the architectural features that would tell us the most about such functions are rings and other devices to tie the animals (from the location of which we could extrapolate such questions as the size, height, and number of animals), and these features were located on walls. This limits the amount of information we can borrow from archaeologists, who most often have to work from collapsed walls. Veronica Kalas, "The Byzantine Kitchen in the Domestic Complexes of Cappadocia," 109.

140. See, for example, MQ 250 and VN 56a.

141. See, for example, VN 77a and IB 277–278. *Waqfiyya*s also offer no hint of (at least permanent) areas specifically designated to hold animals near cities or villages. One narrative passage (VN 52b) specifically mentions a meadow bordering a village that is explicitly devoted to cows, although the same passage's emphasis on the need for someone to watch over the animals at every instant also excludes the possibility that the area may have been fenced in any significant way.

I should point out, however, that Lindner (*Nomads and Ottomans*, 62) refers to a practice by nomadic pastoralists of holding the sheep in pens in the fall, during the mating season. This claim seems to be based on a combination of the name of an Ottoman tax (the *resm-i agıl*, or "penfold tax") and modern anthropological observations. I have no hint that could support this claim in my own sources, although, as I have stated several times already, this does not constitute any form of proof that such practice was unknown.

142. Landscape perception is obviously a broad topic, and one that I hope to tackle as part of an upcoming research project. Still, the reader can get a sense of the range of ways in which modern, "commonsense" assumptions about the landscape need to be

questioned by taking a look at Nico Roymans, "The Cultural Biography of Urnfields and the Long-Term History of a Mythical Landscape," as well as the ensuing discussion in the same issue of the journal.

143. See, for example, BR 234 and, in a more lyrical register, YED 204:7. A reference found in a *waqfiyya* refers to a *maṣīf* that "they call *yaylāq* in Turkish" (WQ32).

As can be seen from a passage of the *Gharib-nama* (GN 2:48b/7), which contrasts it with a mine that produces precious stones, *yaylas* seem to have held the image of relatively desolate places.

144. BR 234, 291, 303; APZ 3; VN 100b.

145. BR 291, 303, 325; VN 98b. Such a designation must certainly have had some ethnolinguistic basis, although it would be simplistic at best to assume a one-to-one relationship between these name tags and the language or cultures with which we commonly associate them. In any case, the impression of political autonomy that the presence of a complex political structure afforded them may not be completely foreign to the reluctance, or even resistance, that they often displayed toward taxes imposed by sedentary authorities (see, for example, BR 325 and APZ 67). On the relationship between the tribal organization of nomads and sedentary political authorities, as well as its evolution through the pre- and early Ottoman period, see Lindner, *Nomads and Ottomans*.

146. Incidentally, it is by depicting nomadic groups as such undifferentiated masses that the *Vilayat-nama* and *Bazm u Razm* convey the impression of large numbers. For example, one of the few references to groups in the *Vilayat-nama* talks of the annual transit of "Tatars" who brought sheep to be slaughtered in Hacı Bektaş's honor (VN 100b). See also YED 294:6.

147. The single reference I could find to an actual destructive effect of nomads on sedentary agriculture refers to deliberate actions, thus rather suggesting that, when there was no such ill intention, the negative impact of nomads may not have been as dramatic as is often thought (APZ 135).

148. VN 77.

149. VN 56a. An episode depicting cows and calves, on the other hand, presents them as staying rather close to the residential areas (VN 52b).

150. ʿĀşıkpaşazāde, when discussing the early Ottomans, both depicts them as "true" nomads and mentions animal products (dairy, but also woolen carpets) they brought back from the *yayla* (APZ 9). Although the possibility of anachronism cannot be ruled out (especially since details such as these can easily be modified from one link to the next in the chain of transmission of a narrative), this passage does imply a strong correlation between nomadism and pastoralism. In the absence of seasonal migrations, the common involvement in an activity such as sheep keeping provides a functional justification to borrow the concept of *yayla* from another group of people, despite the obviously vast differences in geographical scale between the ways either group understood the concept.

Whatever the truth about this issue may be, the presence of a "summer pasture" (designated both as a *maṣīf* and as a *yayla*) as part of the property endowed for the benefit of a *waqf* (WQ32) raises a whole different set of questions, since its position in the document leaves no doubt that it was intended to provide revenues. It may suggest that some form of "rent money" was demanded from the shepherds bringing their sheep to graze on this property or that what was actually endowed was the right to collect a particular tax on sheep (either as rent or as fines) from the village in which it is located, presumably something similar to the *resm-i otlak* said in some *kānūnnāmes* to date from "ancient times" (*kadimden*). See, for example, the Karaman *kānūnnāme* of 1528 (Ömer Lütfi Barkan, *XV ve XVI ıncı arsırlarda Osmanlı İmparatorluğunda zirai ekonominin hukukî ve malî esaslar*, vol. 1, *Kanunlar*, 47); as well as Lindner, *Nomads and Ottomans*, 63; and I. Beldiceanu-Steinherr, "Recherches sur la province de Qaraman au XVIe siècle," 62–63, 93. The fact that *kānūnnāme*s of Meḥmed II (dated 1488) carefully point out that no tax should be collected on *yaylas* and *kışlas* without referring to practices from "ancient times" further suggests that such taxes may have been collected in pre-Ottoman times, thus requiring a legislative effort to cancel them (Barkan, *Kanunlar*, 391). One should remember, however, that the unique status of this endowed property (the only pasture among more than four hundred pieces of revenue-producing property in the *waqfiyya*s I surveyed) is in itself significant and might indicate either that this particular property was obtained by some twist in the regulations (especially since the endower of this particular *waqf* was also the regional ruler, Sulaymān Pāshā of the Candar family, in Kastamonu) or that this kind of property would not normally produce enough revenue to justify including them in such a perpetual endowment.

Another passage, this one taken from Ibn Baṭṭūṭa, also hints at the "private" ownership of a meadow (*marʿā*), this time by a group of Turkmens (IB 315).

151. VN 131b.

152. APZ 67.

153. VN 75a–77b. See also YED 207:4.

CHAPTER TWO

1. As a matter of fact, the kind of detail on which al-ʿUmarī concentrates (regional variations in export products, prices, weights and measures, and currency units) strongly suggests that the section of his encyclopaedic work devoted to Anatolia was in fact intended for merchants.

2. Al-ʿUmarī mentions that sheep were exported to "Shām [i.e., Syria], Diyarbakır, Iraq and Iran" (AU 310). These destinations might seem quite distant for such little legs, but the claim that individual nomadic pastoralists could cover such a distance nicely dovetails with the repeated presence of the "Turkmens of Shām" in Anatolia, which *Bazm u Razm* points out on a number of occasions (see, for example, BR 234, where they graze around Sivas).

3. Ibn Baṭṭūṭa makes only one direct mention of fruit export from central Anatolia (in reference to a variety of apricot that is dried and exported from the regions of both Antalya and Konya [IB 259–260, 281]), but both he and others make it clear that fruit drying was a common practice (see, for example, IB 336 and MA 8/79).

4. See, for example, Anthony McNicoll, *Taşkun Kale: Keban Rescue Excavations, East-*

ern Anatolia, 64–65; Stephen Mitchell, *Aşvan Kale: Keban Rescue Excavations, Eastern Anatolia*, 55, 73–74; John Moore, *Tille Höyük I: The Medieval Period*, 71–74; and Öney, "Pottery from the Samosata Excavations, 1978–81." Similar evidence also appears for glassware, another expensive product. See Scott Redford, "Ayyubid Glass from Samsat, Turkey."

5. See Joanita Vroom, "Some Byzantine Pottery Finds from Kaman-Kalehöyük: A First Observation."

6. This picture is strengthened by the presence, among the findings of the Kaman-Kalehöyük archaeological excavation, of a small amount of camel bones, which Hitomi Hongo associates with long-distance trade (the small amounts are congruent with a transitory presence of this animal, fairly rare in the region at that time). This suggests that the animals belonging to long-distance traders would indeed visit (and sometimes die in) even remote villages. See Hongo, "Patterns of Animal Husbandry in Central Anatolia," 68–71, 159.

7. APZ 64.

8. VN 117a.

9. IB 329.

10. Saffron: IB 329; rice: AU 330.

11. *Khān-i shakar furūshān*: MA 3/10, 3/17.

12. *Khān-i birinj furūshān*: RS 126. Concerning the association between *khān*s and merchants, see also MA 1/21.

13. See note 6.

14. See, for example, MA 3/85, 3/148.

15. *Ṭarīq va libās-i tujjār* (RS 123).

16. Camels appear in scenes taking place on routes between Syria and Anatolia and through limited archaeological evidence from northern central Anatolia. Some passages simply use the Turkish word *davar*, which could refer to any large quadruped (see, for example, VN 117a, 127a). Concerning camels, see MA 3/374 and AU 347 (where al-ʿUmarī directly states that camels are nowhere to be found in the north-central Anatolian region of Kastamonu). Both horse and ox bones from the medieval levels of the Korucutepe excavation show signs of overloads that can be attributed to the use of the animals for transportation (Boessneck and Driesch, "Animal Bones from Korucutepe," 217).

17. "Kanlı kanlı helvalar, dürlü dürlü nimetler akub gelür" (SH 15b). If we expand the scope of the research to Thrace (which at that time was just beginning to slip out of Byzantine rule), we can add to this one more scene also depicting *kañlı*s, although carrying rather less miraculous loads of wheat, barley, and millet (DN 102). Expanding into earlier periods, the geography of Ibn Saʿīd (completed in mid-thirteenth century, but partly based on earlier observations) mentions merchandise transport by ox-drawn carts (*ʿajal*) around Kayseri, Aksaray, and Konya. See Claude Cahen, "Ibn Saʿīd sur l'Asie Mineure Seldjuqide," 46–47.

18. "Ilden ile yükler çeker" (GN 2:89a).

19. VN 116b–117a, 127a.

20. This suggestion is strengthened by the fact that the exceptions indeed correspond

to regions that were chronologically closer to a period of peace and relatively centralized political authority.

21. Discussing trade between the Aegean possessions of Venice and the emirates of Aydin and Menteşe, Elizabeth Zachariadou indeed presents all the cereals exported from Anatolia as being produced in the Aegean coastal region rather than central Anatolia (*Trade and Crusade*, 163–164).

22. APZ 64; VN 83a. The latter depicts a dreamlike scene in which a boat sinks while carrying cereals on the Black Sea; the merchant then goes to the bottom of the sea, only to find that his grain has been stacked and threshed ("yığılmış, çeç olmış"). As I stated in chapter 1, cereals were hauled from the field to threshing grounds located near the village, although the decrease in weight and volume that threshing allowed would render transportation over longer distances more efficient. Such depictions thus betray the worldview of peasants who were mainly used to seeing cereals transported over short distances—and not exported abroad.

23. That story appears in both MA 3/289 and RS 92. The market was also home to numerous dogs, apparently considered as lowly at best and, more generally, as pests (MA 2/19, 3/77, 3/486).

24. QN 16, 18. The fact that both words used in the "Turkish" translation are in fact Arabic (though the syntax follows Turkish grammar) further strengthens the suggestion that this is a deliberate choice of an expression, and not the reflection of lexical limitations.

25. See, for example, MA 4/4, where the setting of the anecdote (a marketplace, though in Baghdad) clearly adds an element of public humiliation to the immorality of consuming wine.

ʿĀşıkpaşazāde implies that "the state," taken in as abstract a sense as possible for that period (i.e., the ruler himself, as representing the office he held), was regarded as responsible for setting up, regulating, and collecting taxes from markets (APZ 9, 14–15, 102). It is nevertheless striking that other authors are completely silent on the issue of market organization and regulation. Perhaps the most common trait between all the scenes in which sources present members of the political elite as interacting with the population is conflict (discontent, injustice). Although rather counterintuitive, it is thus tempting to suggest that such market regulation was in fact, in fourteenth-century central Anatolia, a comparatively marginal source of conflict. A comparative look in the narrative sources for better-documented periods might give us some enlightening insight in this respect.

26. One *waqfiyya* (WQ21), for example, mentions the markets of the drapers (*bazzāzīn*), the grocers (*baqqālīn*), and the saddlers (*sarrājīn*) in Tokat. The *Manaqib al-ʿArifin* also refers to the market of the butchers in Konya (MA 3/486), and Ibn Baṭṭūṭa points out that the various trades are separately located in Konya's markets (IB 281).

27. A *waqfiyya* item (WQ14) points out a particular plot of land that is simultaneously bordered by the cap makers' market (*sūq al-qallānisīn*), that of the jewelers or goldsmiths (*ṣāʾighīn*), that of the butchers (*qaṣṣābīn*), and that of the grocers (*baqqālīn*). Unless this is a truly exceptional location or a very large plot, this does suggest relatively small-size "markets" (or rather market sections), located very close to each other.

28. WQ33. A number of sources (mostly *waqfiyyas*) refer to the shop of people they call *baqqāl* and locate them in urban marketplaces. Although this word is often translated as "greengrocer," the evidence already cited concerning the sale of produce taking place in gardens rather than in the city (see p. 151n) argues for an alternative translation. Edward William Lane, in *The Manners and Customs of the Modern Egyptians*, suggests "a seller of dry fruits," "a seller of eatables (of various kinds, and particularly of dried and salted provisions, cheese, etc.)," and even "a shop-keeper" (the latter is probably not correct, as MA 3/63 puts *baqqāls* in a list that also includes tailors and cloth sellers, as well as shopkeepers).

None of the passages that use the word *baqqāl* makes any reference to the goods they would sell (MA 3/373; WQ14; WQ21; WQ33), although Yûnus Emre points out that the trade of the *baqqāl* requires the use of scales (*terāzū* [YED 417:17]). Erdoğan Merçil, in his thorough and exhaustive though often uncritical catalog of references to crafts in Seljuk Anatolia (*Türkiye Selçukluları'nda meslekler*, 44), also points out that he was unable to identify the exact nature of their work beyond the fact that they sold rose oil and guessing that their trade might be akin to that of perfume sellers.

29. No shop endowed in a *waqfiyya* is presented as bordered by a residential building. In fact, these documents never explicitly refer to residential buildings (either as endowed property or as bordering elements), although almost a quarter of the geographical elements used to delineate shops are designated as "property" (*milk*) or "endowments" (*waqf*), whose nature is impossible to determine. One should also note that more than a third of the delineating elements are specifically designated as other shops. This suggests either that residential buildings were located in altogether separate sections of the city or, perhaps more simply, that they were the same as those housing the shops.

30. See, for example, MA 3/63.

31. IB 333. Likewise, RS 123, for example, employs the verb *bīrūn raftan* (to go outside) to refer to someone leaving a shop. Ibn Baṭṭūṭa also mentions that one of his fellow travelers settled down in an empty shop to watch over the horses on a winter night (IB 333).

32. Out of fifteen mentions, five specify the use of the shop (WQ33 includes references to a baker, a butcher, a leather stitcher, and two grocers; WQ20 mentions a baker), whereas ten others simply designate them as "shops" (WQ33; WQ8, three items; WQ9; WQ14, five items).

33. IB 334.

34. Many historians would point out the presence of *ahi*-led organizations as playing the role of guilds, though it is important to note that for all his mentions of the *ahi*s, Ibn Baṭṭūṭa only once refers to their relation to crafts: "Among them, the *akhī* is a man who gathers the people of his trade *and others* from among the unmarried young men and the celibates" (Wa al-akhī ʿindahum rajul yujtamaʿ ahl ṣanātih *wa ghayrahum* min al-shubbān al-ʿazāb wa al-mutajarridīn [emphasis added]). Such a formulation suggests that, insofar as Ibn Baṭṭūṭa's unique observation is based on a correct understanding of the organizations (something that we should probably not take for granted), the composition of *ahi*-led groups was at least broader than that of a craftsmen's guild (IB 261).

35. MA 3/89, 3/486.

36. MA 2/19, 4/25, 4/97; RS 123.

37. It might be of some relevance to point out a passage in which Yûnus Emre refers to the smells that spread around when a shop is open, betraying to those in the vicinity the goods it offers (YED 121:7).

38. See above, p. 151n.

39. This argument is in large part borrowed from Giovanni Rebora's *The Culture of the Fork*, which depicts a similar situation in medieval Italy.

40. For more on the place of bread in the diet of fourteenth-century Anatolians, see p. 85ff.

41. "Ögidür buğdayı bağlar suvarur" (GN 2:213a). Anthony Bryer mentions the existence of windmills in the Aegean region of Anatolia during the Byzantine thirteenth century, but says nothing concerning central Anatolia ("Means of Agricultural Production," 111). For the particular case of rice mills, see above, p. 29.

42. Bryer, "Means of Agricultural Production," 111. For a thorough survey of mills, see Hill, *History of Engineering*, 155–179.

The same article by Bryer also points out that, in order to compensate for the limited efficiency of the horizontal wheel, in Byzantine mills "development was lateral—to two- or three-'eyed' mills . . . where stones ran together on a bench above the same flume" (ibid.). Two references in *waqfiyya*s, one to a mill with a single stone (WQ20) and another to a mill of two "eyes" (the Turkish-language document uses the word *göz* [eye, WQ34]), suggest that the same system—including the horizontal position of the wheel—continued to prevail in the period discussed here.

The word *ik*, which appears among the mill parts described in the *Gharib-nama* (GN 2:102a–b, quoted later in this section), could in theory be translated as "gear" or "joint" (i.e., a mechanism designed to translate the movement of a vertical paddle wheel to a horizontal millstone). However, it can also mean "axle"—a much-likelier translation given the description that accompanies it.

43. In other words, the paddles driving the mill were not sitting in the water. This is fairly clear from GN 2:103a.

44. See, for example, WQ13, which refers to one "canal of the mill" as a geographical marker. There are also suggestions that devices existed to control—to some extent—the flow of water in such channels. See, for example, MA 8/39 (a metaphor referring to an *amīr-i āb* who is able to cut the flow of water to a mill) and MA 8/34 (which claims that at some periods of the year the wheels could be "drowned" by overflowing water).

45. GN 2:102a–103b. A much more succinct reference also appears as part of a description of bread-making process (GN 1:218b–219a). I would like to thank Dr. Helga Anetshofer for her precious help in fine-tuning the translation of this passage.

46. MA 3/298 also mentions the rhythmic sound that comes out of a working mill.

47. A passage from the *Manaqib al-ʿArifin* presents the building housing the milling machinery as large enough to allow one to dance around the millstone (MA 3/298).

48. A flour-based type of cookie, on which see p. 86.

49. See especially VN 65b.

50. See, for example, WQ4, WQ6, WQ8, WQ14, WQ17, WQ20, WQ31, WQ33, and WQ34. In the European context, Duby (*Rural Economy and Country Life*, 16–17) points out the large investment that the building of a mill would entail, but also its important contribution to economic expansion through the workforce it freed, when compared to hand-milling grain.

51. Incidentally, a passage of the *Manaqib al-ʿArifin* compares a body without knowledge to a city without water. The other comparisons that accompany this one (a person without abstinence is like a tree without fruits, and one without modesty is like a cauldron without salt) strongly suggest that, as undesirable as it was, a city "deprived of" water must have been a distinct possibility for the author of this text (MA 4/59).

52. VN 147a and MA 3/555, respectively. The desirability of running (rather than stagnant) water can be witnessed in the parallel that a passage of the *Gharib-nama* makes between *akar su* (running water) and *uçar kuş* (flying birds), which it presents, respectively, as the ideal drink and the ideal food (GN 2:3a).

53. Some later Ottoman endowments are exclusively dedicated to providing for the maintenance of a single fountain, and it is likely that endowments with a similarly narrow focus existed in the fourteenth century but did not survive to this day. Among extant *waqfiyyas* for the late-medieval period, fountains do appear but always as part of a broader array of services to the population. See, for example, WQ14 (which includes a fountain located near the *khānqāh* that is part of the same endowment), WQ8, MA 3/255 (where a man builds or rebuilds the fountain attached to a mausoleum as a token of gratitude for being accepted as a disciple of a Mavlāvī leader), and MA 6/6 (which apparently refers to the same fountain as the previous item, mentioning that it offered water freely for all, at a very small cost for the endowment).

For a thorough discussion of the interactions between patrons, manual workers, political networks, and plumbing in a different context (Istanbul at the turn of the eighteenth century), see the PhD dissertation of Deniz Karakaş in the Department of Art History, Binghamton University.

54. WQ8. Note also the location of a fountain, on the site of a mausoleum, in an example previously mentioned (MA 3/255, 6/6).

55. MA 3/114.

56. See below, p. 92ff.

57. VN 61a. The best study of the changes that Ottomans brought about in tax practices is a substantial article by Irène Beldiceanu-Steinherr, "Fiscalité et formes de possession de la terre arable dans l'Anatolie préottomane." It is based almost exclusively on a "backward reading" of Ottoman documents, and thus concentrates on practices that Beldiceanu-Steinherr can identify as having continued from earlier periods into Ottoman times. Such a line of approach can obviously say but little about practices that disappeared with the Ottoman conquest.

Rudi Paul Lindner (*Nomads and Ottomans*, esp. 52–54, 57, 63) also discusses taxes in pre-Ottoman Anatolia, but he concentrates on those levied on sheep.

58. See p. 32.

59. However, no obvious pattern of differences appears among the comparatively few cases surveyed here. The question would be worth pursuing in a combined analysis of this and other types of evidence that fall outside the boundaries of this study. Relevant evidence could, for example, include data from narrative political history in the various locales and from the type of documents (mostly cadastral surveys and *kānunnāmes*) used by Beldiceanu ("Fiscalité et formes de possession de la terre arable dans l'Anatolie préottomane").

Based only on the *waqfiyyas*, it seems that in very general terms those *waqfs* that drew revenues from individual pieces of land were concentrated in the Candar and Karaman emirates (respectively, northern and southern central Anatolia), around the 1330s and late 1360s. Table N.1 (located at the end of this notes section) shows the breakdown. *Waqfiyyas* not appearing in this table do not include agricultural real estate among their sources of revenue.

Beldiceanu's article is of no use in this respect, insofar as she does not take into account individual pieces of land: "Nous n'avons pris en considération ni les biens tels que maisons, boutiques et moulins, ni les parcelles de terres situées à proximité des villes" (We have taken into consideration neither properties such as houses, shops, and mills, nor land plots located near cities [296]).

60. APZ 15. The passage concerns the town of Karaca Hisar, which APZ presents as a Christian-ruled bone of contention between the bordering Ottoman and Germiyanid emirates. Lindner, in his field-expanding *Explorations in Ottoman Prehistory* (79), discusses the passage and, pointing out that Byzantine forces and influence were by that time long gone from the region, dismisses it entirely as fabrication, a ploy to justify early Ottoman attacks on the (Muslim) Germiyanid by inventing a Christian enemy where there was none. Although he is clearly right in pointing out that APZ's "Christian" enemy was not the Byzantine Empire, it is rather more difficult to understand why he does not consider the possibility that local Christians may have ruled the castle, acting as a buffer city-state between the Ottoman and Germiyan. Such a hypothesis would fully explain, rather than ignore, the anecdote's apparent incongruities. This is, indeed, the suggestion that Irène Beldiceanu-Steinherr puts forward in her review of Lindner's book ("Dans le labyrinthe des débuts de l'histoire ottoman: À propos d'un ouvrage de R. P. Lindner," 400).

61. BR 196.

62. BR 163.

63. BR 239. The "one hour's walk" figure comes from a scene in which a caravan makes itself safe by alighting one *farsang* farther away from an enemy army (the *farsang* is a unit of distance usually understood to correspond to one hour's walk, a distance that varies depending on the terrain type and the quality of the road). One should, however, note that this anecdote takes place in Syria and involves a Mongol army, two factors that might make it slightly less relevant for the fourteenth-century central Anatolian context (MA 3/374).

64. DN 91–92.

65. BR 204. For more about plunder, see the next section.

66. APZ 73. The possibility of course remains that the locations mentioned were only this—landmarks meant to identify the route to be taken rather than supply points—and thus that they do not correspond to logistically important points.

67. See, for example, APZ 100 and BR 142. The way this statement is presented in sources seems to suggest that this knowledge was obvious only to the military specialists and did not filter into the general consciousness.

68. Bozkurt Ersoy, "Kale-i Tavas (Tabae) 2007 yılı kazısı," 43, 50, 52. See also APZ 119.

69. APZ 100. See also Traian Stoianovich, "Le maïs dans les Balkans," 1039–1040, who points out one case where millet (an admittedly long-lasting grain) was discovered in edible shape after forty-two years of preservation. One could reasonably expect similar if not better figures in the drier central Anatolian climate.

70. APZ 39.

71. APZ 32 (in which an airtight siege is presented as unusual) and 64 (where trade takes place between the besieging force and the people living in the city). See also the section on garden destruction below.

72. This picture cannot be dismissed as the effect of biased sources unwilling to present "their" ruler's forces in a positive light, since authors who were politically more independent present the situation in a similar fashion. For example, despite its pro-Ilkhanid slant, the *Manaqib al-ʿArifin* twice mentions the plunder of the Konya region by the incoming Mongol forces (MA 3/165, 3/524).

73. See, for example, DN 59, 63.

74. APZ 153; DN 63, 102–103, 104; MA 3/165, 3/524.

75. APZ 153; BR 238; DN 95.

76. IB 277–278. See also DN 103, where military protection is given to a cereal convoy.

77. DN 91–92. See also APZ 153.

78. APZ 135.

79. The discussion of this anecdote and the argument I make about it are adapted from a paper presented at the International İznik Conference in September 2005 and published in the proceedings. Nicolas Trépanier, "İznik, the Gardens, and the Starving Enemy?"

80. "ʿAlî Bag bā umarāʾ mushavarrat payvast kih dar shahr bi-cha ṭarīq madkhul sāzad va jang bar cha manvāl andāzad. Ikhtiyār bar ān āmad kih dar ṭaraf-i sharqī, miyān-i shahr va vilāyat bi-nashīnand va bi-kharābī-i mazrūʿāt va qaṭʿ-i darakhtān va qamʿ va qalʿ-i bāgh va būstān mashghūl shavand" (BR 159–160). I wish to thank Eliza Tasbihi for her help in fine-tuning my translation of this passage.

81. The core Iznik anecdote is from APZ 22, although the number of troops is extrapolated from what seems to be a different telling of the same story in the Anonymous Giese (various manuscripts give either forty or one hundred troops, which is at least enough for us to get an order of magnitude; see Halil İnalcık, "Osmān Ghāzī's Siege of Nicaea and the Battle of Bapheus," in *Ottoman Emirate*, edited by Zachariadou, 91). Con-

cerning the Crusader siege, see Bernard S. Bachrach, "Some Observations on Administration and Logistics of the Siege of Nicaea"; and Foss, *Nicaea*, 47.

82. On the central character of bread and meat in meals, see below.

83. Robin Osborne, *Classical Landscape with Figures: The Ancient Greek City and Its Countryside*, 154. See also Scott Redford, with Gil J. Stein, Naomi F. Miller, and Denise C. Hodges, *The Archaeology of the Frontier in the Mediaeval Near East*, 22–23.

84. See p. 24ff.

85. This, of course, does not mean that such discussion never took place. As much as they are decided on the field, debates over the Boston Red Sox and the New York Yankees spread far and wide beyond the teams' players and shareholders.

86. I could find only one passage describing, from the part of a member of the elite, actions that may have elicited peasant gratitude, Ibn Baṭṭūṭa's observations about Tavas, which I mentioned in note 68 above (IB 277–278). The very fact that the traveler takes the pain of describing this practice strongly suggests its unusual character.

CHAPTER THREE

1. I should emphasize that I use the word *consumption* here in its most literal meaning, and not as a reference to the recent historiographical trend of consumption studies. This is by no means a criticism of this fascinating new approach, but rather the admission that it is nearly impossible to apply it in a context where almost all evidence is anecdotal and impressionistic. For a thorough introduction to consumption studies in the Ottoman context, see Donald Quataert, ed. *Consumption Studies and the History of the Ottoman Empire, 1550–1922: An Introduction.*

2. The narrative sources I consulted offer only one hint that goes against this suggestion, ʿĀşıkpaşazāde's reference to someone working as a "kebab-turner" in a *bozahane* (a parent of cafés and taverns, where the mildly alcoholic drink *boza* was sold). This passage, however, is set in Bursa, probably well into the fifteenth century, and may reflect a historical change rather than undermining the point I make here. For more on *bozahanes*, see Selçuk, "State and Society in the Marketplace."

In the more or less contemporary Mamluk Cairo, Amalia Levanoni ("Food and Cooking during the Mamluk Era: Social and Political Implications," 210–211) mentions that urban lower classes overwhelmingly purchased cooked meals, whereas the elite preferred home cooking because it allowed them to avoid a long list of foul adulterants that market cooks included willingly (such as impure meats) or unwillingly (from insects to bodily fluids) in the dishes they sold. One should note, however, that Cairo was then a much larger and more cramped city than any in Anatolia and that Levanoni does not cover the habits of peasants, who constitute the majority of people discussed here.

3. See p. 151n.

4. See p. 48ff.

5. MA 4/23; IB 342.

6. WQ20, WQ33. Whereas most shops appearing in *waqfiyyas* are presented using unspecific terms (*ḥānūt*, i.e., "shop"), these two cases specify *ḥānūt al-khabbāz* (literally, "baker's shop"), thus strongly hinting at the presence of architectural characteristics that made these particular shops more specialized than others, possibly because of the presence of ovens.

7. MA 3/209. The *Vilayat-nama* includes a few passages that, at least indirectly, refer to bread making in villages, but none of them specifies the identity of the people preparing the dough or baking it (rather using a third-person plural pronoun without referent). Their formulation opens up the possibility that these people may have been nonprofessionals selected by the community. See, for example, VN 45b and 65b–66a.

8. This would explain, for example, the mention of an oven (*furn*) as a revenue-producing property for a *waqf* (WQ24). It also offers a way to interpret the statement that Ibn Baṭṭūṭa makes about Anatolia in general, saying that in this region men would bring him and his fellow travelers bread "sent by" women, thus hinting at a family-based rather than commercial production of bread (since in a purely commercial operation, there would be no obvious justification for the separate mention of senders and carriers, a fortiori a gender-based one [IB 256]). On the same issue, see p. 73ff.

9. MA 3/459. See also MA 3/245, 3/490.

10. "Nav ʿarūsī rā bi-khāna avurda budam var as vajh-i kharjī żurūrāt-i ʿaẓīm dāshtam" (RS 90).

11. ʿĀşıkpaşazāde mentions, in an obvious attempt at praising the early Ottomans, that their first ruler created such an atmosphere of trust in the market of Bilecik that the Christians would send women there (APZ 9). Although this seems to suggest that the market was a predominantly male location, the emphasis put on the importance of trust might in fact reflect concerns unique to the especially chaotic Ottoman-Germiyan borderlands in the beginning of the fourteenth century, and may thus not be fully applicable to central Anatolia for the century as a whole.

12. Interestingly, even in an anecdote where conflict occurs over the use of food stored in the house of relatively poor peasants, both of the contenders are female (an older woman and her daughter-in-law [VN 46b]). In both MA 3/340 (urban upper class) and VN 65b (village gentry), a woman is depicted as the "go-to person" for up-to-date information on the status of the house's stockpiles.

13. VN 64b.

14. See, for example, GN 1:104a for dried fruits.

15. Of wine, for example (MA 8/80), or of *ablūj* (sugar [MA 3/94]).

16. VN 46b, 49b, 65b; YED 229–230. Al-ʿUmarī also seems to refer to domestic storage when he says that the inhabitants of Anatolia make reserves of jerked meat (*qadīd*), oils (*adhān*), and wine, then do not come out of their houses during the winter (AU 311).

17. Redford et al., *Archaeology of the Frontier*, 68; Andrew Fairbairn and Sachihiro Omura, "Archaeological Identification and Significance of ÉSAG (Agricultural Storage Pits) at Kaman-Kalehöyük," 17–20.

18. GN 1:178a, 2:64a; MA 3/592. This might in fact be the same thing that is called,

in the *Vilayat-nama*, "un evi" (flour house [VN 65b]). See also above, p. 59, for a discussion of the logistics of military defense structures, another form of storage that involved grain provisioning directly.

19. MA 7/31. See also MA 2/8.

20. One passage of the *Gharib-nama* (GN 1:251b–252b) in fact simply states that the spicy taste (*acı*) makes the eater's tongue and mouth hot but is good for the body. The latter characteristic might be a reference to spices' use as preservatives.

21. MA 3/40. Ice may have been used for cold storage, and perhaps as an ingredient in refreshing drinks or desserts. Redford (*Landscape and the State*, 62) points out the documented existence of two or three icehouses in Konya, dating to Seljuk times, that included structures to capture water into ice in cold weather and then retain it in that form for several months.

22. See, for example, MA 8/79 and IB 336. Commercial treaties also contain provisions concerning the exportation of dried vegetables from the emirates of the Aegean coast to Venetian lands (Zachariadou, *Trade and Crusade*, 59, 155). Although their status as export products might be unique to the Aegean region, it seems probable that both fruits and vegetables were preserved in dried form in central Anatolia as well, if only for local consumption.

Perhaps the most obvious absence from this list is that of salting, which may indeed not have been practiced. As we will see later in this chapter, a number of references suggest that a good dish had to include salt, short of which it was deemed incomplete. There is, however, no reference to anything deemed *too* salty, a judgment one would expect to see at least on a few occasions if food preservation by salting was widely practiced. Though it might have been used in combination with drying, at least for meat, it is nevertheless striking to see that the (rather numerous) references to salt in the sources almost exclusively concentrate on the taste-giving properties of this substance.

23. BR 207.

24. GN 1:147b.

25. BR 285.

26. APZ 159. Although this anecdote falls outside the scope of this study, it aptly exemplifies both the ability for one to find employment in a trade where there obviously were no family antecedents and the personal downfall that working "below one's birth" incarnated.

27. See, for example, MA 8/21, 8/85; and VN 100b.

28. In that respect, it might be significant that one *waqfiyya* (WQ20) provides a salary for someone who was to concurrently perform the duties of *mu'adhdhin*, cook, doorman, and sweeper. Since these appear as part of a description of an employee's duties, they can reasonably be assumed to correspond to his actual occupation. However, it is not impossible that such titles may, in other instances, have been sinecures, or entailed occupations more prestigious than a literal interpretation would suggest.

29. Of the latter four, three in fact receive only marginally less, as shown in Table N.2 (located at the end of this notes section).

30. Respectively, MA 8/85 and 1/21. The latter passage, without being completely explicit, suggests that the two recruits were actually expected to continue practicing the trade in which they were involved before becoming disciples.

31. As opposed, that is, to the preexistence of abstract principles that would have guided the practical organization of the order, as today's members of these organizations are fond to claim. For more on the development of Mavlāvī rituals and symbols, see Nicolas Trépanier, "Starting without Food: Fasting and the Early Mawlawī Order."

32. GN 2:35a.

33. RS 123. This is one of three versions of the same story, in which a saintly ascetic lives off the "juice" that is produced in such shops. Although this specific version (which, unlike the others, is set in Damascus) is the only one that includes the word *ṭabbākh* (cook), the nature of the variations from one version to the next suggests that this was indeed a type of shop that would have been well known in Konya. Other versions can be found in MA 2/19 and 4/25.

34. MA 8/85.

35. VN 49b is such an exception, depicting a mother-in-law cooking while her son's wife is outside washing clothes.

36. IB 342 ("half a sheep"), RS 69 (unwashed tripe), MA 7/31 (what appear to be carrots and beets). Conversely, the only reference that my sources contain to ready-to-eat dishes that would be sold in a public place, roasted meat in a *bozahane*, might in fact reflect a later, western Anatolian, situation (APZ 159).

37. This late-medieval central Anatolian custom therefore stands in contrast with the practice (which has become increasingly common with the democratization of gourmet food in recent decades) to invite friends not only to share a meal, but also to participate in the cooking process.

38. VN 156a–b.

39. As a matter of fact, if Ibn Baṭūṭṭa is correct in claiming the widespread character of shared living quarters for young, unmarried craftsmen (IB 261), these institutions may have played a role in counterbalancing the social fragmentation that would naturally result from such overemphasis on the household as a social unit, in a fashion reminiscent of compulsory military service. This extrafamilial esprit de corps would, in turn, be fully congruent with the seemingly common appearance of *ahi*-led groups as urban militias in that period.

40. MA 3/172; VN 111b. In the latter case, the manuscript included as facsimile in annex of the 1995 edition (which I used in researching this book) presents the man himself as cooking, whereas other manuscripts add a short phrase attributing the cooking to his elderly mother (the man's role being limited to bringing the cookies to his religious master). The discrepancy between manuscripts on this point might be a significant indication of change in gender attitudes, or simply a transcription error.

41. VN 156a–b.

42. See, for example, VN 46b, 49b; and MA 7/31.

43. VN 100b, 147a; MA 3/392, 3/395; WQ14, WQ20. As Ayşil Tükel Yavuz points out

("The Concepts That Shape Anatolian Seljuq Caravanserais," 87–88), even caravanserais didn't have rooms that were exclusively dedicated to cooking.

44. VN 147a. This is a reference to the *maṭbakh* that apparently belonged to the early Bektaşi convent, located in what probably was a small town at the time. Whereas urban *maṭbakh*s may have been equipped with "running water," this passage nevertheless shows that such a feature was not a defining element of this type of architectural structure.

45. It might not have even been limited to a single place in the house, if we are to follow the mention (in reference to what seems to have been an upper-class household) of a nanny who was cleaning vegetables "in her own room" (*dar khalvat-i khūd* [MA 7/31]; the expression can also be translated as "in private," though the two translations are not mutually incompatible).

Living quarters carved into Cappadocian rock, in which the walls have been preserved since Byzantine times, allow us to identify certain rooms as kitchens because they preserved the architectural features that characterize cooking areas. Such features are all but invisible from most archaeological excavations, since walls are rarely preserved. On this subject, see Kalas, "Byzantine Kitchen," 109–112.

46. This explains, for example, why a *waqfiyya* has to mention a *furn* and "a bread house" (*bayt khubz*) as separate architectural structures (WQ21). See also WQ24 and MA 3/536.

47. Two references in the Turkish-language *Vilayat-nama* merely tell us that a *tanūr* could easily be large enough to fit a standing adult (VN 66b, 152a). The Persian-language *Manaqib al-ʿArifin* describes the same structure as something that could be used for drying newly written pages (MA 3/124), burning paper (MA 3/541), baking bread (MA 3/209), and producing an at least limited amount of ambient heat (MA 3/108).

48. Maurits N. van Loon, "Architecture and Stratigraphy," 43–44; Moore, *Tille Höyük 1*, 32, 19–55; McNicoll, *Taşkun Kale*, 9. For ethnological observations by archaeologists, see Bradley J. Parker and M. Barış Uzel, "The Tradition of *Tandır* Cooking in Southeastern Anatolia: An Ethnoarchaeological Perspective," 7–8, 28.

49. As Parker and Uzel point out, "There are no openings that would allow pots or trays to be inserted, the heat cannot be directed to a burner or smoker, there are no racks or access points that might allow skewered foods to be cooked, etc." ("Tradition of *Tandır* Cooking," 29).

50. See, for example, BR 219; MA 3/117 (with a reference to *pukhta*—meat, probably boiled); VN 94a (where the cauldron's lid is sealed off), and VN 100b, 121b (where the food seems to be left to cook for the whole night, something that is easier to imagine with a sealed cauldron that retains moisture than in an oven).

51. VN 49b.

52. The plentiful number and contemporary character of both types of structures are obvious even to the most novice reader of archaeological literature. See, for example, Theresa Goell, "Samosata Archaeological Excavations, Turkey, 1967," 98–99; Timothy Matney et al., "Tenth Preliminary Report on Excavations at Ziyaret Tepe (Diyarbakır

Province), 2007 Seasons [*sic*]," 510–511, 518; McNicoll, *Taşkun Kale*, 9, 11; Moore, *Tille Höyük*, 19–55; and van Loon, "Architecture and Stratigraphy," 43–44.

It is worth noting that the only specialist attempts I could find at a comprehensive analysis of the use of hearths and *tandırs* and the way they related to each other are limited to twentieth-century ethnoarchaeological observations. A thorough synthesis of the medieval material, which would take into account such factors as spatial relationships between these structures and the architecture as well as pottery finds (which tells a lot, among other things, about cooking techniques), remains sorely needed.

53. IB 337–338; MA 3/108, 3/448. In an archaeological context that is slightly outside and earlier than the scope of this book, Redford et al. (*Archaeology of the Frontier*, 48) describe a type of "double-chambered ovens" that seem to have been used for heating only, with no apparent cooking use. They do not, however, fit the description that textual sources give of the *bukhārī*.

54. See, for example, MA 9/8; and DN 91–92, 95. Written sources do not refer to frying as a cooking technique. As for archaeological remains, there do not seem to be any remains of metal frying pans, although the reader should remember that metal objects, especially thin ones, decay relatively rapidly underground. Ceramic frying pans certainly existed in other contexts (see, for example, Paul Arthur, "Pots and Boundaries: On Cultural and Economic Areas between late Antiquity and the Early Middle Ages," 19). However, no archaeologist identifies any of the large number of published cooking-ware examples taken from medieval Anatolian excavations I have seen as a frying pan.

55. See, for example, MA 5/30 as well as APZ 54 and DN 59.

56. Most promising in this respect is the ongoing work of archaeologist Joanita Vroom. See, in particular, her "Medieval Ceramics and the Archaeology of Consumption in Eastern Anatolia." She points out, among other things, that Anatolian examples confirm to some extent the hypothesis put forward by Paul Arthur in "Pots and Boundaries," according to whom the preferred cooking techniques in regions such as Anatolia, where sheep were the main source of meat, involved braising and evaporation in shallower, wider-opened casseroles as well as the use of sauces, as opposed to the pig-based diets of northern and central Europe, where stews were cooked in taller, smaller, narrow-mouthed pots.

For more about medieval Anatolian archaeology, see p. 145ff.

57. VN 49b, 133b. The first must clearly be translated as "meal," whereas the second might in fact have been intended to refer to cooked dishes or even "food" in the broadest sense.

58. Respectively, MA 8/19 and 3/548. The overwhelming majority of passages that we would take as containing references to meals make such direct mention of food or the vessels containing it. The term *öyün* (literally, "what is eaten at a given mealtime") appears only once, in a passage that strengthens the argument presented here by the fragmented depiction of meals it conveys: "Or did I make you hungry by eating your *öyün*?" (YED 417:10).

59. A modern parallel might be, for example, "the morning commute": most of our contemporaries will readily discuss events that occurred during or surrounding the trip

from their homes to their work, placing them in context by using references to parts of the event ("when I got on the bus," "while I was on the bridge") rather than to the event as an independent concept ("during my morning commute").

60. Respectively, MA 4/47 and VN 43b–44b. There are also other, more indirect, suggestions that fresh fruits would regularly be consumed outside regular mealtimes; see, for example, VN 188a and MA 3/457.

61. VN 60b. See also DN 58.

62. MA 3/408.

63. MA 6/7. There might also have been informal food consumption during short stops while traveling (see, for example, MA 6/15).

64. AE 9/97, 13/134; VN 5b, 22b, 33b, 90b, 107b, 127a, 156a; WQ8. It is possible that the Persian word *naṭʿ* designated the same object. *Naṭʿ* occurs twice, once in the guest tent of a nomadic grandee (BR 347) and once in the private house of the leader of a dervish order (MA 8/79). The latter case, however, is problematic since it mentions a vessel filled with water (in which dry apricots are soaked to be rehydrated) that is left *under* the *naṭʿ*—a position difficult to imagine if the object was a piece of leather usually folded between the meals.

65. Obviously, such detail occurs in the prescriptive sections of these documents. Yet far from making the information found in *waqfiyyas* less reliable, the prescriptive character of the passages in fact might make it *more* trustworthy, since any discrepancy between these prescriptions and their application in real life is likely to have arisen from the clash between, on the one hand, a prescription of what was the usual practice and, on the other hand, a failure to provide as many meals as prescribed. In other words, even if we assume, following some of the manuscripts of ʿĀşıkpaşazāde's chronicle (APZ 159), that the institutions thus funded were not always run in accordance with the stipulations of the *waqfiyyas*, it is rather unlikely that this failure was due to their promising to offer more meals than the socially accepted standards and then falling short by limiting themselves to an adherence to these very same standards.

66. WQ8, WQ14, WQ18, WQ20.

67. WQ20.

68. WQ8. It is important to note, however, that this is an exceptional mention, since this level of detail about the types of food to be offered, often appearing in later Ottoman *waqfiyyas*, is generally absent from fourteenth-century documents.

69. QN 16–24. A passage of the *Risala-yi Sipahsalar* quotes a verse from Rūmī that suggests that the evening meal was taken around the time of the sunset prayer ("Chū namāz-i shām har kas bi-nahād chirāgh ū khʷānī" (When [it is the time of] the sunset prayer, everybody puts up the lamp and the food). Given the direct opposition of this statement with all the other evidence found in fourteenth-century Anatolian sources, this in all likelihood reflects a literary tradition rather than the daily environment of its author. This example can thus serve as a warning against too uncritical an acceptance of Persian poetry as a reflection of daily practice.

70. "Asr olındı ve taam getürdiler" (VN 22b).

71. "Ikindü vaktında nöbet ururlar kim halk gelüb taam yiyeler" (APZ 8).

72. IB 261.

73. See, for example, this typical passage from *Bazm u Razm*: "He set up the assembly of pleasure, asked for wine. The singers sat down and the wine-bearers stood up. The water of cups [i.e., wine] erased the dust of grief from the courtyard of the chests" (BR 178–179). The main concern of the author, here, may have been to show his ability to create literary flourishes or praise the lifestyle of his patron, but probably not to accurately describe a scene that he did not in fact witness. Many chronicles surveyed for this book include similar scenes, but none with such high frequency as *Bazm u Razm*, whose title, incidentally, translates as "Banquet and battle."

Religious celebrations, on the other hand, are somewhat more reliably documented, and I will discuss them in the last chapter of this book.

74. See, for example, MA 3/158. On most occasions, references appear through the mention of specific dishes, but few passages using the term *şeker* (literally, "sugar") actually seem to refer to the conceptual category of "sweets" (see, for example, YED 11:7 and 132:2). Fruits, however, do not seem to have been considered as part of the sweet foods that made a festive meal stand out of the ordinary.

75. MA 3/411.

76. VN 10b.

77. See below. Provisions concerning particular expenses to make *ḥalwāʾ* for religious celebrations appear in a number of *waqfiyya*s. See, for example, WQ8 and WQ20.

78. Ibid. These elements, and particularly the latter point, smoothly fit the association of fatty and sweet with pleasure that will be discussed later in this chapter.

79. See, for example, RS 105 and WQ8.

80. Examples of these elements can be found in DN 70 (music), MA 8/41 (poetry), and MA 3/552 and DN60 (wine and *nuql*, the latter word referring to sweetmeats of unspecified nature that often appear in passages that refer to wine consumption).

81. The *Manaqib al-ʿArifin* makes three mentions of foods of above-average quality, twice using the expression "ṭaʿāmhāy-i nafīs" (superb foods). One occurrence serves to praise the cooking aptitudes of a dervish (MA 8/85), whereas the other refers to the particularly high level of quality for the foods served on a special occasion (MA 3/244). It also uses the expression "kh^{w}ān-i khāṣ" (special/select food) likewise in relation to the food served in a festive banquet. All three of these occurrences remain general to the point of meaninglessness, as they refer to "foods" rather than any particular dish.

82. On the conceptual separation between sweets and fruits, see p. 95.

83. As opposed, that is, to the situation of most Western countries today, where even fairly poor individuals can afford to acquire more food than they could possibly consume—at least if they are willing to sacrifice on quality and nutritional value. Fourteenth-century central Anatolia, in other words, offered no equivalent of instant ramen noodles.

84. Levanoni, discussing the contemporary but better-documented context of Mamluk Cairo, also observes that "the banquet was a social event emphasizing the shared status and cultural background of the participants" ("Food and Cooking during the Mamluk Era," 211).

85. MA 3/37, 6/12; IB 268, 304. Ibn Baṭṭūṭa makes similar observations about a religious scholar whom, he claims, he almost mistook for a king (IB 297) and about an *ahi*-led group (IB 264). Strictly speaking, none of these are members of the political elite, but, as we are about to see, his reference to a king's appearance is quite significant in the former case, whereas the latter case may have been an unusual occurrence.

86. See especially MA 3/265 and RS 86–87. Although sources offer no further precision on what the words *takht* and *masnad* might refer to, the former may have been a table-like raised platform (rather than a "throne," a common but probably anachronistic translation for this word) and the latter a cushion, with the understanding that other people in attendance would sit on nothing thicker than carpets.

Some passages use the word *ṣadr*, which refers to the abstract concept of a "place of honor" without entailing any particular physical object or location (see, for example, MA 3/37).

87. IB 268, 276, 297, 341; MA 3/548; RS 85. On seating arrangements and their symbolic meaning, see also Levanoni, "Food and Cooking during the Mamluk Era," 218.

Only one source depicts food being set on the table before the partakers come and sit, a passage that at first glance may seem to refer to some unspecified elite class, but might in fact first and foremost reflect the image that the lower classes had of palace rituals (GN 1:146b).

If we postulate, among the *beylik* elite, a parallel between the (fairly well-documented) relative places of the Persian and Turkish languages and the (largely unknown) relative places of Seljuk court culture and more "popular" influences, then the Turkish translations of the *Qabus-nama* strengthen this hypothesis. A passage of the original Persian text stating that a ruler should not be served before his guests is properly translated in all but the earliest Turkish translation (first half of the fourteenth century [QN 17–25]). It thus leaves us with the impression that the translation arising from the earliest, least Persianized setting is also the only one to suggest that the serving order was not an issue (since the food is already on the table when people arrive). In other words, both the *Gharib-nama* and this early translation of the *Qabus-nama* suggest (without by any means proving) that lower classes may have followed the opposite practice, setting down the food before the partakers sat down.

88. VN 22b, for example, simply mentions that two religious masters "ate with a few dervishes" (bir nice dervişle yidiler), without adding seating-related detail. This contrast cannot be due to the different nature and focus of the various sources, since it is apparent even between passages depicting meals among the political elite and passages depicting meals among dervish brotherhoods within the same source, the *Manaqib al-ʿArifin*.

89. Concerning changes in food-related rituals over the *longue durée* in Sufi orders, see Trépanier, "Starting without Food."

90. GN 1:146b, 147b, 2:66b; MA 3/94, 8/39.

91. IB 288, 336; MA 3/340; VN 5b, 6a, 66b. In MA 3/305, a ruler's wife seems to send food without bringing it in person. Concerning food giving and hospitality, see also p. 92ff.

92. A rare reference to women-only activities can be found in the depiction, in the *Manaqib al-ʿArifin*, of a group of women heading to entertain themselves in a suburban garden (MA 4/43).

93. MA 3/270.

94. See p. 77.

95. AE 9/7; MA 8/93; RS 85; VN 5b, 22b, 156a.

96. GN 1:146b; MA 3/101, 3/457, 3/548; VN 133b, 156a. This seems to occur, at least in formal meals, throughout the social hierarchy.

The idea of beginning a meal with a conventional signal is not without parallels with the fast-breaking collective dinners (*ifṭār*) held during the month of Ramadan, when the fasters sit patiently in front of their ready meal until the call to the sunset prayer allows them to start eating. The word *ifṭār* is indeed used in both my Turkish- and my Persian-language sources, although in many cases the context makes it clear that it means nothing more than to start eating, with no particular reference to fasting—let alone the religious fast of Ramadan (on which see p. 108).

97. VN 5b, 22b, 64b, 65a, 66b, 133b, 134a. Yûnus Emre (YED 184:17) also uses the term *sahha*, which, according to Tatcı (the text's modern editor), is a formula wishing good health addressed to one who is drinking something. This interpretation is perfectly compatible with the use Yûnus makes of this term, which, however, constitutes a hapax legomenon in this text.

98. GN 1:146b; VN 133b. A passing reference to the use of spoons for eating appears in the latest Turkish translation of the *Qabus-nama* (dated 1432 [QN 24]). However, an earlier translation (which Birnbaum attributes to the second half of the fourteenth century) adds an original passage that tells the reader to "eat the big bite with three fingers" (büyük lokma [. . .] üç parmahuñla yi [QN 21]), in a formulation suggesting that the size of the bite imposed a variation in the number of fingers used (rather than imposing the use of fingers as opposed to some utensil). The *Vilayat-nama*'s reference to washing one's hands (VN 67b) *after* the meal is perfectly coherent with a pattern where rural classes and the earlier Ottoman courtiers tended to eat with their fingers, whereas later Ottoman courtiers adopted a more common use of spoons.

The use of spoons and fingers need not, of course, be mutually exclusive. It would make perfect sense that spoons were used for some foods (and not only for liquid foods, if we can trust Ibn Baṭṭūṭa's report of having seen a man drawing *ḥashīsh* powder from a bag with a spoon [IB 351–352]) and fingers for some other. It is also clear that bread was used to pick up food (AE 10/99–102, 11/113).

There is, however, no reference to the table use of knives (their only culinary use appearing in sources takes place when a character snacks on a cucumber while sitting outdoors [VN 60b]) or to forks, which probably were already in use in the upper reaches of Byzantine society during the same period.

99. MA 3/548. It is also possible that licking a plate was deemed socially acceptable. This is at least what Rūmī is depicted as doing after consuming a mix of excessively sour *māst* (on which see p. 87) that causes blisters to appear on the tongue of the baffled narrator (MA 3/340). It is not, however, impossible that this reference to licking plates—the

only one I could find—was in fact intended to add humor (an extremely difficult element to identify in historical texts) to this depiction of the hero's saintly powers, without implying that this was normal or socially acceptable behavior, especially given that the anecdote takes place in his private house.

100. Several sources explicitly mention a chronological separation between the period when discussion is held and the period when food is eaten. Such is the case for Ibn Baṭṭūṭa's account of telling various rulers about his travels before they invite him to eat (IB 300, 341) and of the *Vilayat-nama*'s two references to discussions that take place only after the food is eaten and the table setup taken away (VN 22b, 156b). Although the *Manaqib al-ʿArifin* refers to two characters discussing during a meal (MA 3/548), one should note that the argument occurs precisely because one of the characters inquires about the reasons that prevent the other from eating. Although this passage may indicate that complete silence was not expected, it does not really contradict the argument proposed here insofar as this verbal exchange concentrates on the practicalities of the meal rather than constituting any form of polite conversation.

A passage of the original *Qabus-nama* states that the ruler should always converse while eating ("bar sar-i khʷān bā mardumān hadith hamī kun"), and its Turkish translations also seem to confirm this point of view. Although the earlier three translations keep the spirit of the phrase intact (and a translation's adherence to its original text does not need to be explained away), the later two make the exact opposite statement ("while eating never talk" [QN 17–25]). Birnbaum, the editor of the text, suggests that this may be the result of a misreading of the original ("namī kun" rather than "hamī kun," "never do" rather than "always do"). Although this is not impossible, and while there seems to be a filiation between these two translations, it remains that the slip is a rather obvious one and could hardly have gone unnoticed (let alone repeated by two translators) if it had contradicted both the original text *and* the rules of etiquette that the translators experienced on a daily basis.

101. It is in fact unclear whether BR 178–179 refers to a drinking session or an actual meal; RS 85, on the other hand, specifies that having such a musical accompaniment was a "tradition of the sultan," suggesting that the author did not expect his readers to be familiar with the practice.

102. All the references in the *Manaqib al-ʿArifin* place it before the meal, presenting the scene in a way suggesting that this was the normal order of things (MA 3/39, 3/101, 3/204, 3/264). The situation is more confused in the *Risala-yi Sipahsalar*, where three references that immediately follow each other depict scenes where the *samāʿ* is held *after* eating. In one of these cases the formulation suggests this was the normal way of things (RS 86–87), in another it does not seem to be expected that way (perhaps because it begins after food service—when partakers should be eating—rather than after food consumption [RS 85]), and in the third it is presented in a matter-of-fact tone that does not suggest anything about the normality of putting things in this order (RS 87). The *Manaqib al-ʿArifin* and the *Risala-yi Sipahsalar* are extremely close in origin and share a significant amount of contents. But although the *Risala* is usually taken as one of the sources of the *Manaqib*, their relationship, as I mention in the appendix, deserves to be reexamined. This discrep-

ancy between the two sources, which might reflect a change in Mavlāvī practice between their respective redactions, should be taken into account as part of this reevaluation.

103. BR 217; MA 3/45, 8/19, 8/93; VN 156a–b. Ibn Baṭṭūṭa further mentions dancing, singing, and *samāʿ* among the *ahi*-led groups (IB 261, 264, 273–274, 274, 318–319). He also refers to Qur'an recitations both among these groups and in courtly settings, at least on special occasions such as religious celebrations or the arrival of a noted guest, that is, himself (IB 273–274, 307, 318–319, 341). One should note, however, that for both types of activities, his references follow rather standard formulations that raise some serious questions about the reliability of each individual reference—even if they might depict scenes that he indeed witnessed on several occasions.

104. Respectively, VN 37a–b; BR 94, 156, as well as YED 95:10; and GN 1:139b.

105. For example, the mention of "fattened duck and rice *mufalfal*" (on the latter, see note 159 below) appears as a (sharply) contrasting term to fasting (MA 3/254; another version of the same story appears in RS 100–101 but mentions only "duck and rice"), and Ahi Evren serves "saffron rice and white rice" in a semiphantasmagoric Meccan setting (AE 9/97). See also MA 3/101 (rice served in a golden bowl at a ruler's table) and 3/270 (rice served in an amir's house), as well as IB 300 (where the traveler Ibn Baṭṭūṭa mentions a "Turkish" ruler who serves him rice, flour, and butter in a sheep's stomach).

A number of passages leave us with the impression that rice was a regular occurrence in *zāwiyas* (dervish lodges). See, among others, Ibn Baṭṭūṭa's mention of rice cooked with butter in one of these institutions (IB 348) and the provision of WQ21 that allocates money to buy rice for consumption on Fridays.

This apparent inconsistency with rice's luxury character remains an inconsistency only as long as we assume that all *zāwiyas* were associated with poverty. This association should probably be reconsidered, in part because it squarely contradicts the use that narrative sources make of rice, but also because of internal evidence within the *waqfiyyas*. Note, for example, the presence, among the belongings of a *zāwiya*, of three metal trays (*ṭabaq* [WQ8]), which are in other passages clearly associated with wealth (DN 67; MA 1/11, 3/113).

On rice production, see p. 28ff.

106. This is especially apparent from the fact that this dish occurs in two completely unrelated source traditions, Ibn Baṭṭūṭa, on the one hand (IB 268), and the *Risala-yi Sipahsalar* and *Manaqib al-ʿArifin*, on the other (RS 123; MA 3/10, 4/25).

107. In all likelihood, the word covered a number of variations on the basic principle: a liquid in which bread or other solid food bits (or both) were soaked. Thus, whereas Ibn Baṭṭūṭa describes what he ate in Eğridir as *tharīd* on top of which lentils, butter, and sugar were added (IB 268), other references describe it rather as a mix of feet or head stock with crumbled bread (MA 3/10, 4/25). In fact, in some cases the word *tharīd* is used as nothing more than a part of the verb *tharīd kardan* (the transitive verb *to crumble*), used, for example, in describing Rūmī crumbling old bread in *māst* (MA 3/340).

In her survey of the vocabulary used in medieval Arabic cookbooks, Nawal Nasrallah defines *tharīd* as "broken pieces of bread sopped in rich broth with meat, mostly on the bone, and vegetables," and calls it "the most popular dish ever served at the tables of high and low[; it] is what they put in it and how they serve it that elevate it or keep it a humble dish" (*Annals of the Caliph's Kitchens*, 618–619). She does not, however, refer to the religious connotations it may have had in the contexts she discusses.

108. See, for example, DN 95 and VN 85a.

109. See, for example, VN 37a–b, 146a; and MA 3/89, 3/581. Notice also beef's absence from DN 95, where a feast is said to include "lamb, mutton, goose and duck."

110. As I pointed out above, statistical analysis of bovine bones from the medieval layers of Anatolian excavations suggests that meat production was at best a secondary motivation for raising cattle (far behind providing traction power for plowing and, to a lesser extent, producing milk). Comparing this with earlier periods, Hongo evokes increased "concentrations of complete or almost complete cattle limb bones especially in pits" ("Patterns of Animal Husbandry in Central Anatolia," 64) and notes that an "increase in heavy chop marks . . . indicates both an increase of heavy duty cutting tools and a change in butchery practices" ("Patterns of Animal Husbandry, Environment, and Ethnicity," 299). Unfortunately, she does not elaborate any further on the nature of such practices.

111. MA 4/101.

112. One should, for example, note the presence of duck (*baṭṭ*) as a rich man's meal (MA 3/254; RS 100), as well as a reference to both ducks and geese as part of a delicious feast (DN 95). This hypothesis is further strengthened if we are to take a reference to flying birds ("uçar kuş" [GN 2:3a]) as an ideal or especially exquisite type of food. Hongo ("Patterns of Animal Husbandry in Central Anatolia," 81–82, and "Patterns of Animal Husbandry, Environment, and Ethnicity," 283) is the only archaeologist I could find who mentions chicken eggs.

Passing references also suggest that pork may have been commercially available in Konya (MA 3/380).

113. Tripe: RS 69; *khuṭāb*: MA 3/304, 3/305, 8/82; fat sheep's tails: VN 149a; ground meat: MA 3/548. The latter case is based on the use, in a highly poetic passage, of the word *kūfta*. Although such a context does shed doubt on the reliability of the word's use, it nevertheless is realistic to imagine that the audience would at least have had some idea of the concept of "ground meat" (which is, when we think of it, a potentially odd proposition for those who have never been in contact with such a product).

114. See MA 2/19, 3/10, 4/25, 4/97; RS 123.

115. See, for example, MA 3/329 and WQ8. The word *kabāb*, which generally refers to roasted meat of any kind, sometimes appears in the general sense of "good things to eat" (see, for example, APZ 115; DN 60, 95; and MA 8/34).

116. GN 1:218b–219a; VN 65b. The latter clearly describes a technique that is different from the uses of the *tandır* described earlier in this section, insofar as it requires baking pans rather than sticking the dough directly on the inside ceiling or wall of the oven.

117. There also are mentions of flour in the case of *çörek* (GN 2:103a; VN 111b).

118. See pp. 66–67. This hypothesis could be valid only in urban contexts, since written sources limit their references to bread baking as a specialized professional activity to the cities.

119. See p. 72; and IB 256, respectively.

120. VN 45b and 65b–66a. The word *saç* is used in modern Turkish to refer to a convex metallic surface set over a fire to bake flat bread. The way in which the word is used in VN 65b–66a would clearly admit such a definition, although it is too imprecise to let us exclude other possibilities (such as a flat baking pan to be set inside an oven).

The same passage uses the word *bazlama*, which in modern Turkish refers to a type of flat bread, although the sentence in which *bazlama* appears might be interpreted as mentioning it *as opposed to* the bread that was baked on the *saç*.

121. McNicoll (*Taşkun Kale*, 58, 172, 176) refers to "flat, round platters with slightly upturned edges like a tray," probably designed to be set over a fire using an iron stand in order to bake bread. However, these objects are most likely associated with earlier periods. Tahsin Özgüç ("Samsat Kazıları 1987," 292) also mentions the discovery of a copper pan (*bakır sahan*) in what appears to have been a small, regional palace.

122. See, for example, VN 65b; MA 3/329, 3/459; and WQ8.

123. AE 11/113.

124. AE 10/99–100.

125. A passage from the *Manaqib al-'Arifin* (MA 3/519) uses the expression "lāb-i nānī," which could be translated as "slice of bread."

126. IB 256. For other bread-soaking practices, see also p. 83, as well as MA 1/37 and IB 304.

As Dr. Joanita Vroom pointed out to me (personal communication), such a practice of baking once a week might have had something to do with the limited availability of wood to fuel fires on a more frequent basis.

127. AE 10/105; VN 46b, 65a; MA 3/340.

128. RS 123. Levanoni ("Food and Cooking," 210–211) mentions that manuals intended for Cairo's market inspectors, roughly in the same period, advise them to be aware of ground peas, broad beans, and chickpeas used to cheaply add weight to bread, as well as spoiled flour and an array of unwanted additions to the dough being kneaded, such as insects, straw, hair, or bodily fluids. There is no reason to believe Anatolians did much better in this respect.

129. GN 2:103a; VN 111b.

130. MA 3/10, 4/23, 4/25 (the first and last case are essentially a retelling of the same anecdote).

131. The basic production process is the same for both sour milk and yogurt, the only significant difference being the type of bacteria used. Sources in Persian limit themselves to the word *māst*, whereas a passage from the Turkish *Vilayat-nama* uses the words *māst* and *yoğurt* interchangeably (VN 65b).

132. VN 65b; MA 3/340, 3/403.

133. The ruler Burhān al-Dīn is offered *māst* just after he enters the city of Amasya (BR 414); other references to *māst* do not seem to suggest that it carried a lowly connotation, either.

134. SH 10b. The language of this particular passage, however, is too confusing for us to derive much more information from it.

135. APZ 3. See also APZ 9, which gives a number of other products, such as *kaymak*

katkıları, *tulum*, and *karın*. The latter two can both be translated as "stomach," and it is not impossible that ʿĀşıkpaşazāde uses them (or one of them) to refer to stomachs serving as containers for liquids (as they are for wine in SH 17b) or some other purpose. One should note, however, that the word *tulum* is often also used in modern Turkish to refer to a particular type of cheese traditionally produced in sheep stomachs.

136. "Sa gūna chīz dar khʷast kard ka az ān sa chīz badtar nabuvad" (MA 3/33). This claim is part of an anecdote in which an "olden king" asks another for the worst animal, the worst type of food, and the worst human being possible; he receives a donkey, cheese, and an Armenian slave. The anecdote takes place as part of a discussion of donkeys, and only in the animal's case is the negative character explained (by a claim that, unlike other animals whose cries are mentions of the name of God, the donkey's cries are mere calls for sex). Neither the lowliness of cheese nor that of the Armenian slave receives explanation. Although this anecdote might originate in an earlier Persian literary tradition (which would make it less significant for our context), I have not been able to trace its roots anywhere.

137. BR 271.

138. WQ8. This incidentally is very much reminiscent of a typical breakfast in today's Turkey.

139. On this issue, see p. 42.

140. BR 53; GN 1:236a; MA 3/519, 7/1, 8/8, 8/14, 8/15; and perhaps YED 152:5.

141. See, for example, VN 147.

142. Figs: MA 3/47; watermelon: MA 4/22, 4/47, YED 106:6; honeydew melon or cantaloupe: VN 43b–44a; apples: MA 3/453, VN 58a; pears, apples, peaches: IB 336; apricots: IB 336, MA 8/79; pomegranates: IB 323, AU 335; grapes: GN 1:36b, VN 122a, YED 407; plum: YED 407; *aluca*: VN 118a.

Redhouse translates the last as "a small or wild plum; a bullace or sloe," but also points out that the word is a diminutive of *alu*, whose semantic range covers varieties of plums, cherries, and even apricots. It is thus clear that it refers to a small fruit with a pit (a characteristic that the *Vilayat-nama* passage indeed points out), though given the variety of possible translations it would be unwise to claim that Redhouse's primary meaning of plum was the only possibility for the fourteenth century.

Though the technique of soil flotation allows direct access to evidence such as fruit seeds, the archaeobotanists who analyze floatation samples devote very little attention to fruit consumption and production in their publications, at least in comparison to the much more common cereal grains. See, for example, Fairbairn, Longford, and Griffin ("Archaeobotany at Kaman-Kalehöyük," 154), where a very limited presence of grapes and plums, the only two types of fruits they found, is noted only in the table of results, but entirely absent from the discussion section.

143. See, for example, AU 335, 375; as well as IB 259–260, 273–274, 276, 278, 281, 285, 292, 295–296, 307, 312, 323–324.

144. AU 325.

145. VN 118a.

146. IB 299, 301; VN 159a; YED 407.

147. MA 3/346; GN 1:134b–135a.

148. That nut-bearing trees grew without human intervention does not mean that the products could not be sold, however, as we can see from Ibn Baṭṭūṭa's suggestion that he bought walnuts and chestnuts in Kastamonu (IB 342) and Bursa (IB 323–324).

149. See, for example, MA 3/47 as well as VN 43b–44a, 118a. For more concerning the relationship between snacks and meals, see p. 76.

150. IB 336; MA 8/79. The latter passage uses the word *khūshāb* to refer to the liquid in which are floating apricots in the process of being rehydrated. The same term is defined by Lane as "a sweet drink, commonly consisting of water in which raisins [are] boiled [. . .] and then sugar: when cool, a little rose-water is dropped in it. The water-melon frequently supplies the place of this" (*Manners and Customs*, 151). While commonalities are obvious, the focus on the fruits rather than the liquid and the absence of boiling makes it clear that Lane's definition is not a perfect fit for the late-medieval Anatolian context.

Not much can be said about the fruit-drying process on the basis of either textual sources or archaeological literature, though Goell extrapolates the existence, in the Samsat excavation, of "flat roofs, which could also be used for the storage, cleaning, and drying of grain and fruit and for sleeping during Samsat's long hot summers" ("Samosata Archaeological Excavations," 97).

151. VN 118a.

152. IB 348.

153. VN 60b; MA 8/50; DN95.

154. Respectively, MA 2/8 and 7/31. In her analysis of findings from the Gritille excavation, archaeobotanist Naomi Miller notes that "a few members of the carrot family were seen" among the plant remains found through floatation samples ("Patterns of Agriculture and Land Use," 238).

155. MA 8/50; DN 60. The third reference (DN 58) presents only a metaphorical use ("Everyone he hit, he would cut in two like a cucumber").

156. IB 301.

157. GN 1:251b–252b. For a more thorough discussion of this list, see p. 95.

158. YED 170:6, 263:4, and esp. 294:2.

159. I could find but one reference to pepper, in fact an indirect and probably misleading one, as the adjective *mufalfal* (peppery) is applied to rice (MA 3/254). However, Charles Perry, using both cookbooks and modern usage, argues that the expression has nothing to do with pepper and that it simply designates rice pilaf ("A Thousand and One Fritters: The Food of the Arabian Nights," 492).

160. Although it can be observed directly (for example, in VN 133b), most references take, rather, the form of metaphors. These should be treated carefully since the restricted number of variations and their repetitive character raise the possibility that they could have been literary motifs, with limited if any counterpart in popular imagination (MA 4/59; BR 94, 2:71b; MQ 1708; YED 166:6).

161. VN 37a–b.

162. VN 11b; AE 9/97; WQ8, WQ20. At least two of those (concerning *çörek* and rice) are put in a context suggesting that saffron was a relatively luxurious product. Ibn

Baṭṭūṭa (IB 329) mentions that he visited a village in northwestern central Anatolia where saffron was the only agricultural production.

163. MA 3/252, 3/339, 3/340; RS 101. The *Manaqib al-ʿArifin* also mentions Rūmī's fondness for garlic mixed into *māst* (yogurt). While such a mixture is fairly popular (and commercially available) in Turkey today, it remains unclear to what extent the author implies that this was as widely consumed at the time, or whether it was, rather, a peculiar habit of Rūmī (MA 3/340, 3/403).

164. MA 3/152; RS 71. Both these references use the same metaphor, comparing the one who talks about musk after chewing on garlic to the one who talks about garlic after taking musk. Musk, together with ambergris, also appears in YED 324:2, in reference to breath but not in relation to garlic.

165. Some passages unambiguously show that this was, at the very least, a possibility. See, for example, the use of butter in MA 4/25, IB 301, and VN 49b (where oil is added to a dish cooked in a cauldron). A similar claim can be made in reference to adding oil or butter (the Turkish word *yağ* can refer to either) to bread (AE 10/105; VN 46b, 49a) and to *çörek* (VN 111b). References to "fattened" (*musamman*) "bird" (*murgh*, assumedly chicken [MA 3/592]) and duck (*baṭṭ* [MA 3/254]) may likewise have been meant to imply the particularly delicious character of these dishes.

166. WQ8, WQ20, WQ21.

167. RS 123.

168. MA 4/63. See also VN 23a; QN 21; and YED 171:6, 388:5.

169. GN 2:251b–252a; MA 3/172.

170. See, for example, MA 3/116, 6/7; and AE 7/73.

171. GN 2:39b, 153a. Incidentally, the word *sharāb* seems to be used in a similarly generic sense on a few occasions as well, although it is overall much more commonly used to refer specifically to wine. See, for example, MA 8/38 and 3/204 (described as "ḥalāl" [religiously legitimate] in a passage that would certainly not apply such term to any alcoholic drink), as well as a series of mentions in verse that clearly use *sharāb* to replace *sharbat* when required by the meter (GN 1:126b/9, 127a/8, 127b/2; compare to 127b/9). For more about wine, see p. 101ff.

172. One passage hints at the need for some preparation (GN 2:141b); another (VN 5b) uses the Turkish verb *ezmek* (to squeeze) to describe this preparation, further strengthening the suggestion that fruit juices were part of the product. Ibn Baṭṭūṭa once refers to the addition of lemon juice in diluted syrup (as part of a dessert that also contains crumbled biscuits [IB 304]) and, on another occasion, mentions that the water used to rehydrate dried apricots would also be drunk (IB 336). Al-ʿUmarī's reference to the cultivation of pomegranates in the Germiyan region also refers to both the alcoholic beverage and the syrup made from the fruit, but not to the possibility of drinking fruit juice in its untransformed state (AU 335).

Furthermore, one passage refers to "sharāb-i ḥummāż." It is clear from this particular context that *sharāb* refers to a nonalcoholic drink (otherwise the anecdote, aimed at defending a religious master from accusations of alcoholism, would make no sense) and that *ḥummāż* should be taken as meaning "orange juice" rather than its alternative translation, "wild sorrel." In this case, the need that the author felt to refer to "a drink of orange juice" (rather than merely "orange juice") thus hints at a further transformation, presumably the addition of water to the juice (MA 8/38).

Finally, another passage refers to the *naqūʿī* (infusion or, more probably, dilution) of seven fruits that serves as the base of a medical drug (MA 3/48). Although the number of fruits and the medicinal use may not have been typical, the idea of transformation beyond the mere extraction of juice is still presented in a matter-of-fact tone.

173. MA 3/94, 3/204; IB 304.

174. BR 53; GN 1:236a; MA 8/14, 8/15. Another passage (MA 8/8) shows that at least upper-class households would employ wet nurses.

175. This is a common literary motif. See, for example, GN 1:120b and MA 3/519.

176. As a matter of fact, al-ʿUmarī directly refers to "milk and what is made from it" (laban wa mā yaʿmalu minhu [AU 310]). For more about dairy products, see p. 86ff.

177. MA 3/116, 3/340.

178. On *boza* sellers in early-Ottoman Bursa, see Selçuk, "State and Society," 52–80.

179. Coffee was introduced to the Anatolian population in the early sixteenth century, whereas tea spread even later in the region. That being said, hot drinks were present throughout the Byzantine Empire's geography and chronology, at least since Roman times (Dr. Joanita Vroom, personal communication). In this context, their absence from the sources I used is even more striking and might reflect a cultural contrast between Byzantine and post-Byzantine settings. As much as one should be wary of the simplistic attitude of using nomadism to explain away all the peculiarities of the "Turkish" culture (which often encompasses everything Anatolian), in a context set shortly after the end of the last migration wave from central Asia such an argument is certainly tempting. Further analysis of archaeological material might shed some light on this question, but I have not been able to find vessels explicitly linked to hot drinks in the published articles I surveyed.

180. This scarcity is, of course, mostly because the characters depicted do not need hospitality, since they are residing in their own homes. It is, however, rather interesting that, even in scenes that take place during travels, the hagiographies include very few references to their lodging conditions.

181. IB 273–274, 288, 324; VN 65a. Ibn Baṭṭūṭa's testimony also suggests that gender was no barrier to hospitality, as he mentions that at least three of his hosts were female, from various social conditions (IB 288, 324, 335).

182. IB 285, 297, 310, 317; MA 3/305. RS 18 might be another example if the word *ʿulūfa* (literally, "allowance") is taken in the sense of "food."

183. IB 265, 293. This stands in contrast with the observation of Lewicka concerning medieval Cairo where, she says, "the master of the house, beside looking after his guests, was also supposed to eat with them" (*Food and Foodways of Medieval Cairenes*, 409).

184. IB 265, 273–274, 290–291.

185. It is equally impossible to determine whether serving patterns changed from one group of guests to the other, as it is documented in the case of later Ottoman soup kitchens. IB 276, 310; APZ 33, 102.

186. See, for example, APZ 33, 102; as well as MA 3/85. Aflākī might refer to a parallel attempt at limiting inequality when he describes a Mongol ruler offering some of his own food to a religious master (MA 8/19).

Note also a passage of the *Manaqib al-ʿArifin* where Rūmī is quoted as saying that the most basic form of thanks is the one given by the "ordinary people" (ʿavām-i mardumān) when receiving food and other material goods (MA 3/518). The contrast between this and the other two forms of thanks he mentions, both of a higher and more voluntary level (and directed toward God), strengthens the impression that it was a basic "duty" for recipients of material aid to be thankful—and that sincerity may not have been a sine qua non condition. For more about what food-giving scenes tell us about social status in fourteenth-century Anatolia, see Nicolas Trépanier, "The Giving Divide: Food Gifts and Social Identity in Post-Byzantine Anatolia" (in Christine Isom-Verhaaren and Kent Schull's forthcoming edited volume).

187. See, for example, IB 319, 320; VN 46b, 49a, 51b; and MA 3/214, 3/592. It is interesting to note the prevalence of Arabic in these formulae. This is, of course, easily explained by the liturgical use of that language at the time. However, as Ibn Baṭṭūṭa repeatedly points out, Arabic was essentially unknown as a street language in fourteenth-century central Anatolia. The apparently widespread use of Arabic or semi-Arabic formulations here thus suggests the ritualized and, consequently, widespread character for the practice of begging. In an apparent extension of the meaning of such formulae, one anecdote tells of a blind man (depicted as pious, though not identified as a dervish) as asking bread "for the love of Mavlānā" (MA 3/540).

I should also mention that I did not come across the Turkish word *keşkül* (or *keçkül*), whose usage in later centuries seems to correspond to that of the word *zanbīl* as discussed here.

188. MA 3/214.

189. As Amy Singer pointed out to me (personal communication), a beggar's movements may also be motivated by the potential of various "markets" (e.g., whether people who circulate are more or less likely to give than people, such as shopkeepers, who spend long periods of time in the same location) and, more important, by repressive policing action that might target them. I should add, however, that the sources I used do not suggest the existence of such repression in late-medieval central Anatolia.

190. The only direct exception to this rule is the pleasure (*ẓavq*) experienced by Rūmī's followers when they consume a certain batch of *ḥalwāʾ* (MA 3/85), although a reference to the consumption of honey in the *Manaqib al-ʿArifin* is also worded in a way that implicitly yet unmistakably affirms that it entailed an element of pleasure (MA 3/158). More generally, a passage from the *Gharib-nama* ("Sanki aşdur tuzı yokdur dadı yok" [It is like food, (if) there is no salt, there is no taste]) suggests that one would expect dishes to offer a (presumably good) taste experience to the eater (GN 2:71b).

Concerning the quality of food in the particular case of festive meals, see p. 79.

191. These adjectives can respectively be found in SH 17b–18a; RS 123; MA 3/94, 3/158; and YED 57:5.

192. VN 111b. Just like its modern counterpart, Old Anatolian Turkish uses the word *yağ* to refer to both solid and liquid forms.

193. GN 1:251b–252a.

194. Both MA 3/204 and RS 85 mention the Persian form as part of Rūmī's poetry. In Turkish the combination of honey and oil/fat appears, for example, in SH 17b–19a; AE 10/105; and YED 55:4.

For an extensive discussion of the association between edible fats (mostly butter, lard, and olive oil), taste, and economic factors in a different context, see Jean-Louis Flandrin, "Le goût et la nécessité: Sur l'usage des graisses dans les cuisines d'Europe occidentale (XIV–XVIIIe siècle)."

195. See p. 79, as well as MA 3/158 and numerous occasions in the works of Yûnus Emre (YED 11:7, 13:2, 132:2, 144:6, 164:2, 170:6, 224:5, 263:4, 271:8, 371:5; and YER 325).

196. "Poison" (Turkish *agu* or *zehr*/*zehir*/*zahir*) is often represented as a liquid substance (BR 121; MQ 1685, 1687; VN 97b; YED 140:1, 144:5, 252:2, 258:8, 263:4, 265:5, 279:4). Some passages oppose it to sugar or honey without reference to its consistency (YED 13:2, 144:6, 321:5–6), but none includes further information that might help us associate the mental image of the various authors with a particular poisonous liquid. On this subject, see also Michael Rogers, "The Palace, Poisons, and the Public: Some Lists of Drugs in Mid-16th-Century Ottoman Turkey."

197. It is striking that the only two authors to explicitly associate fruits and sweetness are Ibn Baṭṭūṭa (IB 259–260, 323) and al-ʿUmarī (AU 335). These are, of course, the only two Arabic-language authors in my pool of narrative sources; more important, they were foreigners and should by no means be expected to reflect an Anatolian perspective. The contrast between these and other sources thus strengthens the suggestion that fruits and sweets were part of two different categories in Anatolia, perhaps in contrast to other regions.

I could find only one exception to this rule, in an anecdote where Shams al-Tabrīzī's followers, when asked for watermelon (*kharbuza*), bring him "sweet watermelons" (kharbuzahāy-i shīrīn [MA 4/47]). On the other hand, the same source contains an entire anecdote centering on the temptation that the narrator feels for a pot of dried apricots left in water for moistening without making a single reference to sweetness (MA 8/79).

198. See, for example, MA 3/39 and GN 2:103a.

199. MA 3/94.

200. MA 3/340.

201. MA 3/152. The same anecdote appears in RS 71.

202. The question of wine taste will be discussed in more detail below. Concerning wine's moral implications, see p. 117ff.

203. For example, Rūmī's practice of sucking on a piece of yellow myrobalan (an astringent fruit used in tanning) is presented as a way to ensure that he does not endanger the purity of his fast by swallowing his own "sweet saliva" (MA 3/411; RS 88). See also MA 8/79, 3/411; and RS 123. Quite unsurprisingly, gluttony is also depicted as a sign of weak-

ness (MA 3/113). For more on the tensions that, some argued, exist between physical and spiritual well-being, see also the section on fasting below.

204. A basic introduction to the way Galen's views were understood in medieval Baghdad can be found in Nasrallah, introduction to *Annals of the Caliph's Kitchens*, 56–64.

205. MA 2/8.

206. The "list of tastes" of the *Gharib-nama* (which I discussed earlier, see p. 95; GN 1:251b–252a) mentions that "*acı*" (hot, spicy) foods are healthy (*ten perver*), but this lone exception in fact concerns a characteristic that may occur to a variable extent in various food items, rather than being a comment on a particular food item.

The reference to "*çarb*" (fatty) in the same list might at first glance seem to be a negative equivalent, insofar as the *Gharib-nama* claims that it causes obesity. Neither this nor other sources, however, contain any suggestion that obesity had the negative associations it carries today; a passage from *Gharib-nama* in fact rather seems to equate it with strength (GN 2:66b).

207. See, for example, MA 3/40, 3/116, 8/34. A passage of the *Gharib-nama* (GN 2:214b) also mentions that the body requires all four of water, wind, fire, and earth to live. Although the unique character of this mention as well as its author's habit of creating lists should make us wary of taking this as the expression of some widespread idea, it nevertheless mimics the concept of *mizāj* in its conceptualization of health as a form of equilibrium and, in this sense, strengthens my suggestion that such a conceptualization was widespread.

208. RS 102.

209. MA 3/17, 3/182, 3/252, 6/9; RS 101. The inclusion of almonds in this list is based on the apparent equation made between the health effects of garlic and almonds in MA 3/182. The reference to meat and blood is based on a passage that might in fact be a hadith (the source of which I could not, however, identify), in which case we might question whether the fever-causing effects of these two items were part of popular knowledge. If a cold was conceptualized as the opposite of fever (the passage attributes the unbalance in *mizāj* that caused it to "a change of air and water"), then we should probably add to this list a remedy suggested for this illness, wine (MA 8/34).

210. Respectively, MA 2/8 for the first and MA 8/3 for the second. Pickled beets are designated as "better than the *muḥallilāt*" (solvents of evil fluids [MA 2/8]), water is forbidden to those afflicted with diarrhea (MA 3/40), and poppy milk appears as a cure for an oversleeping individual (although the miraculous context of the story, told thrice with only minor variations, suggests that this may be the opposite of normality, i.e., that people knew the product for its sleep-inducing properties [MA 3/253, 3/377; RS 102]).

More generally, the formulation of two other passages shows that various types of fruits were associated with a variety of (unspecified) effects on the body (GN 1:82a, 2:57a; GN 2:88b might also imply the same). Yet another passage further suggests that edible plants may have been divided between the "wet" and the "dry" ones (GN 2:88a), although without offering much insight as to the way this galenic-sounding classification was understood.

211. The formulation of this reference (MA 8/2) suggests that this was not widely known information.

212. Incidentally, the latter anecdote goes further to tell of a man who had the unwise idea to swallow two of these cereal seeds, got pregnant, and, unable to give birth for obvious physiological reasons, died in awful pain—although his two sons survived (VN 61a–62a). This second part thus depicts an otherwise positively connoted food item as having very negative effects when consumed by someone whose body is not in a proper state to receive it.

213. VN 37a–b. Another passage (GN 1:148a) further specifies that the stomach can get "blocked" (*tutulmış*) and not digest what is eaten, in which case drinking *sharbat* (probably meaning any drinkable liquid here) "opens it up."

214. To the point of allowing one to "digest away" the effects of poison (MA 3/470). As a matter of fact, this also shows how changes such as digestion were seen as capable of transforming the very nature of the edibles. The greater assimilative capacity of an empty stomach also explains why, in one of the three tellings of the anecdote mentioned earlier, poppy milk is given as medication with the recommendation of drinking it on an empty stomach (*ʿalā al-rīq* [MA 3/377]).

215. GN 1:95b. Other references to digestion include suggestions that the ability of young children to eat solid foods was developed through practice (as opposed to arising naturally with age [MA 3/110]), that women have a weaker digestive capacity than men (VN 37a–b), that constant hunger over a long period can cause loss of teeth (MA 2/5), that hunger is a sure sign of health (MA 3/546; one should remember, however, that this particular source strongly advocates the practice of fasting), and that purer (*khāliṣtar*) wine is easier to digest (*khūsh-guvārtar* [BR 156]). In view of the importance of liquids in digestion, I would tend to assume that the "pure" character as it is used in the latter mention should be understood to mean "devoid of impurities" rather than "undiluted," especially given that another passage claims that insufficiently diluted wine "burns [or scorches] one's stomach" (göyündürür kursağını [GN 1:121a]).

216. VN 131a; IB 320.

217. Both references appear as part of the same passage (SH 24b–25a).

218. MA 3/262, 3/275; APZ 81.

219. MA 3/275.

220. RS 81 depicts one as preparing purgatives for dervishes, and MA 3/116 seems to suggest that their services were available to the "people of Anatolia" (the anecdote uses both *ahl-i Rūm* and *mardum-i Rūm*).

221. It might be significant that one of the few cases of injury (as opposed to illness) I could find, which involves a man who breaks his foot by falling off a donkey, is treated by miraculous means with no reference to what could have been the medical alternative—or even *whether* there would have been a medical alternative (MA 2/3).

222. See esp. MA 3/275 and RS 82. MA 3/157 refers to the *dukkān* (shop) of the physicians, although its being set in the somewhat "intemporal time" of Moses should make us wary of taking the details too literally.

The few passages that can be understood as including references to alchemy (such as MA 3/56) make no explicit link between the latter and medicine.

223. See MA 3/40, 3/262, 3/275; and RS 82, the latter two being the most explicit examples.

224. For example, in MA 3/275, the physician seems to be asked to produce several drugs at the same time, with no reference to any specific health problem that the sultan (who gave him the order) may have encountered. This is all the more significant, given that such a reference to an illness would have been a typical and very useful literary device to introduce the anecdote.

225. Only one passage refers to what may have been an "active ingredient," a flower called "maḥmūda" (MA 3/48). See also MA 3/157; APZ 81; and AE 7/74.

226. RS 81; MA 3/275.

227. MA 3/48, for example, includes a reference to the addition of active ingredients in a fruit-based infusion or (more probably) diluted fruit juice. See also MA 3/262 (referring to "medicines," adviya); RS 82 (mentioning "ingredients and compounds," ajzāʾī va maṣāliḥ).

In MA 6/7, "miraculous" honey served in *sharbat* seems to play the part that active ingredients usually play in the work of physicians.

228. MA 3/83, 3/116, 3/262, 3/275, 8/3; RS 81. Conversely, the word *sharbat* is sometimes used in a way that clearly entails a medical use (see, for example, AE 7/73; APZ 122; GN 1:126b–127b; and MA 3/116).

229. Respectively, MA 8/71, 3/157, 3/40, 8/3. The latter case, abortion, seems to have combined the use of these drugs with "violent movements."

230. This is particularly obvious in AE 7/74; APZ 81; and MA 3/157.

231. MA 3/116. See also Abdullah Ghouchani and Charyar Adle, "A Sphero-conical Vessel as *Fuqqāʿa*, or a Gourd for 'Beer,'" where the authors use archaeological and literary evidence to identify a particular type of container as a "beer gourd" that was used until the thirteenth century (and might correspond to the type of container to which Rūmī refers here) but fail to notice that the *boza* consumed in later centuries might be the same liquid as the *fuqāʿ* they describe.

232. MA 5/23. This statement adds more than a pinch of irony to the classification of Rūmī's works in the "Turkish literature" section of university libraries in today's Turkey.

Another anecdote refers to the builder of a "bukhārī" oven as "miʿmārī Rūmī" ("a [Greek] architect" [MA 3/448]).

233. BR 206.

234. For example, when "a Greek architect" (miʿmārī Rūmī) is asked why he is not Muslim, the formulation makes no explicit reference to Christianity, thus strongly suggesting that the word *Rūmī* would by itself have been taken as sufficient indication that he was a Christian (MA 3/448).

235. It would have made no sense for Aflākī to use the expression "faqih-i Turk" (Turkish jurists) if "Turk" meant nothing more than "Anatolian Muslim," since the word

faqih itself entails that they were Muslim. The context of this particular reference also strongly suggests that this ethnic tag carried a connotation of poverty (MA 3/219).

236. The narrative line of a passage from the *Gharib-nama* describes an Arab, an Armenian, a "Persian" (*Acem*), and a "Turcoman" (*Türkmen*), when faced with hunger, each suggesting in his own language that they should collectively go and buy grapes and, because the linguistic divides prevent them from realizing that they all want the same thing, eventually breaking into a fight over what they should do (GN 1:36b).

237. Whereas the (very urban) *Manaqib al-ʿArifin* includes a number of such ethnic references, they are much less common in the (very much rural) *Vilayat-nama*. The latter even describes the population of a particular village as "zimmi" (non-Muslim "People of the Book," meaning either Christian or Jewish). This somewhat downplays the importance of ethnic differences (insofar as they existed at all between this and other villages [VN 45b]).

238. It might be worth noting the more common presence of Persian than Greek speakers in Turkish sources and the greater number of Turks than Armenians in Persian sources.

The *Manaqib al-ʿArifin* contains an anecdote presenting the conquest of Baghdad by the Mongols (whom it designates as *kuffār al-dīn*, "unbelievers of the Faith") as successful but only after fasting, in a fashion strongly reminiscent of Mavlāvī practices (MA 3/112). Rather than a downplaying of the importance of ethnic differences, this passage should probably be read as a way to emphasize the universality of Mavlāvī practices, here presented as so valid that they cross religious and ethnic lines. On the other hand, one should also remember that the early Mavlāvīs had a particular sympathy for the Ilkhanid Mongol, who were the overlords of Anatolia for several of the early decades of the order's existence.

239. An anecdote that appears in three versions (MA 3/253, 3/377; RS 102) contains a reference to poppy milk, but the latter is mentioned only in relation to its curative effects for sleep problems. The only direct reference to opium I could find is part of a verse from Rūmī that almost certainly derives from his literary background rather than social environment (RS 56).

240. BR 178–179, 339, 376–377, 409–410, 522; DN 73; IN 271–272; MA 1/20, 8/38, 8/80.

241. Astarābadī very often makes this claim; see, for example, BR 141, 178–179.

242. "Khāṣiyyat-i sharāb ānast ka mast kunad" (MA 3/388). See also BR 141; DN 60; and GN 1:121a, 37b. This perception of bad taste seems to have been the result of the actual bad quality of the product (i.e., a defect that would be recognized as such by a modern wine-loving palate) rather than of different standards in taste, if we can give credence to Rūmī when he suggests that there is no difference between alcohol-less wine and vinegar (MA 3/388).

One should also note that the use of water to dilute drinkable liquids extended to nonalcoholic drinks as well (see p. 91).

243. All mentions of wine that refer to color describe it as red (and often compare it to ruby). Furthermore, a passage in the *Gharib-nama* states that, although there are dif-

ferent varieties of grapes, the wine from all of them looks the same (GN 1:37b). However, we do know that white wine was produced in the Loire and Rhineland regions at the time (James L. Newman, "Wine," 732).

244. One passage refers to "old wine" as especially praiseworthy, and it is worth pointing out that it does so in a heavily rhyming formulation: "Bi-tanāvul-i raḥīq-i ʿatīq va jām-i ʿaqīq mashghūl shuda" (They busied themselves with the consumption of old wine in red gemstone goblets [MA 8/38]). Literary concerns no doubt played a large part in this choice of word, yet it remains significant. After all, even an exquisite literary effect would not be sufficient to push an author to describe his master as drinking "old" milk.

245. See, for example, BR 178–179; GN 1:46b; and MA 8/80 (in the latter case, the role of *sāqī* is played by a "beloved friend" who is the grandson of Sultān Valad). Indeed, there was a certain honor in serving wine, which is most clearly expressed in a verse where Yûnus Emre depicts God as offering a wine cup (YED 164:7). While this passage is as metaphorical as can be, one never encounters a metaphor where Yûnus presents God engaged in activities deemed "lowly" for human beings, such as sweeping the floor or washing the dishes.

246. MA 4/11. The reliability of this depiction is supported by the fact that the story takes place in a city, Konya, which was the very place of residence of a good part of the text's intended audience. In the typical fashion of the Muslim religious poets of his time, Yûnus Emre also presents, on a number of occasions, "wine houses" (şarabhane, meyhane) as so many incarnations of an unholy place (YED 148:6, 267:5, 328:4).

247. AU 311. In a short passage describing Anatolia, early-fourteenth-century Armenian historian Hayton notes that wine (along with wheat and fruits) was abundantly produced in the region. Though his focus is primarily on a region stretching between Egypt, Lesser Armenia, and Iran, his and al-ʿUmari's references show that Anatolia did have in neighboring regions the image of a wine-producing area (Hayton, *La fleur des histoires de la terre d'Orient*, 817).

Furthermore, Redford (et al., *Archaeology of the Frontier*, 164) notes the presence of a stone that looks like one used in olive presses among the material excavated from the Gritille site. As he points out, in the absence of olives from the region, it most likely was used to press grapes to produce wine or the sweet jelly called today *pekmez*, or both.

248. AU 335. Even though distilled alcohol may have been known as an experimental product at that time, there is no indication that it was consumed on any significant scale. See James Comer, "Distilled Beverages," 655.

249. The setting, a "fairy-tale-esque" Baghdad, somewhat reduces our ability to claim that this reflected a general situation in Anatolia, but it is clear that the author expected his audience to be familiar with such moral views (MA 4/4).

250. IB 257, 351–352.

251. IB 257, 351–352. BR 169 mentions another case.

252. MA 4/31. The next anecdote (MA 4/32) further associates cannabis consumption with sodomy, but the care it takes in arguing that both of these are blameworthy deeds in fact suggests that there might have been divergent opinions floating around on the moral value of these activities.

253. Ibn Baṭṭūṭa further points out that it was consumed with the help of a spoon (IB 351–352).

Directly eating the untreated plant would have strongly limited its psychotropic effect, whereas there was no reason to take the process one step further by heating and compressing the substance into what modern usage calls "hashish" (a thick, dark resin whose main advantages over "*kief*" are its slow burning rate and concentration in active ingredients).

One source uses the expression "ot içmek" (AE 7/74), which exactly corresponds to a modern Turkish slang expression to refer to smoking marijuana. However, the context makes it clear that, in this particular context, the expression should rather be translated as "drinking [a compound of medicinal] herbs."

254. One passage describes hallucinogenic effects (and does present the visions as invented by the beholder, rather than manifestations of another realm of reality [MA 4/31]), whereas another mentions the paranoia-inducing effects of cannabis (IB 169).

255. As I pointed out when discussing "snack" foods, the volumes consumed depended more on the availability and the spur of the moment than on any (even roughly) set levels of demand.

256. Its presence in the region is attested through historical and archaeological evidence since ancient times (Harry Godwin, "The Ancient Cultivation of Hemp," 42).

257. For an excellent demonstration of the social importance of population density (although in an altogether different context), see Darrett B. Rutman, "People in Process: The New Hampshire Towns of the Eighteenth Century."

CHAPTER FOUR

1. Obviously, most serious scholars recognize that there was a multiplicity of heterodoxies and variations on religious creeds among Muslims and among Christians. However, even a scholar such as Sara Wolper, who devotes most of her attention to this very issue (*Cities and Saints*, 75), seems to take for granted that for all the fluidity and negotiation room that existed in the various possible layers of identity, "being Christian" or "being Muslim" was an unavoidable dichotomy and a (or perhaps *the*) important element in any individual's social localization.

2. SH 22a. Other examples can be found in VN 37a–b, 50b–51; and YED 106:8, 109:2, 302:13–14, 303–4 (though some of Yûnus Emre's passages are presented in the first person or as abstract statements, they do follow the same pattern).

Besides spiritual retreats, fasting accompanies oath taking (VN 23a), votive prayers (MQ 1470ff), and the rain prayer (MA 3/466, this being one of the few passages in the *Manaqib al-ʿArifin* that depicts the religious practices of people unconnected to the Mavlāvī order; see also below). A similarly "atmospheric" use of fasting occurs in the passages of Mavlāvī sources that refer to the *samāʿ* (MA 3/201, 3/403, 3/461; RS 68). See also BR 220, where a political character's decisions are partly justified by the pious and clear-sighted state of mind that fasting allows him to reach.

I should also point out the facetious suggestion by Hacı Bektaş that it is "womanly" to deny oneself both eating and drinking, whereas a "manly" practice entails eating beef stew every day without drinking a single gulp of water (VN 37a–b). It is rather unlikely that this passage describes a regular (or regularly imagined) practice, both because it is a unique proposition and because its formulation suggests, rather, that it would have been unexpected for its intended audience.

3. This opposition between worldly desires and fasting is common in most sources that refer to fasting (see, for example, SH 24b; GN 1:222a, 2:218a, 234a; the latter is actually a Qur'anic reference to "the men who fast and the women who fast," *al-ṣā'imīn wa al-ṣā'imātī* [33/35]). As we will see in the next section, this same dichotomy also plays a central part among the arguments appearing in Mavlāvī sources, although the latter, unlike the *Gharib-nama*, enjoin their audience to engage in fasting.

4. GN 1:148b–152a.

5. Trépanier, "Starting without Food."

6. On the Qalandar movement, see Karamustafa, *God's Unruly Friends*.

7. Of course, Ramadan is also a calendar month, but, unlike *waqfiyya*s, the narrative sources used here seldom give specific dates that could refer to this month for strictly chronological purposes.

I should also note here that, although it is a common practice among Alevis in today's Turkey to fast for ten days at the beginning of the month of Muharram, I did not find references to this month in relation to food (either depicting, implying, or excluding the practice of fasting) in the Alevi-affiliated *Vilayat-nama* or any other source.

8. Perhaps most striking is MA 3/555, one of the few anecdotes in the *Manaqib al-ʿArifin* that explicitly takes place during Ramadan, and in which Rūmī disappears from his disciples to hide in a well in order to devote himself entirely to spiritual exercises. Although the narration clearly entails a particular sacredness to the month of Ramadan (it starts with the unusually chronologically specific mention that "it was the first day of the blessed month of Ramadan . . . ," *ghurra-i māh-i Ramadan-i mubarak shuda būd* . . .), the anecdote makes no reference, direct or indirect, to fasting.

A number of anecdotes also mention the fast of Ramadan, along with the five daily prayers, either as *farḍ-i ʿayn* (individual religious duty) or as conditions that make for a perfect religious master. However, the formulations suggest that these passages could have been copied directly from theological treatises devoid of any particular association with late-medieval Anatolia (see, for example, MA 3/96 and 4/63).

It might be worth adding that the word *Ramadan* does *not* appear in the concordance that Mustafa Tatcı collected from the complete works of Yûnus Emre, a remarkable detail given that each one of these four hundred or so poems centers on Muslim religious themes (by contrast, the word *namāz*, one of several types of prayers, appears on more than three dozen occasions).

9. IB 268, 275; BR 169, 170. Aqsarāyī is the only author from the period I could find explicitly criticizing someone for not fasting during Ramadan (the Seljuk sultan ʿAlā al-Dīn Kayqubād III), and he does so as part of a long list of recriminations (AQ 282).

10. WQ21 (candles) and WQ1 (Qur'anic recitations). It would at first glance seem

logical to assume that the provision for supplemental candles entails a change in habits congruent with the daytime fast of Ramadan (namely, remaining awake later than usual after sunset). However, one should also note that the provision demands that candles be lighted not only on the nights of Ramadan, but also on a number of other days (including every Friday, which would seem to exclude a systematic association with fasting). This provision closely parallels the request, in another document (WQ8), to light candles on a limited list of festive days, without any mention of Ramadan.

11. VN 155a. Such hyperbole is reminiscent of the yearlong fasts I discuss in my article "Starting without Food: Fasting and the Early Mawlawī Order."

12. VN 100b, 112b.

13. See esp. pp. 36–39ff above.

14. MA 3/466, 6/8, 7/11.

15. It appears along with either giving charity money (BR 174; MA 6/11, 8/3, 8/14) or distributing the meat for charity (VN 159b).

16. As thanks: MA 6/11, 8/14; VN 155a. As part of a request: MA 8/3, VN 112b.

17. VN 61a, 85a, 100a, 100b.

18. VN 45b.

19. MA 3/466, 3/592, 6/8, 7/11.

20. See p. 82.

21. MA 3/45, 3/77, 3/94.

22. MA 3/305.

23. Perhaps most obvious in this respect are MA 3/45 and 3/94.

24. See, for example, MA 3/542; RS 68 (the expression "*samāʿ* of our companions" suggesting that other versions existed); VN 75a; and IB 273–274.

25. Abdülbâki Gölpınarlı (*Mevlânâ'dan sonra Mevlevîlik*, 375–379) offers a prime example of a detailed yet "hopelessly timeless" description of the performance of *samāʿ*, projecting what is probably the early-twentieth-century incarnation of the practice on to the history of the Mavlāvī order as a whole.

26. MA 3/244.

27. See, for example, MA 3/411; APZ 11, 51; and, indirectly, MA 2/5.

28. See p. 112ff.

29. The full definition of a festival proposed by Alessandro Falassi, from which I have derived my formulation, goes beyond religious celebrations: "a periodically recurrent social occasion in which, through a multiplicity of forms and a series of coordinated events, participate directly or indirectly and to various degrees, all members of a whole community, united by ethnic, linguistic, religious, historical bonds, and sharing a worldview" ("Festival: Definition and Morphology," 2).

30. See especially IB 332 (in which an elite-oriented author depicts a village gathering) and VN 121b (depicting an elite crowd for a lower-class audience). MA 3/592 and VN 61 involve miracles that take place on a Thursday, thus suggesting a widely agreed-upon sacred character for that day.

31. WQ1, WQ8, WQ19, WQ20. All call for such recitations on Mondays and Thursdays, in formulations variable enough to lessen the risk that these would be merely for-

mulaic provisions. WQ17 also clearly refers to Thursday, along with an illegible word that should probably be read as "Monday."

WQ8 also goes beyond recitations, as it allocates funds for the acquisition of extra food (meat, bread, *ḥalwāʾ*) for "Friday nights." WQ21 prescribes the acquisition of rice, butter, and meat "every Friday," although it is unclear whether these were to be served on that particular day, or rather that Friday was the day when provisioning for the week would take place.

32. MA 8/92 in the first case and MA 3/85 and VN 10b in the second. The latter is specifically a reference to making *bişi* (cookies?) on the day of *ʿArafa*, which is the eve of the *ʿĪd al-Aḍhā* in the strictest sense.

33. IB 276. He also claims to have witnessed an *ahi*-hosted feast on *ʿAshuraʾ*, though in Bursa and therefore outside the geographical scope of this study (IB 318–319).

34. "A seven-day week prevailed throughout the Byz[antine] world" (Brian Croke and Anthony Cutler, "Day").

35. MA 3/45, 3/94; VN 85a. See also IB 276 (on the *ʿĪd al-Fiṭr*), 332 (communal "*dhikr* and dinner"); MA 3/85 (*ḥājj* and *ʿĪd-i Qurbān*), 3/581 (*qurbān* upon a saint's death).

36. MA 3/438. See also VN 151a, as well as DN 60, 70, and 95 (which include wine drinking).

37. MA 3/580. See also VN 150b ("*muhayyā*" as a chronological counterpoint to the more explicitly Muslim "*bayrām*"), 121b, 131b; IB 354 (mourning); and MA 1/10 (feast offered to a visiting religious scholar).

38. Neither does the vocabulary used to refer to these feasts show any strong pattern of consistency that could betray an essential difference in the perception of religious and unreligious feasts. In fact, one expression, "muhayyā va aḥiyā," is used to describe the yearly feast offered by an as yet unrepentant brigand on one occasion (VN 151b) and the feast given by a new disciple of a saint on another (VN 85a). In Turkish, both the nouns *muhayyā* and *aḥyā* are attested (at least in later centuries) but separately, respectively, meaning "prepared, existing" and "animating, making (a night) alive with religious exercises, etc."

39. Examples include *khūshāb* (water in which dried apricots were left to moisten [MA 8/79]), *raughān* (butter or oil [MA 4/25]), almond sweets (MA 3/411), as well as sweet foods (RS 88) and good foods in general (MA 3/438). For more about "the fatty and the sweet," see p. 95.

40. MA 3/552.

41. See p. 28.

42. This is mostly because the scenes that depict the consumption of barley bread for ascetic purposes tend to include few references to the acquisition of the bread or other forms of social interaction, as can be seen, for example, in MA 2/5, 39, and 4/41. Furthermore, some of the passages that associate barley with asceticism invoke hadiths; as I pointed out in my earlier discussion of the subject, the authors probably selected hadiths that reflected their opinions rather than developing their opinions after reading the hadiths. See p. 156n above, as well as MA 3/219, 3/487, 3/515, and 3/557.

43. Feet: MA 3/10; head: MA 2/19, 4/25, 4/97, RS 123; *girda*: MA 3/10, 4/23, 4/25.

44. As a matter of fact, Ibn Baṭṭūṭa notes (with what could perhaps be interpreted as amusement) that "Turks" give precedence to *tharīd* because they see it as the favorite food of the Prophet (IB 268). However, other references to that dish suggest that if its name and basic principle (bread crumbled in liquid) were fairly standard, the exact recipe could vary. See also MA 3/10 and RS 123. For more on *tharīd*, see p. 83.

45. It is true that dates appear in the *Manaqib al-ʿArifin* only as part of references to hadiths (MA 3/219, 3/515). However, the presence of "forty dates" in a passage of the *Vilayat-nama* (VN 24a) strongly suggests that, even if dates were not widely available, the population at large was at least aware both of the existence of dates and of the part that they play in the theological discourse since the very beginning of Islam.

46. GN 2:7b/9.

47. See, for example, RS 21 (fruits), as well as GN 1:120b and 2:4b (references to the Qur'anic statements that one of the rivers of Paradise is made of milk) and MA 3/281, RS 46, and GN 2:4b–5a (all of which contrast theological milk with mystical wine).

48. MA 3/519 and 7/1.

49. For example, MA 4/41 presents wine as *ḥarām* and implies that barley bread is nearly universally *ḥalāl*, but it can hardly be a coincidence that these two consumables are heavily loaded with religious symbolism (respectively, negative and positive) in the sources I have used in this research.

50. MA 3/101, 3/204.

51. MA 3/156; DN 108; SH 25a; YED 124:10, 154:4.

52. IB 352–353.

53. MA 4/11. It is, of course, not uncommon that a type of food be produced and sold by a small segment of the population yet consumed by all, whereas the opposite is rather unusual.

54. This is assuming that the originally Persian word *jānavar* specifically meant "pig" (either wild or domestic pigs) in the Turkish of the *Vilayat-nama* and of ʿĀşıkpaşazāde. The context of these mentions suggests that this was indeed the case (see in particular VN 76a, in which a shepherd who mocked Hacı Bektaş is punished by being sent to "Frengistan," where he has to look after pigs). However, the semantic range of the word could also be wider in Turkish at that time, as evidenced by the use of the expression "dörd ayaklu canavar" (four-legged beasts; it would, of course, be pointless to specify the number of legs if the word could refer only to swine) in a ca. 1380–1387 translation of the *Qabusnama* (QN 18).

55. VN 76a; APZ 42; VN 126b. See also the passage in which Ibn Baṭṭūṭa points out that the name of Denizli originally meant "City of the Pigs" and, shortly thereafter, points out the large Christian community in the region (IB 271). Perhaps the only "orthodox" view of the animal appears in an anecdote from the *Manaqib al-ʿArifin* (a man who had pledged to do whatever his wife orders finds himself asked to eat pork), which serves as a setup for a theological debate (MA 3/380). Among all the anecdotes mentioned here, this is by far the one that gives the strongest "canned," abstract, and lifeless impression, especially since it is resolved by a witticism.

56. The faint character of some of these hints suggests that some of these practices

(if they indeed were practices) may not have been codified or even voiced at all. MA 3/581 shows a mule being sold in order to buy food (rather than slaughtering it for meat); GN 2:89a identifies the use of horses as being "for riding"; IB 336 depicts a greedy man skinning a dead horse in order to squeeze all the profit he can (without any mention of selling the meat, even though it would have strengthened the author's argument on that character's greed); MA 5/4 depicts a fishing community as a symbol of low status, though without making direct reference to fish consumption; and MA 3/486 and 3/497 contrast (edible) sheep, which are slaughtered, with dogs, which are not.

Concerning a ban on fish eating among later Mavlāvīs, see also Uzunçarşılı, *Mevlânâ'dan sonra Mevlevîlik*, 291–292. Hongo ("Patterns of Animal Husbandry in Central Anatolia," 105) does notice some bones bearing cut marks that suggest that dogs were butchered in earlier centuries, but finds no such markings from the time period discussed here. She adds, "Although they seem to have been discarded rather than buried, [complete dog skeletons from the time periods relevant to this book] suggest that dogs were often treated in different manner from other animals" (112).

57. In support for the argument of diversity in the possible forms of *ḥalwāʾ*, I should mention the use of the word in the plural (MA 8/58) and one passage that specifies "sweet" (*dadlu*) *ḥalwāʾ* (suggesting that sweetness was not necessarily entailed by the very use of the word *ḥalwāʾ* [SH 16b]). It is, however, possible that the word *dadlu* is merely understood as "good-tasting" here. Other references to *ḥalwāʾ* do not offer decisive insight into its shape or texture: it is in turn presented as cut in pieces (IB 283), carried as "a handful" (*mushtī* [MA 3/79]), served on a tray (IB 283; MA 3/378), likened to *kireç* (lime, i.e., a powdery substance [SH 16b]), and carried in carts (in miraculously large quantities [SH 15b]). One mention also appears in which it is stored in a *khumm* (which, in another anecdote from the same source, appears to be a kind of pitcher used to carry *julāb*), suggesting a liquid or semiliquid consistency (MA 8/80).

Waqfiyyas contain a number of references to the ingredients to be bought in order to make *ḥalwāʾ* on special occasions, including honey (WQ6, WQ8, WQ14), wheat flour (WQ20), butter or fat (*duhn* [WQ8]), saffron (WQ20), and perhaps, in one case, rice (*thamann*, which might very well be a misspelling of *samn*, meaning butter [WQ14]). The prescriptive nature of the documents suggests that rather than a complete list of what was necessary to make *ḥalwāʾ*, these were the most central or unique ingredients or those that were the most likely to be substituted with cheaper products. Still, it seems reasonable to assume that the definition of *ḥalwāʾ* entailed its containing both flour and a sweetener or flavoring agent.

The few passages that refer to other sweets (such as "almond sweets" [shakar-i bādām] in MA 3/411 and *çörek* in VN 111b) never mention these along with *ḥalwāʾ*, leaving open the possibility of an overlapping semantic range, with *ḥalwāʾ* being used in a generic sense (i.e., something along the lines of the word *dessert* in modern English). Yet it does seem counterintuitive to imagine that the numerous passages depicting people as "eating *ḥalwāʾ*" would be so nonspecific about the scene they describe. The one exception in this respect may be the Arabic-language travelogue of Ibn Baṭṭūṭa, who mentions having eaten *ḥalwāʾ* in a number of locations in Anatolia (mostly *ahi*-run *zāwiyas*) in a repetitive, formulaic fashion that systematically lists "*ḥalwāʾ*" along with "food and fruits" (IB 264, 273–274, 285, 307, 348). Such a generic use is attested in the Arabic language of medieval Cairo (Levanoni, "Food and Cooking during the Mamluk Era," 217). On the other hand, a cookbook from Abbasid Baghdad, rather, seems to use the term as I interpret it, in a way that is closer to the modern Turkish use (Arbery, "A Baghdad Cookery-Book," 210–212).

58. MA 3/172. See also 3/85, 3/378, 8/23, and 8/80. *Ḥalwāʾ* also miraculously appears in large quantities, along with other unspecified "bounties" (*nimetler*), when the followers of Sayyid Hārūn are building a city (SH 15b). The "spiritualizing effect" of mentioning *ḥalwāʾ* is not without parallels with the use of fasting and sacrifice (*qurbān*), as I pointed out earlier in this chapter.

59. Respectively, MA 5/11 and 8/58.

60. See MA 9/9, in which the expression "to eat someone's *ḥalwāʾ*" is used to mean outliving them (although this passage is in Persian, a similar expression does exist in modern Turkish), VN 159b (Hacı Bektaş telling his followers to eat *ḥalwāʾ* seven and forty days after his death), and MA 8/41 (with a feast, *ʿurs*, held forty days after a woman from the political elite passes away). Ibn Baṭṭūṭa likewise notes that forty days is the normal length of mourning "among them" (*ʿindahum*, which might refer to Anatolians in general, to the people of Sinop, or to the local elite), suggesting this was a regional peculiarity; he does not, however, make direct mention of *ḥalwāʾ* (IB 354).

In a broad-ranging but rather disorganized survey of medieval references to *ḥalwāʾ*, Irène Mélikoff ("Le rituel du ḥelvâ: Recherches sur une coutume des corporations de métiers dans la Turquie médiévale") notes an association between the latter and mourning. However, she seems to ignore its survival in today's Turkey and downplays the funeral aspect of the issue in favor of what she perceives as a particular association between the dish and craftsmen's guilds.

61. MA 3/567.

62. Amalia Levanoni ("Food and Cooking in the Mamluk Era," 203) notes a similar pattern in the same period in Egypt.

63. See, for example, AE 10/98 and MA 3/567.

64. Homemade: MA 3/85, 3/172, 3/378. References to buying ready-made *ḥalwāʾ* appear in IB 342 ("*ḥalwāʾ* of honey") and MA 3/79. Ibn Baṭṭūṭa also points to an anecdote he heard, involving a street peddler of *ḥalwāʾ*, and whose reliability should probably not be overestimated if we consider the combination of the chronological distance between his informants and the story (the anecdote—a folk interpretation of the meeting between Rūmī and Shams Tabrīzī—takes place three or four generations before Ibn Baṭṭūṭa's visit to Anatolia) and the cultural distance between Ibn Baṭṭūṭa and his informants (which is likely to have affected such details along the way) (IB 283).

65. A disconnect between production and consumption certainly existed when *ḥalwāʾ* was bought ready-made, though it also seems to have taken place in at least some cases when the product was homemade. See, for example, the unspecified third party that distributes *ḥalwāʾ*, after a woman has made it, in the cat anecdote discussed above.

66. There is one reference to the practice (said to be relatively common around Denizli) of making pomegranate wine (AU 335), but if we define "wine" as "fermented

fruit juice," then it is the only alcohol appearing in the sources I used. The drink called *fuqāʿ* (see p. 91) may have been made of mildly fermented barley, but the authors that refer to it clearly did not conceive of it as an alcoholic drink. On distilled alcohols, see p. 203n above.

67. Examples of metaphorical uses of wine to represent mystical knowledge can be found GN 1:120b, 121a, 2:5a; RS 46 and MA 3/281 (both of which oppose it to milk); and MQ 2049 and MA 8/34 and 8/96 (all three of which refer to Sufi "intoxication").

68. For example, APZ 26, 63. Ahmedi's reference to refraining from alcohol and music posits such attitudes as making one a better Muslim than usual (IN 271–272).

69. APZ 68, 96, 99, 115; MA 1/11. On the other hand, Aflākī goes to great lengths to justify the apparent drinking habit of his own spiritual master (ʿĀrif Çelebi). One of the ways in which he does so is by characterizing such a behavior as "Jesus-like" (*ʿĪsāvār* [MA 8/80]), which could perhaps be interpreted as a way to downplay the breach of Islamic ban on alcohol by pointing out theological commonalities with Christian piety.

70. For example, when Rūmī invites a group of Christians and Jews visiting him to abandon wine in order to protect their intellect, his discourse is rendered in Arabic and takes a form that carries a strong scent of import from a theological treatise rather than actual oral conversation (MA 3/597).

71. For example, BR 138 mentions that drinking leads to fighting, but BR 141 and 179 as well as DN 60, rather, associate it with happiness, pleasure, and other types of worldly enjoyments, and BR 205 presents it in the context of polite interaction between enemies. The *Dustur-nama* depicts military troops ("the *gazis*") drinking (*içmek*) with their leaders on several occasions (e.g., DN 73, 95), although only a few of these cases clearly refer to wine or drunkenness. Even when the central character's refraining from alcohol appears as a laudable example of piety, the depiction of his troops' drunkenness is at most presented as a benign sin.

72. AU 311. There is an element of irony in al-ʿUmarī being our best informant in this respect (insofar as, on this issue as much as on pretty much any other, he makes only a limited number of short relevant statements), but this certainly goes to show the extent to which popular wine consumption is conspicuously absent from the sources.

73. AU 335. He also praises the complexion of the inhabitants of the region of Tavas (south of Denizli) as resembling a mixture of milk and wine (AU 339), an image we should obviously relate to the author's literary universe rather than to the drinking habits of late-medieval Anatolians.

74. MA 8/38.

75. GN 1:12a, 2:4b. Both passages use exactly the same formulation, which suggests it might in fact be a set expression—which would limit the degree of extrapolation it is possible to make on its basis.

76. He does, after all, point out with obvious disappointment the widespread and socially accepted consumption of hashish among Anatolians (IB 257).

I should also mention that, when ʿĀşıkpaşa describes the various ages of human life, he refers to "eating and drinking" as a characteristic of the youth (GN 1:64b). Yet while the implication here is clearly that young people are interested in worldly enjoyments, there is no indication that this use of the verb *to drink* necessarily entailed the consumption of alcohol in particular.

77. The closest sources come to offering an explicit condemnation in this respect include MA 3/552, which depicts a religious character whose alcohol consumption leads him to give in to his carnal soul (*nafs*), and SH 28a–b, where Adam's drunkenness is blamed for his yielding to Eve's insistence that he eat the forbidden grain of wheat.

78. Respectively, BR 179 and 138.

79. APZ 26, 96, 99, 115; BR 90–91.

80. DN 70.

81. APZ 68.

CONCLUSION

1. As opposed, say, to the character of Umberto Eco's *Name of the Rose*, William of Baskerville. This character's protoscientific outlook, which represents a possible but highly unusual perspective for its fourteenth-century setting, creates in the modern reader a feeling of empathy for him at the expense of the other characters. We are thus tempted to dismiss the perspectives of the latter as the worldviews of merely ignorant obscurantists. In other words, even though this character's worldview was possible in that period, its being unusual in the very context when most readers first learn about this period has the ultimate effect of *obscuring* rather than conveying the worldviews that actually prevailed in the world where the story is set.

2. "Khidmatgār rā bi-Rūmī guftām . . ." (I said in Greek to the servant . . .) (MA 3/270). It is, of course, possible to formulate a number of guesses, but in view of the multiplicity of mutually exclusive possibilities (ranging from a particular kindness toward the language of the humble to a stark refusal to even let the lowly servant learn the poetic stronghold that was Persian) and the apparent absence of further relevant information, none of these guesses could reasonably be termed "educated."

3. Deciphering the publications, however, may prove rather challenging for the nonspecialist. See, for example, this article on the squatting habits of some late Byzantines: I. H Oygucu et al., "Squatting Facets on the Neck of the Talus and Extensions of the Trochlear Surface of the Talus in Late Byzantine Males."

4. Piero Camporesi, *Bread of Dreams: Food and Fantasy in Early Modern Europe.*

5. IB 277–278.

6. The image of time passing remains fuzzy to the modern reader even when it takes a central place in a narrative. See, for example, the anecdote in which a shepherd, exiled for a year in "Frengistan" after insulting Hacı Bektaş, is woken up by his brother, who claims he had left home the same morning and merely slept through the day (VN 76a–77a).

7. The only exceptions in this respect, the only realms of investigation for which we have sufficient material to discuss alternative approach strategies to "ignorance," are those areas having become the topic of intellectual debates that translated into a significant volume of polemical literature. Partakers in debates about theological issues, for example,

actively explored and explicitly discussed the limits of their knowledge and understanding. Needless to say, these debates were usually topics of concern for a tiny fraction of the population and by no means central components in the worldviews of ordinary people.

APPENDIX

1. Original Persian edited by Tahsin Yazıcı, who also published a Turkish translation (under the title *Āriflerin Menkıbeleri*). There also exists a much-earlier French translation based on a different set of manuscripts (Clément Huart, *Les saints des derviches tourneurs: récits traduits du persan et annotés*), as well as a slightly disappointing but much more recent English one (John O'Kane, *The Feats of the Knowers of God: Manāqeb al-ʿārefīn*). References to the *Manaqib* in this book take the shape of the abbreviation "MA" followed by the paragraph number in Yazıcı's Persian edition.

2. In the absence of a much-needed improved critical edition of this text, I have used the edition by Saʿīd Nafīsī (*Risalay-i Faridun b. Ahmad Sipahsalar dar Ahval-i Mavlana Jalal al-Din Mavlavi*). The only translation I am aware of is an early-twentieth-century Ottoman Turkish one by Midhat Bahari Husami (*Tarjama-yi Risala-yi Sipahsalar ba-Manaqib-i Hazrat-i Khudavandigar*), itself republished in simplified Latin script (Tahir Galip Seratlı, ed., *Sipehsalar Risalesi: Hz. Mevlana ve Yakınları*); neither of those should be used for academic purposes. References to the *Risala* in this book take the shape of the abbreviation "RS," followed by the page number in the Nafīsī edition.

3. There are 162 pages in the Nafīsī edition, as opposed to the 1,000 pages of Yazıcı's edition of the *Manaqib al-ʿArifin*.

4. Compare, for example, RS 100–101 and MA 3/254.

5. It argues, of course, the strength and legitimacy of Rūmī's religious authority, both through displays of miracles (as proofs of his sainthood) and demonstrations of his knowledge of theology.

6. There also exists a written verse version, which I have not used in this research in order to limit the risks associated with the greater frequency at which style influences the choice of vocabulary in verse than in prose. For Gölpınarlı's account of the origins of the written text as well as a discussion of the extant manuscripts, see pages xxiii–xxxix of his edition. Assumedly reaching for a general public audience, Gölpınarlı's simplified Latinized version fails in several ways to meet scholarly standards, most notably due to the significant transformation that Gölpınarlı imposed on the text in order to render it in something close to modern Turkish. I have thus decided to rely on the MS facsimile provided as an appendix to the 1995 edition (the original 1958 edition offered a different, earlier, and more reliable MS as facsimile, but the abysmal print quality makes it mostly illegible). References to the *Vilayat-nama* in this book take the shape of the abbreviation "VN" followed by the folio number in this manuscript.

I should add that I became aware, after the completion of this book, of a new and critical edition of the text, which should be used for any further research: Hamiye Duran, ed., *Velāyetnāme Hacı Bektāş-I Veli.*

7. This text was published in an excellent edition by Cemâl Kurnaz as *Makâlât-i Seyyid Hârûn: Tenkitli Basım*. References to the *Maqalat* in this book take the shape of the abbreviation "SH," followed by the MS folio number as given by Kurnaz.

8. See Franz Taeschner, "Gülshehrī," in *The Encyclopaedia of Islam*, edited by H. A. R. Gibb et al., 2:1138.

9. Franz Taeschner edited and translated the text (to German) twice, once in 1930 (under the title *Ein Mesnevi Gülschehris auf Achi Evran*) and again, with expanded notes and an improved translation, in 1955 (*Gülschehrîs Mesnevi auf Achi Evran, den Heiligen von Kirschehir und Patron der türkischen Zünfte*). References to the *Karamat* in this book take the shape of the abbreviation "AE," followed by the page and line number shared in both these editions.

10. Although there is only one extant manuscript of this work, it is the subject of two editions in Latin script: one by İsmail Erünsal and Ahmet Yaşar Ocak (*Menâkıbu'l-Kudsiyye fî Menâsıbi'l-Ünsiyye*) and one by Mertol Tulum (*Tarihi Metin Çalışmalarında Usul Menakıbu'l-Kudsiyye Üzerinde bir Deneme*). I have primarily used the Tulum edition, but since both editions follow the same line-numbering system, references to the *Manaqib al-Qudsiyya* in this book take the shape of the abbreviation "MQ," followed by the line number.

11. This work is available in a generally excellent facsimile / critical edition / modern Turkish translation by Kemal Yavuz (*Garib-nāme: Tıpkıbasım, kaşılaştırmalı metin ve aktarma*), although the modern Turkish translation tends to be a rather free one and should be approached carefully. References to the *Gharib-nama* in this book take the shape of the abbreviation "GN," followed by the MS page number as given in the Yavuz edition.

12. I provide a full translation of this passage above, as part of my discussion of mills (pp. 51–53).

13. Yûnus Emre, *Divan* and *Risalah al-Nushiyyah*, edited by Mustafa Tatcı as *Divān ve Risâletü'n-Nushiyye*. References to the *Divan* will appear in the format "YED x:y," where *x* is the poem number and *y* is the line number, as given by Tatcı. References to the *Risalah* will appear in the format "YER x," where *x* is the line number.

14. For the purposes of this study, I surveyed only this last section for relevant content. It is available in Kemal Sılay's edition that also includes an English translation, index, and facsimile of the second oldest-known manuscript ("Aḥmedî's History of the Ottoman Dynasty"). References to the *Iskandar-nama* in this book take the shape of the abbreviation "IN," followed by the line number according to the Sılay edition.

15. Edited by Friedrich Giese as *Die altosmanische Chronik des ʿĀšiḳpašazāde* (Leipzig, 1929). References to this chronicle in this book take the shape of the abbreviation "APZ," followed by the chapter (*bāb*) number.

16. For a thorough discussion of this topic, see Kafadar, *Between Two Worlds*, 99–105.

17. APZ 29.

18. I have used the Persian edition by Fuad Köprülü (*Bazm u Razm*). References to the *Bazm u Razm* in this book take the shape of the abbreviation "BR," followed by the page number in the Köprülü edition.

19. For more about the author, see the relevant section of the introduction to Osman Turan's edition of the text (32–40). References to the *Musamara al-Akhbar* in this book take the shape of the abbreviation "AQ," followed by the page number of the Arabic script section in Turan's edition (*Müsāmeret ül-Ahbār: Mogollar zamanında Türkiye Selçukluları tarihi.*) I have not had access to the more recent edition and Turkish translation of this work (*Müsāmeretü'l-ahbār*, edited and translated by Mürsel Öztürk [Ankara: Türk Tarih Kurumu, 2000]).

20. Irène Mélikoff published a superb edition and French translation of the text (*Le Destān d'Umur Pacha*). References to the *Dustur-nama* in this book take the shape of the abbreviation "DN," followed by the page number in the Mélikoff edition.

21. The first part is a history of the prophets and of the kings of Persia, and the third is an Ottoman history. See the introductory notes by Mélikoff (28), who edits and translates only the second part, leaving out the first and third.

22. Whether *Dustur-nama* is correct in attributing to him the leadership of his dynasty is still the subject of debate.

23. I have used the nineteenth-century edition and French translation by C. Defrémery and B. R. Sanguinetti (*Voyages d'Ibn Batoutah*). References to the *Tuhfat* in this book take the form of the abbreviation "IB," followed by the page number in this Defrémery-Sanguinetti edition. The more widely used English translation (H. A. R. Gibb, trans., *The Travels of Ibn Battuta, A.D. 1325–1354*) is indeed based on the Defrémery-Sanguinetti edition and contains page references to it.

24. On this issue, see p. 108.

25. I have used the edition by Aḥmad ʿAbd al-Qādir al-Shādhālī (*Masalik al-Absar fi Mamalik al-Amsar*), though it is worth mentioning that Fuat Sezgin published an excellent manuscript in facsimile without, unfortunately, editing it (*Routes toward Insight into the Capital Empires: Masalik al-Absar fi Mamalik al-Amsar*). References to the *Masalik al-Absar* in this book take the shape of the abbreviation "AU," followed by the page number in the Shādhālī edition.

26. Eleazar Birnbaum, ed. *The Book of Advice by King Kay Kā'us ibn Iskander: The Earliest Old Ottoman Turkish Version of His Ḳābūsnāme.* The edition includes a substantial introduction as well as a facsimile of the manuscript used. References to these translations will take the shape of the abbreviation "QN," followed by the relevant page number in Birnbaum's publication.

27. See, for example, Birnbaum's introduction, 24.

28. They are not state documents, at least in the strictest sense. Although is true that many (though certainly not all) of the endowers were high-ranking state officials, and while the independence of the shariʿa-based judicial apparatus (the structure that supported the *waqf*'s existence as an institution) from political authorities may have been more theoretical than actual, it remains that the establishment of a *waqf* (the act that is recorded in a *waqfiyya*) was an individual's decision rather than any form of state policy and that no state decision could, at least in theory, modify the *waqf*-related laws.

29. I should point out that the word *waqf* actually has two meanings. In the broader sense, as it is used here, it refers to the entire endowment, including both the revenue-

producing and the service-giving property. In the narrower sense, however, it is limited to the revenue-producing property. Although both meanings occur in *waqfiyya*s, it seems that the word *waqf*, when referring to a geographical feature, is limited to the narrower sense.

30. Lefort ("La représentation de l'espace et du paysage dans les documents de l'Athos") discusses more or less contemporary documents from the Mount Athos monasteries that also described agricultural land for surveying purposes. Based on his account, the documents he describes seem to contain a greater degree of detail, including such elements as the nature of the vegetation and, more important, estimates of distances and surface areas for some plots. None of these appears in the *waqfiyya*s consulted for the present study.

31. There are also a few examples of "family *waqf*s," where the revenues are solely meant to provide a livelihood to the descendants of the endower.

32. However, in reality very few medieval *waqfs* survive to this day, in large part because these endowments tend to "die" when, because of mismanagement or other reasons, the revenues grow insufficient, but also due to the *waqf*-cancellation policies of rulers such as Meḥmed II.

33. The catalog of Ankara's *Vakıflar Genel Müdürlüğü* contains as many as a hundred entries that fall within the relevant geographical and chronological range. Detailed examination, however, led me to reduce dramatically this number by weeding out duplicates and catalog entries for which the corresponding documents were impossible to find. By further excluding the few among these *waqfiyya*s that were not directly located in central Anatolia as well as two or three examples that were simply illegible, I arrived at the list of thirty-five documents that I have used here.

A careful comparison between two of these that appear to be subsequent copies of the same document (WQ10 and WQ11, the former corresponding to approximately the first half of the latter) suggests that the copy was indeed a literal one and not a paraphrase. The few differences between these two documents were seldom more than transcription errors, generally substituting for each other two letters that would have been read in the same way by a native Turkish speaker (*ḥā* for *khā*, *tā* for *tā marbūṭa*, and so on). In a few cases entire words were omitted (*lā*, *wa*), although this case study did not contain any change that could have remained unnoticed when put in relation with its context.

References to *waqfiyya*s in this book take the shape of the abbreviation "WQ," followed by a reference number corresponding to the table located in the bibliography.

34. An example of excellent quality can be found in Irène Beldiceanu-Steinherr's *Recherches sur les actes des règnes des sultans Osman, Orkhan et Murad I.*

35. As Amy Singer, one of the leading specialists of *imaret*s, pointed out (personal communication), a comparison between these prescriptive clauses of *waqfiyya*s and other accounting documents emanating from the same institutions suggests that there might have been significant differences between the prescriptions of the founders and the actual functioning of an *imaret*. A close comparison of foundation and accounting documents would be likely to yield considerable insights into the nature of these institutions. Unfortunately, such accounting documents are not available for fourteenth-century Anatolia.

36. There are countless ways in which an inventive crook could have created a gulf between the way the document requires the money to be spent and the way it was actually spent, but even an endower bent on appropriating someone else's agricultural estate had every reason to describe the landscape as accurately as possible.

37. If there is a trait of character that most of today's Ottoman historians share with their medieval counterparts, it may be a general lack of interest for the setting of the stories they tell. By this, I refer not to social contexts or abstract political backgrounds, but rather to the very physical and visual world in which these stories take place, the landscape and the human geography. Quite unsurprisingly, those who have attempted to compensate for this shortcoming generally are scholars who share a strong background in art history. See, for example, Redford, *Landscape and the State* (incidentally, the only study I could find that uses *waqfiyya*s for anecdotal evidence in a discussion of agricultural practices); Redford, "Just Landscape in Medieval Anatolia," esp. 317; and Wolper, *Cities and Saints*. However, even fewer scholars have made a "geographical" use of *waqfiyya*s. One exception (for an urban context) is Çiğdem Kafesçioğlu ("The Ottoman Capital in the Making: The Reconstruction of Constantinople in the Fifteenth Century").

For an early attempt at an all-encompassing review of *waqfiyya*s as historical sources (interesting, yet prone to rather naive generalizations), see Köymen, "Selçuklu devri kaynakları olarak vakfiyeler."

38. The others are usually followed by a mention such as "does not need delineation due to its being well-known where it is" (al-mustaghnī al-taḥdīd li-shuhratihā fī makānihā). Especially considering that many documents contain both delineated and non-delineated items, the choice of those that deserve such a detailed treatment is in itself an interesting issue that remains to be further explored.

39. Different categories of endowed property tend to be surrounded by different categories of bordering elements: this is precisely what allows us to estimate the location of different types of property based on the features surrounding them, making this analysis worthwhile. Yet it is generally the *frequency of occurrence* of given bordering elements, rather their very nature, that changes from one endowed property type to the other. Gardens, for example, are more often (though not exclusively) bordered by other gardens than cereal fields.

Furthermore, although there are individual exceptions, each type of delineated property is associated with a relatively equal number of bordering elements, the average ranging from 3.2 borders given for cereal fields to 4.7 for commercial property.

40. The following excavations or archaeological projects have a significant medieval component, although the extent to which material from the relevant level has been analyzed and published widely varies from one to the other: Amorium, Aşvan Kale, Avkat (a promising, large-scale project still in its early stages), Gritille (perhaps the most thoroughly published site, by Scott Redford), Hattuşa/Boğazkale, Horum Höyük, Kaman-Kalehöyük (which has the most extensive zooarchaeological study, by Hitomi Hongo), Korucutepe, Kubadabad, Sagalassos, Samsat Höyük, Taşkun Kale, Tille Höyük, Yumuktepe, and Zeytinlibahçe.

41. Scott Redford, perhaps the dominant figure in the field, has kindly acted as an

archaeological mentor over the years, but I was also fortunate enough to get help from Joanita Vroom, Canan Çakırlar, and a number of others.

42. Culling pattern analysis tells us, for example, that if sheep of both sexes are kept alive long into adulthood, wool production is likely their main function, whereas if most males are slaughtered young, milk and meat production are probably higher priorities. For a thorough discussion of this approach, see Payne, "Kill-Off Patterns in Sheep and Goats."

TABLE N.1 SEE CHAPTER 2, NOTE 59

Waqfiyya	*Year*	*Region*	*Village*	*Land*	*Mazraʿa*
WQ1	1300/1301	Konya	Y		
WQ4	1306/1307	Amasya	Y		
WQ5	1314/1315	İskilip (Çorum)	Y		
WQ6	1319/1320	Tokat	Y		Y
WQ7	1321	Uşak (Germiyan)	Y		
WQ8	1323	Niksar	Y	Y	
WQ9	1324/1325	Kütahya	Y		
WQ11	1324/1325	Tokat	Y		Y
WQ12	1332/1333	Kastamonu		Y	
WQ13	1336/1337	Bozkır (Konya)		Y	
WQ14	1337/1338	Ankara	Y	Y	Y
WQ15	1339/1340	Amasya?	Y		
WQ16	1344/1345	Tokat?	Y		
WQ17	1344/1345	Larende		Y	
WQ19	1354	Amasya	Y		
WQ20	1362/1363	Tokat	Y		Y
WQ21	1363/1364	Tokat	Y	Y	
WQ22	1363/1364	Konya			Y
WQ23	1363/1364	Kastamonu		Y	
WQ24	1364/1365	Larende		Y	
WQ25	1366/1367	Çorum		Y	
WQ26	1367/1368	Larende	Y		
WQ27	1368/1369	Ankara	Y		
WQ28	1368/1369	Amasya	Y		
WQ29	1368/1369	Konya			Y
WQ31	1370/1371	Niksar/Tokat	Y		
WQ32	1372/1373	Kastamonu		Y	Y
WQ33	1372/1373	Tokat	Y		
WQ34	1373/1374	Çankırı	Y		

TABLE N.2 SEE CHAPTER 3, NOTE 29

Waqfiyya	*Official title*	*Percentage of cook's salary*
WQ8	Shaykh & imam	333
WQ21	*Nāẓir* (endowment overseer)	300
WQ20	Shaykh	225
WQ21	*Farrāsh* (sweeper)	200
WQ21	*Ḥākim* (judge)	200
WQ21	*Jābī* (revenue collector)	200
WQ21	*Naqīb* (manager?)	200
WQ14	Muezzin	117
WQ14	*Bawwāb* (doorman)	100
WQ21	Imam	100
WQ21	*Khabbāz* (bread baker)	100
WQ21	Muezzin	100
WQ21	*Muraqqim* (bookkeeper?)	100
WQ8	*Khādim* (servant)	80
WQ8	*Qannā* (plumber)	80
WQ8	*Ḥammām* (worker)	67
WQ8	*Nāṭūr* (bath attendant)	13

Bibliography

PRIMARY SOURCES

*Waqfiyya*s

ANKARA, *VAKIFLAR GENEL MÜDÜRLÜĞÜ*

Reference (in this book)	*Defter (volume)*	*Sayfa (page)*	*Sıra (serial)*	*Date (hicrī)*	*Location (region)*
WQ1	596	151	134	700	Konya, Niğde, Larende, Akşehir
WQ2	591	12	16	703	Kastamonu
WQ3	582/1	271	183	705	Kastamonu
WQ4	607	10	11	706	Amasya
WQ5	610	36	45	714	İskilip (Çorum)
WQ6	608/2	63	52	719	Tokat
WQ7	592	139	116	721	Uşak
WQ8	581/2	198	300	723	Niksar
WQ9	608/2	296	240	725	Kütahya
WQ10	484	137	226	725	Tokat
WQ11	484	309	20	725	Tokat
WQ12	606	193	246	733	Kastamonu
WQ13	581	232	231	737	Bozkır (Konya)
WQ14	593	255	201	738	Ankara
WQ15	609	226	269	740	Amasya?
WQ16	581/2	332	325	745	Tokat?
WQ17	579	363	159	745	Larende
WQ18	593	255	201	753	Ankara
WQ19	590	51	35	755	Amasya

Reference (in this book)	*Defter (volume)*	*Sayfa (page)*	*Sıra (serial)*	*Date (hicrī)*	*Location (region)*
WQ20	581/2	20	11	764	Tokat
WQ21	611	93	79	765	Tokat
WQ22	2178	77	59	765	Konya
WQ23	582/1	286	195	765	Kastamonu
WQ24	579	362	158	766	Larende
WQ25	601	175	230	768	Çorum
WQ26	579	360	157	769	Larende
WQ27	582/2	328	236	770	Ankara
WQ28	608/1	235	255	770	Amasya
WQ29	608/1	123	151	770	Konya
WQ30	608/1	223	238	770	Akşehir
WQ31	734	324	157	772	Niksar and Tokat
WQ32	580	121	74	774	Kastamonu
WQ33	589	256	423	774	Tokat
WQ34	612	6	8	775	Çankırı
WQ35	595	103	96	795	Afyon Karahisar

NARRATIVE SOURCES

ʿAbd al-Karīm b. Shaykh Mūsa. *Maqalat-i Sayyid Harun.* Edited by Cemâl Kurnaz as *Makālāt-i Seyyid Hârûn: Tenkitli Basım.* Ankara: Türk Tarih Kurumu Basımevi, 1991.

Aflākī, Shams al-Dīn Aḥmad. *Manaqib al-ʿArifin.* Edited by Tahsin Yazıcı. 2 vols. Ankara: Chāpkhānah-i Anjuman-i Ta'rīkh-i Turk, 1959–1961.

Ahmedī. *Iskandar-nama.* Edited and translated by Kemal Sılay as "Aḥmedi's History of the Ottoman Dynasty." *Journal of Turkish Studies* 16 (1992): 129–200.

al-Aqsarāyī, Karīm al-Dīn Maḥmūd. *Musamarat al-Akhbar.* Edited by Osman Turan as *Müsāmeret ül-akhbar: Mogollar zamanında Türkiye Selçukluları tarihi.* Ankara: Türk Tarih Kurumu Basımevi, 1944.

ʿĀşıkpaşa. *Gharib-nama.* Edited by Kemal Yavuz as *Garib-nāme: Tıpkıbasım, karşılaştırılmalı metin ve aktarma.* 4 vols. Istanbul: Türk Dil Kurumu, 2000.

ʿĀşıkpaşazāde. *Tavarikh-i Al-i Osman.* Edited by Çiftçioğlu Nihat Atsız in *Osmanlı Tarihleri.* Istanbul: Türkiye Yayınevi, 1949.

Astarābādī, ʿAzīz b. Ardashīr. *Bazm u Razm.* Edited by Fuat Köprülü. Istanbul: Evkaf Matbaası, 1928.

Elvan Çelebi. *Manaqib al-Qudsiyya fi Manasib al-Unsiyya.* Edited by İsmail Erünsal and Ahmet Yaşar Ocak as *Menākıbu'l-Kudsiyye fī Menāsıbi'l-Ünsiyye.* Istanbul: Türk Tarih Kurumu, 1984. Also edited by Mertol Tulum as *Tarihi Metin Çalışmalarında Usul Menakıbu'l-Kudsiyye Üzerinde bir Deneme.* Istanbul: Deniz Kitabevi, 2000.

Enverī. *Dustur-nama.* Edited and translated by Irène Mélikoff as *Le destan d'Umur Pacha.* Paris: Presses Universitaires de France, 1954.

Gülşehri. *Karamat-i Akhi Avran.* Edited by Franz Taeschner as *Ein Mesnevi Gülschehris auf Achi Evran.* Hamburg: Buchdrucker Heinrich Augustin, 1930.

Ibn Baṭṭūṭa. *Rihla.* Edited and translated by C. Defrémery and B. R. Sanguinetti as *Voyages d'Ibn Batoutah.* Paris: Société Asiatique, 1877.

Kay Kā'us b. Iskandar. *Qabus-nama.* Sample of five early Turkish translations edited by Eleazar Birnbaum in *The Book of Advice by King Kay Kā'us ibn Iskander: The Earliest Old Ottoman Turkish Version of His Ḳābūsnāme,* 16–25. Cambridge, MA: Sources of Oriental Languages and Literatures, 1981.

Sipahsālār, Farīdūn b. Aḥmad. *Risāla.* Edited by Sa'īd Nafīsī as *Risalay-i Faridun b. Ahmad Sipahsalar dar Ahval-i Mavlana Jalal al-Din Mavlavi.* Tehran: Kitābkhāna ve Chāpkhāna-yi Iqbāl, 1325 (1946).

al-ʿUmarī, Ibn Faḍl Allah. *Masalik al-Absar fi Mamalik al-Amsar.* Edited by Aḥmad ʿAbd al-Qādir al-Shādhālī. Vol. 3. Abu Dhabi: al-Majmaʿ al-Saqafī, 2003.

Vilayat-nama-yi Haji Baktash Veli. Edited by Abdülbâkî Gölpınarlı (with a manuscript facsimile) as *Vilāyet-nāme: Manākıb-ı Hünkār Hacı Bektāş-ı Veli.* Istanbul: İnkılâp, 1995.

Yūnus Emre. *Divân ve Risâletü'n-Nushiyye.* Edited by Mustafa Tatcı. Istanbul: Sahhaflar Kitap Sarayı, 2005.

OTHER SOURCES

Afshar, Iraj. *Kar-nama ve Maddat al-Haya: Matn-i Du Risala dar Ashpazi az Davra-yi Safavi: ʿAsr-i Saltanat-i Shah Ismaʿil-i Avval ve Shah ʿAbbas-i Avval.* Tehran: Surūsh, 1360 (1981).

Akın, Himmet. *Aydın Oğulları tarihi hakkında bir araştırma.* Istanbul: Pulhan Matbaası, 1946.

Albala, Ken. *Eating Right in the Renaissance.* Berkeley: University of California Press, 2002.

Algar, Ayla. "Food in the Tekke." In *The Dervish Lodge: Architecture, Art, and Sufism in Ottoman Turkey,* edited by Raymond Lifchez, 296–303. Berkeley: University of California Press, 1992.

ʿÂlī, Muṣṭafā. *Mawaʾid al-Nefaʾis fī Qawaʾid al-Majalis.* Edited by Mehmet Şeker. Ankara: Türk Tarih Kurumu, 1997. English translation by Douglas S. Brookes under the title *The Ottoman Gentleman of the Sixteenth Century: Mustafa Āli's Mevāʾidüʾn-Nefāis fī Kavāʿidʾl-mecālis.* Cambridge, MA: Department of Near Eastern Languages and Civilizations, Harvard University, 2003.

Alvaro, Corrado, Francesca Balossi R., and Joanita Vroom. "Zeytinli Bahçe, a Medieval Fortified Settlement." *Anatolia Antiqua* 12 (2004): 191–213.

Arbery, A. J. "A Baghdad Cookery-Book." *Islamic Culture* 13 (1939): 21–47, 189–214.

Arthur, Paul. "Pots and Boundaries: On Cultural and Economic Areas between Late Antiquity and the Early Middle Ages." In *Late Roman Coarse Wares, Cooking Wares, and Amphorae in the Mediterranean: Archaeology and Archaeometry*, edited by Michel Bonifay and Jean-Christophe Tréglia, 15–27. Oxford: Archaeopress, 2007.

Ashtor, Eliyahu. "Essai sur l'alimentation des diverses classes sociales dans l'Orient medieval." *Annales: Économies, sociétés, civilisations* 23, nos. 5–6 (1968): 1017–1053.

Aubaile-Sallenave, Françoise. "Al-Khishk: The Past and Present of a Complex Culinary Practice." In *A Taste of Thyme: Culinary Cultures of the Middle East*, edited by Richard Tapper and Sami Zubaida, 105–139. New York: Tauris Parke, 2000.

Bachrach, Bernard S. "Some Observations on Administration and Logistics of the Siege of Nicaea." *War in History* 12, no. 3 (2005): 249–277.

Bakırer, Ömür. "The Medieval Pottery and Baked Clay Objects." Chapter 8 in *Korucutepe: Final Report of the Excavation of the Universities of Chicago, California (Los Angeles), and Amsterdam in the Keban Reservoir, Eastern Anatolia, 1968–1970*, edited by Maurits N. van Loon, 3:189–249. Amsterdam: North-Holland, 1980.

Barkan, Ömer Lütfi. *XV ve XVI ıncı asırlarda Osmanlı İmparatorluğunda ziraî ekonominin hukukî ve malî esasları*. Vol. 1, *Kanunlar*. Istanbul: Burhaneddin Matbaası, 1943.

Bartosiewicz, László. "Animal Remains from the Excavations of Horum Höyük, Southeast Anatolia, Turkey." In *Archaeozoology of the Near East VI: Proceedings from the Sixth International Symposium on the Archaeozoology of Southwestern Asia and Adjacent Areas*, 150–162. Groningen: ARC, 2005.

Beldiceanu, Nicoara, and Irène Beldiceanu-Steinherr. "Riziculture dans l'empire ottoman (XIVe–Xve siècle)." *Turcica* 9–10, no. 2 (1978): 9–28.

Beldiceanu-Steinherr, Irène. "Dans le labyrinthe des débuts de l'histoire ottomane: À propos d'un ouvrage de R. P. Lindner." *Turcica* 40 (2008): 395–407.

———. "Fiscalité et formes de possession de la terre arable dans l'Anatolie préottomane." *Journal of the Economic and Social History of the Orient* 19, no. 3 (1976): 233–322.

———. "Recherches sur la province de Qaraman au XVIe siècle: Étude et actes." *Journal of the Economic and Social History of the Orient* 11, no. 1 (1968): 1–129.

———. *Recherches sur les actes des règnes des sultans Osman, Orkhan et Murad I*. Munich: Societatas Academica Dacomana, 1967.

Bell, Rudolph M. *Holy Anorexia*. Chicago: University of Chicago Press, 1985.

Bloch, Marc. "Avènement et conquête du moulin à eau." *Annales ESC* 7, no. 36 (1935): 538–563.

Boessneck, J., and A. von den Driesch. "The Animal Bones from Korucutope Near Elâzığ, Eastern Anatolia: Finds from the 1968–1969 Excavation" [English summary]. In *Korucutepe: Final Report on the Excavations of the Universities of Chicago, California (Los Angeles), and Amsterdam in the Keban Reservoir, Eastern Anatolia, 1968–1969*, edited by Maurits N. van Loon, 1:193–220. Amsterdam: North-Holland and American Elsevier, 1975.

Bolens, Lucie. "Le haricot vert en Andalousie et en Méditerranée médiévales (phaseolus, dolichos, lubia, judia)." *Al-Qantara: Revista de estudios Arabes* 8, nos. 1–2 (1987): 65–86.

Bordaz, Jacques. "The Threshing Sledge." *Natural History* 74, no. 4 (1967): 26–29.

Brant, James. "Journey through a Part of Armenia and Asia Minor, in the Year 1835." *Journal of the Royal Geographic Society of London* 6 (1836): 187–223.

Bryer, Anthony. "The Means of Agricultural Production: Muscles and Tools." In *The Economic History of Byzantium: From the Seventh through the Fifteenth Century*, edited by Angeliki Laiou, 101–113. Washington, DC: Dumbarton Oaks, 2002.

Bryer, Anthony, and Heath Lowry, eds. *Continuity and Change in Late Byzantine and Early Ottoman Society*. Washington, DC: Dumbarton Oaks, 1986.

Buitenhuis, Herman. "Archaeozoology of the Holocene in Anatolia: A Review." In *Archaeometry 94: The Proceedings of the 29th International Symposium on Archaeometry*, edited by I. Demirci, A. Özer, and G. Summers Ankara, 411–421. Ankara: Tübitak.

———. "Preliminary Report on the Faunal Remains of Hayaz Hoyuk from the 1979–1983 Seasons." *Anatolica* 12 (1985): 61–74.

Bynum, Caroline Walker. *Holy Feast and Holy Fast: The Religious Significance of Food to Medieval Women*. Berkeley: University of California Press, 1987.

Cahen, Claude. "Ibn Saʿīd sur l'Asie Mineure Seldjuqide." *Tarih Arastirmalari Dergisi* 6, no. 10 (1968): 41–50.

———. "Notes pour une histoire de l'agriculture dans les pays musulmans médiévaux." *Journal of the Economic and Social History of the Orient* 14, no. 1 (1971): 63–68.

———. "Sur les traces des premiers Akhis." In *60. Yıldönümü münasebitiyle Fuad Köprülü armağanı (Mélanges Fuad Köprülü)*, 81–91. Istanbul: Dil ve Tarih-Coğrafya Fakültesi, 1953.

Camporesi, Piero. *Bread of Dreams: Food and Fantasy in Early Modern Europe*. Cambridge: Polity Press, 1989.

Canard, Marius. "Le riz dans le Proche Orient aux premiers siècles de l'Islam." *Arabica* 6 (1959): 113–131.

Caneva, Isabella, and Gülgün Köroğlu. *Yumuktepe: A Journey through Nine Thousand Years*. Istanbul: Ege Yayınları, 2010.

Carroll, Lynda, and Uzi Baram, eds. *A Historical Archaeology of the Ottoman Empire: Breaking New Ground*. New York: Kluwer Academic / Plenum, 2000.

Charanis, Peter. *Studies on the Demography of the Byzantine Empire: Collected Studies*. London: Variorum Reprints, 1972.

Comer, James. "Distilled Beverages." In *The Cambridge World History of Food*, edited by Kenneth F. Kiple et al., 1:653–664. Cambridge: Cambridge University Press, 2000.

Croke, Brian, and Anthony Cutler. "Day." In *The Oxford Dictionary of Byzantium*, edited by Alexander P. Kazhdan. Oxford: Oxford University Press, 2005.

Cunbur, Müjgan. "Mevlana'nın Mesnevi'sinde ve Divan-ı Kebir'inde Yemekler." In *Türk Mutfağı Sempozyumu Bildirleri 31 Ekim–1 Kasım 1981*, 69–85. Ankara: Kültür ve Turizm Bakanlığı, 1982.

Danti, Michael D. *The Ilkhanid Heartland: Hasanlu Tepe (Iran) Period I*. Philadelphia: University of Pennsylvania Museum of Archaeology and Anthropology, 2004.

Delahaye, Hippolyte. *Cinq leçons sur la méthode hagiographique*. Subsidia Hagiographica no. 21. Brussels: Société des Bollandistes, 1934.

———. *Les légendes hagiographiques*. Subsidia Hagiographica no. 18. Brussels: Société des Bollandistes, 1905.

Douglas, Mary. "Deciphering a Meal." In *Myth, Symbol, and Culture*, edited by Clifford Geertz, 61–81. New York: W. W. Norton, 1971.

Duby, Georges. *Rural Economy and Country Life in the Medieval West*. Translated by Cynthia Postan. Columbia: University of South Carolina Press, 1968.

———. "La seigneurie et l'économie paysanne, Alpes du Sud 1338." *Études Rurales*, no. 2 (June–July 1961): 5–36.

Eastwood, Warren J., Osman Gümüşçü, Hakan Yiğitbaşıoğlu, John F. Haldon, and Ann England. "Integrating Palaeoecological and Archaeo-historical Records: Land Use and Landscape Change in Cappadocia (Central Turkey) since Late Antiquity." In *Archaeology of the Countryside in Medieval Anatolia*, edited by Tasha Vorderstrase and Jacob Roodenberg, 46–69. Uitgave: Nederlands Instituut voor het Nabije Oosten, 2009.

Eilers, Wilhelm, Marcel Bazin, and William L. Hanaway. "Bāg." In *Encyclopaedia Iranica*, edited by Ehsan Yarshater, 3:392–396. London: Routledge and Kegan Paul, 1982.

Ersoy, Bozkurt. "Kale-i Tavas (Tabae) 2007 yılı kazısı." *Kazı Sonuçları Toplantısı* 30, no. 3 (2008): 41–56.

Fairbairn, Andrew, Catherine Longford, and Bronwyn Griffin. "Archaeobotany at Kaman-Kalehöyük 2006." *Anatolian Archaeological Studies* 16 (2007): 151–158.

Fairbairn, Andrew, and Sachihiro Omura. "Archaeological Identification and Significance of ÉSAG (Agricultural Storage Pits) at Kaman-Kalehöyük." *Anatolian Studies* 55 (2005): 15–23.

Falassi, Alessandro. "Festival: Definition and Morphology." In *Time Out of Time: Essays on the Festival*, edited by A. Falassi, 1–9. Albuquerque: University of New Mexico Press, 1987.

Faroqhi, Suraiya. "Supplying Seventeenth- and Eighteenth-Century Istanbul with Fresh Produce." In *Nourrir les cités de Méditerranée: Antiquité—temps modernes*, edited by Brigitte Marin and Catherine Virlouvet, 273–301. Paris: Maisonneuve et Larose, 2003.

———. "The Tekke of Hacı Bektaş: Social Position and Economic Activities." *International Journal of Middle East Studies* 7 (1976): 183–208.

Faroqhi, Suraiya, and C. Neumann. *The Illuminated Table, the Prosperous House: Food and Shelter in Ottoman Material Culture*. Istanbul: Orient-Institut, 2003.

Flandrin, Jean-Louis. "Le goût et la nécessité: Sur l'usage des graisses dans les cuisines d'Europe occidentale (XIV–XVIIIe siècle)." *Annales ESC* 38, no. 2 (1983): 369–401.

———. "Mealtimes in France before the Nineteenth Century." *Food and Foodways* 6, nos. 3–4 (1996): 161–192.

Flandrin, Jean-Louis, and Massimo Montanari, eds. *Histoire de l'alimentation*. Paris: Fayard, 1996.

Foss, Clive. *Nicaea: A Byzantine Capital and Its Praises*. Brookline, MA: Hellenic College Press, 1996.

Frangipane, Marcella, Corrado Alvaro, Francesca Balossi R., and Giovanni Sirucasano. "The 2000 Campaign at Zeytinlibahçe Höyük." In *Ilısu ve Karkamış Baraj Gölleri Altında Kalacak Arkeolojik Kültür Varlıklarını Kurtarma Projesi: 2001 Yılı Açılış Çalış-*

maları [Salvage project of the archaeological heritage of the Ilısu and Carchemish Dam Reservoirs activities in 1999], edited by Nurman Tuna, Jean Öztürk, and Jâle Velibeyoğlu, 57–99. Ankara: Orta Doğu Teknik Üniversitesi, 2001.

Frangipane, Marcella, Francesca Balossi R., Gian Maria Di Nocera, Alberto Palmieri, and Giovanni Sirucasano. "The 2001 Excavation Campaign at Zeytinlibahçe Höyük: Preliminary Results." In *Ilısu ve Karkamış Baraj Gölleri Altında Kalacak Arkeolojik Kültür Varlıklarını Kurtarma Projesi: 2001 Yılı Açılış Çalışmaları*, 20–56. Ankara: Orta Doğu Teknik Üniversitesi, 2004.

Geertz, Clifford. *Islam Observed: Religious Development in Morocco and Indonesia*. New Haven, CT: Yale University Press, 1968.

Geyer, Bernard, and Jacques Lefort, eds. *La Bithynie au moyen-âge*. Réalités Byzantines. Paris: P. Lethielleux, 2003.

Ghouchani, Abdullah, and Charyar Adle. "A Sphero-conical Vessel as *Fuqqāʿa*, or a Gourd for 'Beer.'" *Muqarnas* 9 (1992): 72–92.

Godwin, Harry. "The Ancient Cultivation of Hemp." *Antiquity* 41, no. 1 (1967): 42–49.

Goell, Theresa. "Samosata Archaeological Excavations, Turkey, 1967." *National Geographic Society Research Reports 1967* (1974): 83–109.

Gölpınarlı, Abdülbâki. *Mevlânâ'dan sonra Mevlevîlik*. Istanbul: İnkılâp Kitabevi, 1953.

Goody, Jack. *Cooking, Cuisine, and Class: A Study in Comparative Sociology*. Cambridge: Cambridge University Press, 1982.

Grimm, Veronika E. *From Feasting to Fasting: The Evolution of a Sin; Attitudes to Food in Late Antiquity*. London: Routledge, 1996.

Hall, Gerald, Sam McBride, and Alwyn Riddell. "Architectural Study." *Anatolian Studies* 23 ["Special Number: Aşvan 1968–1973"] (1973): 245–269.

Hayton. *La fleur des histoires des la terre d'Orient*. Translated to modern French by Christiane Deluz in *Croisades et Pèlerinages: Récits, chroniques et voyages en terre sainte, XIIe–XVIe siècle*, edited by Danielle Régnier-Bohler, 803–878. Paris: Robert Laffont, 1997.

Hendy, Michael F. *Studies in the Byzantine Monetary Economy, c. 300–1450*. Cambridge: Cambridge University Press, 1985.

Higgs, Eric S., ed. *Papers in Economic Prehistory*. Cambridge: Cambridge University Press, 1972.

Hill, Donald. *A History of Engineering in Classical and Medieval Times*. London: Routledge, 1984.

Hillmann, Gordon. "Agricultural Productivity and Past Population Potential at Aşvan." *Anatolian Studies* 23 (1973): 217–224.

———. "Agricultural Resources and Settlement in the Aşvan Region." *Anatolian Studies* 23 (1973): 225–240.

Hobsbawm, Eric, ed. *The Invention of Tradition*. Cambridge: Cambridge University Press, 1983.

Hongo, Hitomi. "Patterns of Animal Husbandry, Environment, and Ethnicity in Central Anatolia in the Ottoman Empire Period: Faunal Remains from the Islamic Layers at Kaman-Kalehoyuk." *Japan Review* 8 (1997): 275–307.

———. "Patterns of Animal Husbandry in Central Anatolia from the Second Millennium BC through the Middle Ages: Faunal Remains from Kaman-Kalehoyuk, Turkey." PhD diss., Harvard University, 1996.

Huart, Clément. *Les saints des derviches tourneurs: Récits traduits du persan et annotés.* 2 vols. Paris: Éditions Ernest Leroux, 1918–1922.

Humphreys, R. Stephen. *Islamic History: A Framework for Inquiry.* Princeton, NJ: Princeton University Press, 1991.

Imber, Colin. "The Status of Orchards and Fruit Trees in Ottoman Law." In *Studies in Ottoman History and Law*, 207–216. Istanbul: Isis, 1996. Reprinted from *Tarih Enstitüsü Dergisi* 12 (1982): 763–774.

Inalcik, Halil. "How to Read APZ's History." In *Studies in Ottoman History in Honor of Professor V. L. Ménage.* Istanbul: Isis Press, 1994.

———. "Rice Cultivation and the Çeltükci-Reʿâyâ System in the Ottoman Empire." *Turcica* 14 (1982): 69–141.

Isaac, Rhys. *The Transformation of Virginia, 1740–1790.* Chapel Hill: University of North Carolina Press, 1982.

Kafadar, Cemal. *Between Two Worlds: The Construction of the Ottoman State.* Berkeley: University of California Press, 1995.

Kafesçioğlu, Çiğdem. "The Ottoman Capital in the Making: The Reconstruction of Constantinople in the Fifteenth Century." PhD diss., Harvard University, 1996.

Kalas, Veronica. "The Byzantine Kitchen in the Domestic Complexes of Cappadocia." In *Archaeology of the Countryside in Medieval Anatolia*, edited by T. Vorderstrasse and Jacob Roodenberg, 109–127. Leiden: Nederlands Instituut voor het Nabije Oosten, 2009.

Kaplan, Michel. *Les hommes et la terre à Byzance du VIe au XIe siècle.* Paris: Publications de la Sorbonne, 1992.

Karamustafa, Ahmet. *God's Unruly Friends: Dervish Groups in the Islamic Later Middle Period, 1200–1550.* Salt Lake City: University of Utah Press, 1994.

Kazhdan, Alexander. "'Сколько eJm Византийцы?" [How much did the Byzantines eat?]. *Voprosy Istorii* 9 (September 1970): 215–218.

Köprülü, Mehmed Fuad. *Türk edebiyatı'nda ilk mutasavvıflar.* 1918. Reprint, Ankara: Türk Tarih Kurumu Basımevi, 1976.

Korobeinikov, Dimitri. "Orthodox Communities in Eastern Anatolia in the Thirteenth and Fourteenth Centuries." Pt. 1, "The Two Patriarchates: Constantinople and Antioch." *Al-Masāq* 15, no. 2 (2003).

———. "Orthodox Communities in Eastern Anatolia in the Thirteenth and Fourteenth Centuries." Pt. 2, "The Time of Troubles." *Al-Masāq* 17, no. 1 (2005): 1–29.

Köymen, Mehmet Altay. "Selçuklu devri kaynakları olarak vakfiyeler." In *Studi Preottomani e Ottomani, Atti del Convegno di Napoli 24–26 Settembre 1974*, edited by Aldo Gallotta. Naples: Istituto universitario orientale, 1976.

———. "Selçuklular zamanında beslenme sistemi." In *Türk Mutfağı Sempozyumu Bildirileri (31 Ekim–1 Kasım 1981, Ankara)*, 35–45. Ankara: Ankara Üniversitesi Basımevi, 1982.

Kut, Günay. "Tabîat-nâme ve Tatlılar Üzerine Bir Yazma Eser 'et-Terkîbât Fî Tabhi'l-Hulviyyât.'" *Folklor ve Etnografya Araştırmaları* (Istanbul) (1985).

———. "13. yüzyıla ait bir yemek kitabı." *Kaynaklar* (Şekerbank) 3 (1984): 50–57.

Kut, Turgut. *Açıklamalı Yemek Kitapları Bibliyografyası: Eski Harflı Yazma ve Basma Eserler.* Ankara: Kültür ve Turizm Bakanlığı, 1985.

Lagardère, Vincent. "Structures agraires et perception de l'espace à travers les recueils de consultations juridiques (XIe–XVe siècles)." In *Castrum 5: Archéologie des espaces agraires méditerranéens au moyen-âge*, edited by André Bazzana, 137–150. Madrid, Rome, and Murcie: Casa de Velazquez / École française de Rome / Ayuntamiento de Murcia, 1999.

Laiou, Angeliki. *Economic History of Byzantium.* Washington, DC: Dumbarton Oaks, 2002.

Landsberg, Sylvia. *The Medieval Garden.* London: Thames and Hudson, 1995.

Lane, Edward. *Arabic-English Lexicon.* Cambridge: Islamic Texts Society, 1984.

Lane, Edward William. *The Manners and Customs of the Modern Egyptians.* London: J. M. Dent and Sons / New York: E. P. Dutton, 1908.

Lefort, Jacques. "La représentation de l'espace et du paysage dans les documents de l'Athos." In *Castrum 5: Archéologie des espaces agraires méditerranéens au moyen-âge*, edited by André Bazzana, 102–112. Madrid, Rome, and Murcie: Casa de Velazquez / École française de Rome / Ayuntamiento de Murcia, 1999.

Levanoni, Amalia. "Food and Cooking during the Mamluk Era: Social and Political Implications." *Mamluk Studies Review* 9, no. 2 (2005): 201–222.

Lévi-Strauss, Claude. *Le cru et le cuit.* Paris: Plon, 1964.

Lewicka, Paulina B. *Food and Foodways of the Medieval Cairenes: Aspects of Life in an Islamic Metropolis of the Eastern Mediterranean.* Leiden: Brill, 2011.

Lewis, Franklin D. *Rumi Past and Present, East and West.* Oxford: Oneworld, 2000.

Lightfoot, Chris S. "Amorium-Hisarcık'ın Selçuklu ve Osmanlı Dönemlerine ait Yerleşim ve Arkeolojisi." *Ege Üniversitesi Sanat Tarihi Dergisi* 9 (1998): 75–84.

Lindner, Rudi Paul. *Explorations in Ottoman Prehistory.* Ann Arbor: University of Michigan Press, 2007.

———. *Nomads and Ottomans in Medieval Anatolia.* Bloomington: Research Institute for Inner Asian Studies, Indiana University, 1983.

Littlewood, Antony, Henry Maguire, and Joachim Wolschke-Bulmahn, eds. *Byzantine Garden Culture.* Washington, DC: Dumbarton Oaks, 2002.

Lowry, Heath W. *The Nature of the Early Ottoman State.* Albany: SUNY Press, 2003.

Macbeth, Helen, and Jeremy MacClancy. *Researching Food Habits: Methods and Problems.* New York and Oxford: Berghahn Books, 2004.

Maqrīzī. *Ighathat al-Umma bi-Kashf al-Ghumma.* Edited by Muḥammad Muṣṭafā Ziyāda and Jamāl al-Dîn Muḥammad al-Shayāl. Cairo, 1940. French translation by Gaston Wiet as *Le traité des famines de Maqrīzī.* Leiden: Brill, 1962.

Matney, Timothy, et al. "Tenth Preliminary Report on Excavations at Ziyaret Tepe (Diyarbakır Province), 2007 Seasons [*sic*]." *Kazı Sonuçları Toplantısı* 30, no. 1 (2008): 507–520.

Mayeur-Jaouen, Catherine. *Al-Sayyid al-Badawi: Un grand saint de l'Islam égyptien*. Cairo: Institut français d'archéologie orientale, 1994.

McNicoll, Anthony. *Taşkun Kale: Keban Rescue Excavations, Eastern Anatolia*. Ankara: British Institute of Archaeology, 1983.

Meisami, Julie Scott. *Persian Historiography to the End of the Twelfth Century*. Edinburgh: Edinburgh University Press, 1999.

Mélikoff, Irène. *Hadji Bektach: Un mythe et ses avatars; Genèse et évolution du soufisme populaire en Turquie*. Leiden and Boston: Brill, 1998.

———. "Le rituel du ḥelvâ: Recherches sur une coutume des corporations de métiers dans la Turquie médiévale." *Der Islam: Zeitschrift für Geschichte und Kultur des Islamischen Orients* 39 (February 1964): 180–191.

Merçil, Erdoğan. *Türkiye Selçukluları'nda meslekler*. Ankara: Türk Tarih Kurumu, 2000.

Miller, Naomi F. "Patterns of Agriculture and Land Use at Medieval Gritille." In *The Archaeology of the Frontier in the Medieval Near East: Excavations at Gritille, Turkey*, edited by Scott Redford, 211–252. Philadelphia: University of Pennsylvania Museum of Archaeology and Anthropology, 1998.

Mitchell, Stephen. *Aşvan Kale: Keban Rescue Excavations, Eastern Anatolia*. Vol. 1, *The Hellenistic, Roman, and Islamic Sites*. Oxford: BAR, 1980.

Moore, John. *Tille Höyük I: The Medieval Period*. Ankara: British Institute of Archaeology, 1993.

Nasrallah, Nawal, trans. *Annals of the Caliph's Kitchens: Ibn Sayyār al-Warrāq's Tenth-Century Baghdadi Cookbook*. English translation with introduction and glossary. Leiden: Brill, 2007.

Nesbitt, Mark. "Grains." In *Cultural History of Plants*, edited by Ghillean Prance, 45–60. New York and London: Routledge, 2005.

Nesbitt, Mark, and G. D. Summers. "Some Recent Discoveries of Millet (*Panicum miliaceum l.* and *Setaria italica [L.] P. Beauv.*) at Excavations in Turkey and Iran." *Anatolian Studies* 38 (1988): 85–97.

Newman, James L. "Wine." In *The Cambridge World History of Food*, edited by Kenneth F. Kiple et al., 1:730–737. Cambridge: Cambridge University Press, 2000.

Ocak, Ahmet Yaşar. *La révolte de Baba Resul; ou, La formation de l'hétérodoxie musulmane en Anatolie au XIIIe siècle*. Ankara: Turk Tarih Kurumu, 1989.

O'Kane, John. *The Feats of the Knowers of God: Manāqeb al-ʿārefīn*. Leiden: Brill, 2002.

Öney, Gönül. "Pottery from the Samosata Excavations, 1978–81." In *The Art of the Saljuqs in Iran and Anatolia*, edited by Robert Hillenbrand, 286–294. Costa Mesa, CA: Mazda, 1994.

Önler, Zafer, ed. *Celālüddin Hızır [Hacı Paşa]: Müntahab-ı Şifā*. Vol. 1, *Giriş, Metin*. Ankara: Türk Dil Kurumu, 1990.

Osborne, Robin. *Classical Landscape with Figures: The Ancient Greek City and Its Countryside*. London: Sheridan House, 1987.

Oygucu, I. H., M. A. Kurt, I. Ikiz, T. Erem, and D. C. Davies. "Squatting Facets on the Neck of the Talus and Extensions of the Trochlear Surface of the Talus in Late Byzantine Males." *Journal of Anatomy* 192 (February 1998): 287–291.

Özgüç, Tahsin. "Samsat Kazıları 1987." *Türk Tarih Kurumu Belleten* 52, no. 202 (1988): 291–294.

Parker, Bradley J., and M. Barış Uzel. "The Tradition of *Tandır* Cooking in Southeastern Anatolia: An Ethnoarchaeological Perspective." In *Ethnoarchaeological Investigations in Rural Anatolia*, edited by Turan Takaoğlu, 4:7–43. Istanbul: Ege Yayınları, 2007.

Payne, Sebastian. "Kill-Off Patterns in Sheep and Goats: The Mandibles from Asvan Kale." *Anatolian Studies* 23 (1973): 280–303.

Peirce, Leslie. *Morality Tales: Law and Gender in the Ottoman Court of Aintab*. Berkeley: University of California Press, 2003.

Perry, Charles. *A Baghdad Cookery Book: The Book of Dishes (Kitab al-Tabikh)*. Blackawton, UK: Prospect Books, 2005.

———. "A Thousand and One Fritters: The Food of the Arabian Nights." In *Medieval Arab Cookery*, 489–496. Blackawton, UK: Prospect Books, 1999.

Quataert, Donald, ed. *Consumption Studies and the History of the Ottoman Empire, 1550–1922: An Introduction*. Albany: SUNY Press, 2000.

Rebora, Giovanni. *The Culture of the Fork: A Brief History of Food in Europe*. New York: Columbia University Press, 2001.

Redding, Richard. "Decision Making in Subsistence Herding of Sheep and Goats in the Middle East." PhD diss., University of Michigan, 1981.

Redford, Scott. "Ayyubid Glass from Samsat, Turkey." *Journal of Glass Studies* 36 (1994): 81–91.

———. "Just Landscape in Medieval Anatolia." *Studies in the History of Gardens and Designed Landscapes* 20 (2000): 313–324.

———. *Landscape and the State in Medieval Anatolia: Seljuk Gardens and Pavilions of Alanya, Turkey*. Oxford: Archeopress, 2000.

———. "Medieval Ceramics from Samsat, Turkey." *Archéologie Islamique* 5 (1995): 55–80.

Redford, Scott, with Gil J. Stein, Naomi F. Miller, and Denise C. Hodges. *The Archaeology of the Frontier in the Medieval Near East: Excavations at Gritille, Turkey*. Philadelphia: University of Pennsylvania Museum of Archaeology and Anthropology, 1998.

Redhouse, James W. *A Turkish and English Lexicon*. Beirut: Librairie du Liban, 1974.

Riché, Pierre. *Daily Life in the World of Charlemagne*. Translated from *La vie quotidienne dans l'empire carolingien*, by Jo Ann McNamara. Philadelphia: University of Pennsylvania Press, 1978.

Rock, Paul. "Some Problems in Interpretative Historiography." *British Journal of Sociology* 27 (1976): 353–386.

Rodinson, Maxime. "Recherches sur les documents arabes relatifs à la cuisine." *Revue des Études Islamiques* 17 (1949): 95–165.

Rogers, J. Michael. "Waqf and Patronage in Seljuk Anatolia: The Epigraphic Evidence." *Anatolian Studies* 26 (1976): 69–103.

Rogers, Michael. "The Palace, Poisons, and the Public: Some Lists of Drugs in Mid-16th-Century Ottoman Turkey." In *Studies in Ottoman History in Honour of Professor V. L. Ménage*, edited by Colin Heywood and Colin Imber, 273–296. Istanbul: Isis Press, 1994.

Romagnoli, Daniela. "*Guarda no sii vilan*: Les bonnes manières à table." In *Histoire de l'alimentation*, edited by Jean-Louis Flandrin and Massimo Montanari, 511–523. Paris: Fayard, 1996.

Roymans, Nico. "The Cultural Biography of Urnfields and the Long-Term History of a Mythical Landscape." *Archaeological Dialogues* 2, no. 1 (1995): 2–24.

Rutman, Darrett B. "People in Process: The New Hampshire Towns of the Eighteenth Century." In *Small Worlds, Large Questions: Explorations in Early American Social History, 1650–1850*, edited by Darrett B. Rutman and Anita H. Rutman, 113–133. Charlottesville: University Press of Virginia, 1994.

Sakaoğlu, Necdet. "Sources for Our Ancient Culinary Culture." In *The Illuminated Table, the Prosperous House: Food and Shelter in Ottoman Material Culture*, edited by Suraiya Faroqhi and Christoph K. Neumann, 35–49. Würzburg: Ergon Verlag, 2003.

Schioler, Thorkild. *Roman and Islamic Water-Lifting Wheels*. Odense: Odense University Press, 1973.

Şehsuvaroğlu, Bedi N., ed. *Eşref Bin Muhammed: Hazā'inü's-Sa'ādāt*. Ankara: Türk Tarih Kurumu, 1961.

Selçuk, İklil Oya. "State and Society in the Marketplace: A Study of Late Fifteenth-Century Bursa." PhD diss., Harvard University, 2009.

Silibolatlaz, Derya. "Animal Bone Studies on Byzantine City of the Amorium [*sic*]." Master's thesis, Middle East Technical University, 2009.

Simoons, Frederick J. *Eat Not This Flesh: Food Avoidances from Prehistory to the Present*. Madison: University of Wisconsin Press, 1994.

Singer, Amy. *Constructing Ottoman Beneficence: An Imperial Soup Kitchen in Jerusalem*. Albany: SUNY Press, 2000.

Stein, Gil J. "Medieval Pastoral Production Systems at Gritille." In *Archaeology of the Frontier in the Medieval Near East: Excavations at Gritille, Turkey*, edited by Scott Redford, 181–209. Philadelphia: University of Pennsylvania Museum of Archaeology and Anthropology, 1998.

Steingass, F. *A Comprehensive Persian-English Dictionary*. New Delhi: Oriental Books Reprint, 1973.

Stoianovich, Traian. "Le maïs dans les Balkans." *Annales ESC* 21, no. 5 (1966).

Taeschner, Franz. "Beiträge zur Geschichte der Achis in Anatolien (14.–15. Jht.) auf Grund neur Quellen." *Islamica* 4 (1929): 1–47.

Tannahil, Reay. *Food in History*. New York: Crown, 1996.

Tapper, Richard, and Sami Zubaida. *A Taste of Thyme: Culinary Cultures of the Middle East*. New York: Tauris Parke, 2000.

Tarama Sözlüğü. 8 vols. Ankara: Türk Dil Kurumu, 1977.

Trépanier, Nicolas. "Iznik, the Gardens, and the Starving Enemy?" In *Uluslararası İznik Sempozyumu, 5–7 Eylül 2005*, edited by Ali Erbaş et al., 225–234. İznik: Belediyesi Kültür Yayınları, 2006.

———. "Starting without Food: Fasting and the Early Mawlawī Order." In *Starting with Food: Culinary Approaches to Ottoman History*, edited by Amy Singer, 1–23. Princeton, NJ: Markus Wiener, 2011.

Ünver, Süheyl. "Selçuklular, beylikler ve osmanlılarda yemek usûlleri ve vakitleri." In *Türk Mutfağı Sempozyumu Bildirileri (31 Ekim–1 Kasım 1981, Ankara)*, 1–13. Ankara: Ankara Üniversitesi Basımevi, 1982.

Uzunçarşılı, İsmail Hakkı. *Anadolu beylikleri ve Akkoyunlu, Karakoyunlu devletleri*. Ankara: Türk Tarih Kurumu Yayınlar, 1937.

van Loon, Maurits N., ed. "Architecture and Stratigraphy." In *Korucutepe: Final Report on the Excavations of the Universities of Chicago, California (Los Angeles), and Amsterdam in the Keban Reservoir, Eastern Anatolia, 1968–1970*, edited by Maurits N. van Loon, 2:3–45. Amsterdam: North-Holland and American Elsevier, 1978.

———. Conclusion to *Korucutepe: Final Report on the Excavations of the Universities of Chicago, California (Los Angeles), and Amsterdam in the Keban Reservoir, Eastern Anatolia, 1968–1970*, edited by Maurits N. van Loon, 3:271–277. Amsterdam: North-Holland and American Elsevier, 1980.

———. *Korucutepe: Final Report on the Excavation of the Universities of Chicago, California (Los Angeles), and Amsterdam in the Keban Reservoir, Eastern Anatolia, 1968–1970*. 3 vols. Amsterdam: North-Holland and American Elsevier, 1980.

———. "The Other Medieval Objects." Chapter 9 in *Korucutepe: Final Report on the Excavations of the Universities of Chicago, California (Los Angeles), and Amsterdam in the Keban Reservoir, Eastern Anatolia, 1968–1970*, edited by Maurits N. van Loon, 3:251–267. Amsterdam: North-Holland and American Elsevier, 1980.

Varlık, Mustafa Çetin. *Germiyan-oğulları tarihi (1300–1429)*. Ankara: Sevinç Matbaası, 1974.

Vroom, Joanita. *After Antiquity: Ceramics and Society in the Aegean from the 7th to the 20th Century A.C.: A Case Study from Boeotia, Central Greece*. Leiden: Archaeological Studies, Leiden University, 2003.

———. "Medieval Ceramics and the Archaeology of Consumption in Eastern Anatolia." In *Archaeology of the Countryside in Medieval Anatolia*, edited by Tasha Vorderstrasse and J. J. Roodenberg, 235–258. Leiden: Nederlands Instituut voor het nabije Oosten, 2009.

———. "Some Byzantine Pottery Finds from Kaman-Kalehöyük: A First Observation." *Anatolian Archaeological Studies* 15 (2006): 163–170.

Vryonis, Speros. *The Decline of Medieval Hellenism in Asia Minor and the Process of Islamization from the Eleventh through the Fifteenth Century*. Berkeley: University of California Press, 1971.

———. "The Muslim Family in 13th–14th Century Anatolia as Reflected in the Writings of the Mawlawi Dervish Eflaki." In *The Ottoman Emirate (1300–1389)*, edited by Elisabeth A. Zachariadou, 213–223. Rethymnon: Crete University Press, 1993.

Waines, David. "Dietetics in Medieval Islamic Culture." *Medical History* 43 (1999): 228–240.

———. "Prolegomena to the Study of Cooking in Abbasid Times: A Circuitous Bibliographical Essay." *Occasional Papers of the School of Abbasid Studies* 1 (1986): 30–39.

Watson, Andrew M. *Agricultural Innovation in the Early Islamic World: The Diffusion of*

Crops and Farming Techniques, 700–1100. Cambridge: Cambridge University Press, 1983.

Wehr, Hans. *A Dictionary of Modern Written Arabic.* Edited by J. Milton Cowan. Wiesbaden: Otto Harrassowitz, 1979.

Wittek, Paul. *Das Fürstentum Mentesche: Studie zur Geschichte Westkleinasiens im 13.–15. Jh.* Istanbul: Universum druckerei, 1934.

———. *The Rise of the Ottoman Empire.* London: Royal Asiatic Society, 1938.

Wolper, Ethel Sara. *Cities and Saints: Sufism and the Transformation of Urban Space in Medieval Anatolia.* University Park: Pennsylvania State University Press, 2003.

Yavuz, Ayşil Tükel. "The Concepts That Shape Anatolian Seljuq Caravanserais." *Muqarnas* 14 (1997): 80–95.

Yazıcı, Tahsin. *Āriflerin Menkıbeleri.* 2 vols. Istanbul: Hürriyet Yayınları, 1973.

Yürekli-Gökay, Zeynep. "Legend and Architecture in the Ottoman Empire: The Shrines of Seyyid Gazi and Haci Bektaş." PhD diss., Harvard University, 2005.

Yusufoğlu, Mehmet. "Selçuk devri ekmek adları: Bazlama-Bazlamaç." *Anıt* (Konya) 2, no. 18 (1950): 2.

———. "Selçuk devri yemeklerinden herise ve tutmaç." *Anıt* (Konya) 2, no. 16 (1950): 9–11.

Zachariadou, Elizabeth, ed. "Notes sur la population de l'Asie Mineure au XIVe siècle." *Byzantinische Forschungen* 12 (1987): 223–231.

———. *The Ottoman Emirate (1300–1389).* Rethymnon: Crete University Press, 1993.

———. *Trade and Crusade: Venetian Crete and the Emirates of Menteshe and Aydin (1300–1415).* Venice: Instituto Ellenico di Studi Bizantini e Postbizantini, 1983.

Zaouali, Lilia. *Medieval Cuisine of the Islamic World: A Concise History with 174 Recipes.* Berkeley: University of California Press, 2007.

Index

Note: The letter *t* following a page number denotes a table.

www.ingramcontent.com/pod-product-compliance
Ingram Content Group UK Ltd.
Pitfield, Milton Keynes, MK11 3LW, UK
UKHW041848020425
457001UK00002B/219

9 781477 309926